THE MEANING OF
HUMAN SUFFERING

THE MEANING OF HUMAN SUFFERING

Flavian Dougherty, C.P., Editor

U.S. Director,
Stauros International

HUMAN SCIENCES PRESS
72 Fifth Avenue   3 Henrietta Street
NEW YORK, NY 10011 ● LONDON, WC2E 8LU

Printed in the United States of America
123456789 987654321

Editorial/Production Services
by **Harkavy Publishing Service**

Library of Congress Cataloging in Publication Data

International Ecumenical Congress on the Meaning of
    Human Suffering (1st : 1979 : University of Notre Dame)
    The meaning of human suffering.

    Bibliography: p.
    Includes index.
    1. Suffering—Congresses. I. Dougherty, Flavian,
1923-   . II. Title.
BT732.7.I57 1979   233   81-6267
ISBN 0-89885-011-8   AACR2

CONTENTS

CONTRIBUTORS

DR. LOWELL G. COLSTON, an ordained minister of the Christian Church (Disciples of Christ), is Professor of Pastoral Care at Christian Theological Seminary, Indianapolis. He is also the director of the program "Continuing Education in Mental Health of Aging Persons." He is a diplomate of the American Association of Pastoral Counselors and is a member of the American Psychological Association, certified for private practice in psychology. He is also a member of the International Transactional Analysis Association. Professor Colston received a B.A. from Drake University, the M.D.D. from Union Theological Seminary, and his Ph.D. from the University of Chicago. He is the author of: *The Context of Pastoral Counseling* (with Seward Hiltner), 1961; "Pastoral Theology and Clinical Training," a chapter in *The New Shape in Pastoral Theology*, 1969; *Wake-up, Self*, a layman's retreat manual, 1969; *Judgment in Pastoral Counseling*, 1969; *Personality and Christian Faith* (with Paul E. Johnson), 1972; and *Pastoral Care with Handicapped Persons*, 1978. Dr. Colston does much of his writing during the 18 hours he spends on a kidney machine each week.

DR. JOHN W. BOWKER is Head of the Department of Religious Studies at the University of Lancaster, England, where he has worked out a new approach to religious studies based on the expansion of the Department. After his university education at Oxford, he went to Sheffield as a Research Fellow and then to Cambridge as Dean of Corpus Christi College. In 1972 he was elected Wilde Lecturer at Oxford, and in 1974 became Professor of Religious Studies at Lancaster. Dr. Bowker has also given recent lectures in Rome, Vancouver, and the U.S. He has served on Commissions on Religious Education and on Marriage and Divorce, and has recently been appointed to the Archbishops' Commission on Doctrine. Dr. Bowker has been a frequent contributor to publications such as *Religious Studies, Humanitas, Concilium*, and others. His books include *Problems of Suffering in Religions of the World*, 1970; *The Sense of God: Sociological, Anthropological and Psychological Approaches to the Origin of the Sense of God*, 1973; *The Religious Imagination and the Sense of God*, 1978; and others. Among his many articles, the following on the phenomenon of suffering should be noted: "Suffering in the Qur'an," *Religious Studies*, IV, 1969; "Suffering and the Origins of Religion," *Humanitas*, IX, 1973; "Assimilation or Rejection? Christian Understanding of Suffering in Eastern Religions," *Concilium*, Feb. 1977; and "Suffering: the Religious Perspective," in the forthcoming Encyclopedia of Bioethics.

PAUL STANISLAS BRETON, a member of the Passionist Congregation since 1928, is Professor of Philosophy at the Catholic Faculties of Lyon, France, and at the Institut Catholique of Paris. He also holds a Conference Chair at the Ecole Normale Supérieure of Paris. From 1939 to 1945 he was a war prisoner in Austria. He took a Ph.D. at the Angelicum in Rome (1947) and a year later was appointed Professor of Philosophy at the Pontifical University de Propaganda Fide in Rome. After taking a Licentiate in Theology at the Catholic Faculties of Lyon, he became a Doctor in Theology in 1978. Father Breton has held visiting professorships at the Universities of Laval and Montreal in recent years has participated in various scholarly meetings in Japan, Morocco, Tunis, and Madagascar. Besides his many articles in French and international periodicals, his books include: *L'esse in et l'esse ad dans la métaphysique de la relation*, 1951; *La Passion du Christ et les philosophies*, 1954; *Situation de la philosophie contemporaine*, 1959; *Approches philosophiques de l'idée d'être*, 1959; *Mystique de la Passion*, 1962; *Du principe*, 1971; *Foi et raison logique*, 1971; and *Ecriture et révélation*, 1979.

CARROLL STUHLMUELLER, a member of the Passionist Congregation since 1943, is Professor of Old Testament Studies at Catholic Theological Union, Chicago. After taking a Licentiate in Theology at the Catholic University, Washington, he obtained a Licentiate in Sacred Scripture and a doctorate at the Pontifical Biblical Institute in Rome. Fr. Stuhlmueller has also served on the faculty of the Passionist Theologate, Louisville, Kentucky; St. Meinrad Seminary, St. Meinrad, Indiana, and St. John's University, New York. He has held lectureships at St. Mary's Graduate School of Theology, Notre Dame; the Theological Coalition, Dubuque; Dayton University; St. Louis University; The Ecole Biblique et Archeologique, Jerusalem, and the Winter Theological School, Southern Africa. From 1973 to 1977 he was Associate Editor of the Catholic Biblical Quarterly. He is currently Associate and Book Review Editor of *"The Bible Today,"* Associate Editor of the "Old Testament Reading Guide," and president of the Catholic Biblical Association. He has contributed to many biblical periodicals and his books include: *The Gospel of St. Luke*, 1960; *The Prophets and the Word of God*, 1964; *The Book of Isaiah*, 1965; *Creative Redemption in Deutero-Isaiah*, 1970; *The Books of Jeremiah and Baruch*, 1973; *Thirsting for the Lord. Essays in Biblical Theology*, 1977; and *Biblical Meditations for Lent*, 1978.

ARTHUR CHUTE McGILL is Professor of Theology at the Harvard Divinity School and is an ordained minister in the United Church of Christ. He graduated from Harvard in 1947, received his B.D. from Yale Divinity School in 1951, ·studied with the theological faculty of the University of Louvain in 1957 and 1958, and received his Ph.D. from Yale in 1960. He has been a member of the Amherst College faculty, Wesleyan University faculty, and the Department of Religion at Princeton University. Professor McGill was elected a Kent Fellow in the National Council on Religion in Higher Education in 1953 and was awarded the Vedder Prize in 1959 for distinguished undergraduate teaching in a private American college. He was appointed a Senior Fellow of the Humanities at Princeton and is a member of the American Theological Society. In 1969 he gave the Cadbury Lectures at the University of Birmingham in England. Professor McGill is a founding member of the board of trustees for the Ecumenical Institute for Advanced Theological Study in Jerusalem. At the time of the Congress on Suffering, he was suffering the after-effects of a kidney transplant, and thus was able to speak from personal experience, as well as his scholarship, on suffering. His publications include: *Reason in a Violent World*, 1958; *The Celebration of the Flesh*, 1964; *The Many Faced Argument*, 1967; and *Suffering: A Test of Theological Method*, 1967.

ROBERT JAY LIFTON holds the Foundations' Fund for Research of Psychiatry professorship at Yale University and has taken an active part in the formation of the new field of psychohistory. He is best known for his study of the psychological effects of the atomic bomb in Hiroshima. His book on this, *Death in Life*, received the National Book Award in the Sciences and the Van Wyck Brooks Award in 1969. Dr. Lifton has written on problems of nuclear weapons, on Chinese thought reform, on psychological trends of contemporary or "Protean" man and woman, and on the

Vietnam War experience. In recent years he has been developing a general psychological perspective around the paradigm of death and the continuity of life and a stress upon symbolization and "formative process." His most recent studies, yet to be published, are on the behavior of those in the medical profession who participated in the atrocities of the "Holocaust." Dr. Lifton has received several honorary doctorate degrees and the Hiroshima Gold Medal in 1975. He has been the recipient of numerous other awards including the 1970 Public Service Award from the New York Society of Clinical Psychologists; 1970 Alumni Medal from New York Medical College; and the William V. Silverberg Memorial Lecture Award from the American Academy of Psychoanalysis, 1971. His books include *The Life of the Self*, 1976; *Explorations in Psychohistory: the Wellfleet Papers*, 1975; and *Home From the War: Vietnam Veterans—Neither Victims Nor Executioners* (which was nominated for the National Book Award in 1974). He has authored many others as well as numerous articles. He even has produced a book of humorous bird cartoons published by Random House in 1969.

DR. WAYNE E. OATES is Professor of Psychiatry and Behavioral Sciences at the University of Louisville School of Medicine. He has also served on the faculty at the Southern Baptist Theological Seminary, Union Theological Seminary in New York, and Princeton Theological Seminary. He studied at Duke Divinity School, at the Southern Baptist Theological Seminary, Louisville, and did postgraduate study at the Union Theological Seminary, New York, and the University of Louisville Medical School. He became Litt.D. at Wake Forest University in 1962. Dr. Oates has held pastorates and chaplaincies in North Carolina and Kentucky and is Certified Supervisor of the Association of Clinical Pastoral Education, Diplomate of the American Association of Pastoral Counselors, and Supervisor of the American

Association of Marriage and Family Counselors. He is the author of 36 books and over 200 articles and chapters in books. Among those books which relate so closely to the subject of suffering are: *Religious Factors in Mental Illness*, 1955; *The Revelation of God in Human Suffering*, 1959; *Pastoral Counseling in Social Problems*, 1966; *Where to Go For Help*, 1971; *Anxiety in Christian Experience*, 1972; *Pastoral Care and Counseling in Grief and Separation*, 1976; *Religious Care of the Psychiatric Patient*, 1978; and *Nurturing Silence in a Noisy Heart*, 1979.

DR. JOEL GAJARDO-VELASQUEZ, Director of the Latin American Department of the National Council of Churches and former Director of the Committee on United States Latin American Policy Study at Cornell, is a citizen of the Republic of Chile. Dr. Gajardo studied at the University of Chile in Santiago, Theological Evangelical Seminary in Buenos Aires, and Princeton Theological Seminary. He has served pastorates in the Presbyterian church in Chile, and has held professorships in Systematic Theology, Ethics, and Anthropology in the Evangelical Theological Community and in the Catholic University of Santiago, Chile. Dr. Gajardo has been actively involved in the ecumenical movement through the World Council of Churches and the Christian Peace Conference, and is widely regarded as one of the most effective interpreters of Latin American Church life and thought in North America. From 1958 to 1960 Dr. Gajardo was the editor of the official journal of the Presbyterian church in Chile and has contributed to several Latin American theological and ecumenical periodicals. He is the author of *La Biblia—Un Libro Desconocido*, 1958, and of *Forma Presbiteriana de Gobierno*, 1960. He also wrote "How the Other American Looks at Us" in a book edited by Dana Green, 1967.

HENRY JAMES YOUNG is a Senior Research Director at

the Center for Parish Development, Naperville, Illinois. He
has majored in philosophy and religion and received his
Ph.D. in systematic theology from the Hartford Seminary
Foundation in Hartford, Connecticut. Dr. Young has wide
experience as a black activist in the civil rights movements,
teacher, administrator, editor, pastor, and guest lecturer.
Some of his previous positions are: Dean of Academic Af-
fairs, Edward Waters College; Editor-in-Chief, The Journal
of the Interdenominational Theological Center; Teaching
Fellow in Religion, Trinity College; Assistant, Special Assis-
tant to the Commissioner of Welfare, Hartford, Connecticut;
Pastor, Union Baptist Church, Pawtucket, Rhode Island;
and Coordinator of YMCA Youth Program, Boston. He has
been active in the Society for the Study of Black Religion,
National Congress of Black Churchmen, and has been a guest
lecturer at the University of North Carolina, University of
Tennessee, Nebraska Wesleyan University, and others.
Among Dr. Young's publications are the following:
Preaching the Gospel, 1976; *Major Black Religious Leaders*:
1755-1940, 1977; *Preaching on Suffering and a God of Love*,
1978; *Major Black Religious Leaders: 1940 to the Present*,
1979. Dr. Young's published articles have appeared in
Religion in Life, *The Duke Divinity School Review*, and *The
Journal of the Interdenominational Theological Center.*

CATHERINE DE HUECK DOHERTY, Foundress of the
Friendship Houses and the Madonna House Apostolate, was
born in 1900 in a pullman car standing on the sidings of a
town by the Volga in Russia. Her father was sent on government business to Egypt, and there she grew up learning the
many languages that would be of such help to her in later life.
After further education in Paris, she finally arrived back in
Russia where she attended the University of Petrograd.
World War I interfered and brought nursing into her life.
Catherine was married to Baron Boris de Hueck at the age of
15 and was forced to flee Communist Russia with him in 1920

and finally settled in Canada. Although they were both in poor health, they struggled to earn a living for themselves and their infant son by a variety of low-paying jobs. Within a few years Catherine had risen to an executive position and was once again wealthy. But she was haunted by the words of Christ, "Sell all that you have and give to the poor, and come, follow me." Catherine did just that in 1930 and founded the First Friendship House in the slums of Toronto. Other foundations in Harlem and Chicago followed, and soon her intense faith and sincere love attracted many helpers. Four years after marrying Eddie Doherty, the well-known newspaperman, they founded Madonna House in Combermere, Ontario, which became a training center for the lay apostolate. The present community there numbers 150. They live a community life based on prayer, work, silence, and the honest love of all who come to share their life. She is the author of several notable books on prayer and spirituality. Her most recent work is *Strannik: The Call to Pilgrimage for Western Man*, 1978.

FLAVIAN DOUGHERTY, the Director of the First International Ecumenical Congress on the Meaning of Human Suffering, is a member of the Passionist Congregation. He served as the provincial of the Eastern Province of the U.S. Passionists from 1968 to 1978, and was the first president of Stauros International. At present, he is the director of the U.S. Stauros office.

INTRODUCTION

Mankind's most common, most persistent, and most puzzling problem is suffering. Death, war, famine, pestilence, violence, oppression, imprisonment, poverty, sickness, loneliness, headaches, and heartaches are all particular parts of this puzzle. Even modern technologies, which have done so much to bring relief from this scourge, have in many instances become instruments of the most insidious and threatening kinds of suffering in history. Witness the technologies of war which have the capacity to destroy mankind.

The problem of suffering is particularly challenging to religions. As Professor John Bowker of the University of Lancaster, England, writes:

> To talk of suffering is to talk not of an academic problem but of the sheer bloody agonies of existence, of which all men are aware and most have direct experience. All religions take account of this; some, indeed, make it the basis of all they have to say. Whatever theoretical constructions may be built, the foundations are laid in the apparent realities of what it is like to be alive. Thus what a religion has to say about suffering reveals, in many ways more than anything else, what it believes the nature and purpose of existence to be.[1]

To reaffirm and revitalize Christianity's approach to suffering, the Passionist Religious Order founded an international, ecumenical organization to promote modern research and study on the "Gospel of Christ's Passion," which is the essence of Christianity's doctrine concerning suffering. Accordingly, the organization is aptly entitled "Stauros," the Greek word for cross.

While necessarily and seriously studying the contributions of other religious persuasions on suffering, Stauros has initiated several projects which focus particularly on the Christian tradition and its current scholarship and practice on the subject.

The most unique and successful project of Stauros thus far was "The First International, Ecumenical Congress on the Meaning of Human Suffering" held at the University of Notre Dame, April 22-26, 1979. It was unique in that it brought together for the first time a group of 300 persons intensely involved with suffering: "suffers" themselves, scholars and practitioners, men and women from different religious persuasions, different disciplines, different social positions and from different parts of the world. For example, of the speakers, Canada, England, France, and Chile were represented. Three were Roman Catholics, six Protestants, and one Jewish. Among the participants were representatives from Italy, France, Spain, Germany, Holland, Belgium, England, Mexico, Brazil, Argentina, Chile, Zaire, Japan, and Australia.

The Congress reexamined through current scholarship and personal experience the relationship between religion and suffering. It did so by focusing on certain critical themes from a philosophic, theological, and existential/practical point of view. Eight of the ten principal resource persons prepared research papers on assigned topics. The other two resource persons spoke from their own background and experience in personal suffering and their career identification with suffering persons in particular conditions.

It was successful not only because it produced scholarly work, as incorporated in this volume, but because it advanced the ecumenical movement among Chritians and provided inspiration and motivation for the participants. On the ecumenical aspect, one participant expressed it:

> Never before, so far as could be discerned, has such a diversity of Christians met to discuss what they all had so profoundly in common: a deep sensitivity to the problem of human suffering. The irony was . . . that it has taken so long for the followers of that crucified Jesus, who is no stranger to anyone, to cease being strangers to one another.

On the inspirational/motivational aspect, another, who works in a social service organization, confessed: "I had decided to quit this work—I was so frustrated—but this gave me the incentive to continue."

In this volume the addresses of our 10 principal resource persons are given together with the question and answer sessions which we were able to record. Dr. Lowell Colston's address, which was the conclusion of the Congress, is placed here at the beginning since it provides an excellent overview of the contents of the presentations. The book is divided into three major divisions as the Congress itself divided the material: 1 a philosophic approach to the problem of suffering; 2 a scriptural/theological approach; and 3 an existential/practical approach. Obviously, not everything that could be said on the subject or on any one of these categories is given here, but what is presented is very definitely a profound contribution to the quest for the meaning of suffering.

Flavian Dougherty, C.P.
Editor

NOTES

[1]John Bowker, *Problems of Suffering in Religions of the World,* Cambridge University Press, 1975, p. 2.

A SUMMARY OF THE CONGRESS
Dr. Lowell G. Colston

I don't envy my task. It is like asking a person to summarize his life in 25 words or less. And I can do that in these words, "Thank God I am here, that I am who I am, and that I am becoming what I shall be." I want to express my appreciation to the Stauros organization for this significant conference, and express appreciation for the whole conference, including the various aspects of it that may be unmentioned.

During this week, we have been vigorously confronted by our speakers, by the challenge to think and to feel again about the nature of our Christian vocation. We are called to a witness of our accountability and responsibility for the way we use and abuse the land, our natural resources, and the people of the land. We are called to become involved in the sufferings of others, to achieve an integrity of mind and heart that enables us to see the sufferings of other people. It is interesting to me that Jesus said, "Seeing, we see," while I recognize that many of us have looked at suffering and pain around us over a period of time and have never seen it. "Hearing, we hear," said Jesus. How is it we can look upon pain and suffering in our world for such a long time and never see or be exposed to the plaintive cries of people and never hear them? And when finally their pain becomes our pain and we discover the nature of their suffering and we suffer, we begin to discern the prototype for all suffering, at the

1

very heart of the gospel itself, Jesus Christ on the cross. We are called to this witness in a world torn with strife and suffering. We may not have to lay our lives upon the line, but if we are to be the Church in the world, we will enter into the sufferings of people and understand them. This is what I am hearing from our speakers.

IN LOVE WITH GOD

The first significant statement that I want to make is in the form of a question actually: "What is it like to identify with a people and to take on their sufferings and their pain?" The grand lady who introduced the Congress, Catherine de Hueck Doherty, exemplified the profound courage and great faith in her identification with the people of Harlem. Most of us cannot enter literally into such experiences, but we can develop what is an important development of what I would call "sympathetic imagination," or perhaps better, "empathic imagination." Her own life reflects the meaning of the Incarnation, which she implicitly interprets in the words, "We are suffering as we walk with Him." "I am in love with God," she said exuberantly, out of her own consistently devoted life "because I follow Him." That was evident. The gift of her own life to the people of Harlem profoundly shows her affirmation of suffering and grace as the gift of Christ to the world. The kind of person she is and our response to that magnificent life reflects the faith and divine trust in the promises of God that where we go He will be with us and that we can have courage and trust in that fact. It is in that spirit that she dedicated her life, as I know it, to the task of entering in and identifying with the sufferings of the people of Harlem.

MARX, FREUD, AND RELIGION

One of the challenges, perhaps *the* challenge in this century to the religions, and especially Christianity, has come from Karl Marx and Sigmund Freud. In a comprehensive and well-documented approach, acknowledged by the implication that the most effective challenges to our religious faith, to the thought and feeling of people around us, judging by the response to them over the current century, has been presented by Marx and Freud. Dr. John Bowker, a most able and comprehensive speaker, engaged in a polemic against them on the basis of his own well-thought out affirmations of a fact which I would like to support, i.e., that neither Freud nor Marx denied the power of religion, but regarded them as illusory and compensatory. The basic problem in religions for Freud and Marx, says Dr. Bowker, is their stance regarding suffering. But there is a rigorous reality in religious views of suffering and evidence that rather than being illusory and compensatory, religions are profoundly realistic in dealing with suffering humanity and have been truly in touch with reality from their very inception; in fact, their origins came from deep confrontation of the reality of suffering. So suffering, says Dr. Bowker, creates an opportunity for religions. Religions have engaged in cautious explanations of the meaning of suffering, taking their cues from observations of the natural order in which they saw the continuities of life and the continuity of the possibility of life beyond death. In this, religions have made cautious statements about such possibilities, but have affirmed them in all faith and trust. In fact, to be redundant, there is a matter of factness in the religions of the world which reflects a rigorous realism regarding suffering and death, which is at the very heart of the religions of the world.

SUFFERING AND TRANSCENDENCE

We were next led in our explorations of suffering by Dr. Stanislaus Breton. Expressions of this intense and enthusiastic gentleman for his subject transcended the barriers of language, and communicated the vitality and richness of the message and the man; he was inspiring even beyond his own topic. In discussing "Suffering and Transcendence," he said there is an enigma or a mystery in suffering that invites us to a modest silence before it. We're so prone to opt to explain, that before suffering we are often silent. He presented his material in three parts: the experience of suffering, the problem of suffering, and the nature of transcendence. The experience of suffering includes three aspects: first, suffering which exposes us to the threatening forces which always surprise and wound us. This anonymous threat takes its form and name in a definite evil, in a sickness, which in every historical age is situated at the summit of the negative that represents an evil which cannot be changed. The sickness puts an organic imbalance in us, which is expressed for knowledge by a contradiction of privation, in which the inevitability of death is manifest. To these three aspects of suffering, as he developed it, there are as many aspects of an action which correspond: first, a knowledge and a will to endeavor to dominate them and to change them; second, by a way, original for each one of us, of bearing one's own evil, and that's an interesting recognition—that we have evil within us and that we do bear it; and third, by a solution also original for each one of us, of the contradiction which divides us inwardly. The problem of suffering rises from the mere fact that man never resigns himself to the inevitability of the suffering. The response to this problem is developed along two very different lines: that of knowledge, as to say, that of doing what we can about the situation. As a dialysis patient, I know that there are some things that in my own understanding I can do about the situation. There are other things that I cannot do and must accept. But, when I do accept these, I discover what I found very early in my experience with kidney disease, that I am not alone. The act of transcendence, the act of transcending or a reality that cannot be reduced to this act of transcendence—the transcended itself—is expressed in the suffering in the shadow of the cross. The foolishness and the weakness which limit each condition, sensitize this universal human capacity to suffer. The cross of Christ recapitulates the human experience of suffering in the world.

NUMBED OR FEELING?

What is the clinical evidence of the meaning of suffering? Dr. Robert Lifton, a dedicated researcher who gave us a report of an extremely significant study he had done among the survivors of Hiroshima, led us in the discussion of that. Departing from the psychoanalytic predilection to reduce explanations to sexual geneses, Dr. Lifton's concern is with the reality of death. He discovered that to protect themselves from the awful threat to their sanity the survivors of Hiroshima became psychically numb. He also learned, after a while, that he, i.e. Dr. Lifton, developed a professional numbing. As a psychotherapist, I think I understand that distance sometimes between one's self and the other is a protective device. This produced some distancing from the survivors to protect him from the grotesque details. He called this "selective professional numbing." The danger in this for us, for our tendency to put distance between ourselves and other people in their suffering, is too much numbing and not enough feeling. Experiential transcendence and symbolic immortality, says Dr. Lifton, are factors which enable us to engage in a feeling response to those who aren't in the midst of suffering, yet maintaining the distance that will enable us to remain sane.

LIBERATION IN THE OLD TESTAMENT

We were next led by an erudite scholar and dramatic portrayer of the events of the Old Testament—I feel that the Old Testament is a dramatic book. Dr. Stuhlmueller challenged us to see the prophetic possibilities within a secular event of our time. Drawing upon his analysis of both the captivity of Israel and Egypt and the Babylonian exile, he deftly emphasized that there was a correspondence between Israel's experience of secular violence and the divine message and the divine consciousness; that Israel celebrated with religious rituals her liberation, saying that religion addressed itself to secular violence, Israel liturgically celebrated her liberation. Other religions reached back to creation and were apparently more supernatural. Biblical religion seems more secular and imminent. Dr. Stuhlmueller referred to what he called the violence of waiting, indicating the apparent restlessness and agitation that waiting upon the Lord was in Israel. Israel's land was a sign of the Lord's generosity, a temptation, a task, a threat, and a sign of destruction. Speaking of the Babylonian exile, Dr. Stuhlmueller sees again the secular oppression and the prayers directed to it, the new exodus out of misery, which is announced by the second Isaiah. The remembrance of that deliverance is celebrated again liturgically. So again is the secular oppression amingle with the divine hopes and the memory of what is constantly given in prayers. Human agony and divine pathos are mingled in suffering and contemplative prayer—this is the nature of Israel's response to her life in the land. Some of the most beautiful literature that ever has been written regarding human agony and the divine pathos is in the "Suffering Servant Songs," which issue a new calm, a calm communication with the ideals of the nation, and tell of the weariness and the resting of the Lord. Israel is schooled by weariness and shame, passive, yet challenging all persecutors, with a contemplative vision and a recognition of the paradox of life in the midst of death. Israel was a homeless people, seeking the Lord; and then a landed people, resting in the Lord; a sinful people, and we cannot point toward the evil in others without acknowledging it in ourselves, because likewise, we are a sinful people.

"INTO YOUR HANDS, I COMMIT MY SPIRIT"

I felt a special collegiality with the one who presented next and admire him for his persistence in character—Dr. Arthur McGill. In a thoughtful presentation, he pointed out that the middle-class people tend, as a whole, to avoid suffering. Discussing the problem of suffering, he noted that we deaden sensitivity through the development of anesthetics and narcotics. In fact, he said, we have committed ourselves to a flight from suffering more than any other generation. Prior to technology, the lessons were to learn to bear suffering, through courage, fortitude, and patience. Related to the desire to increase ways to avoid suffering is the failure to teach our children about failure itself. We believe suffering is incompatible with being genuinely human. We need to discern, says Dr. McGill, that sin, not suffering, is the problem. We are holding ourselves behind walls. Openness to others and the tearing down of the walls which will give us opening to others is required. We cannot help our neighbor from behind walls, and, so to speak, playing it close to the vest, taking no risks, being careful to protect ourselves or to deaden our sensitivity, keeps us behind walls. If there is no wall, we are vulnerable; but without vulnerability, there is no love. Dr. McGill asks, "What do the gospels portray regarding beatitude to human suffering?" He cites the words of Jesus as an example: "Father, into Thy hands I commend My Spirit." The weak reading of this is, "I can't bear this anymore, you take over," which is a way of resignation. A strong reading of this puts the whole matter into the context of an ongoing relationship, "Into Your hands, I commit My Spirit," he re-reads this. This is indicative of the trust and the care of the Father, a trust which has previously existed and continues in its strength. Being a person means taking down the walls and committing one's self to God's care. Letting one's self be vulnerable even to suffering, even when he felt abandoned by God, Jesus continued to exercise His humanity.

SUFFERING AND DEATH

My very good friend over the years, Wayne E. Oates, whom I've admired and respected for a long time, led us in a consideration of death and grief. Death, he said, becomes the prototype for the other sufferings of life. The critical issue in death is the fear of the unknown and the agony of separation from those whom we know who provide security, love, and meaning to the process of life. Moving beyond Kübler-Ross, Dr. Oates distinguishes the kinds of grief as anticipatory, acute or traumatic, chronic sorrow, near-miss, pathological grief, and the tragic sense of life itself. *Anticipatory grief* usually accompanies an incurable illness; family and friends deadline each other through patterned meanings of non-religious and religious rituals, such as urging, diagnosis, resistance, family gathering and leave-taking, prolongation, death virgil, notification of the next of kin, the planning of the funeral and the funeral itself, visitation to the cemetery, thinning of the crowd, and the division of effects; these rituals enable people to move through the suffering of grief. Then there is *acute* or *traumatic grief* which has meanings not present in other kinds of grief, consists of physiological and psychological shock, psychological loss of feeling, a numbness, the sight and the identification of the body of the dead person, and the delay of grief work itself. *No-end grief* is the necessity of living with a heartbreaking set of circumstances that are unalterable, unending, and ever demanding. *Near-miss grief* is the kind in which the person narrowly escapes being killed; people who go through this still have to face the issues of life as though they were as good as dead. *Pathological grief* is an extended form of grief which must be carefully diagnosed; the patient is given an opportunity to re-grieve and to re-experience what perhaps in the past he could not adequately experience. The *tragic sense of life* is the kind of grief which arises from a sense of being human, limited and subject to death ourselves. Facing death is apparent suffering of which the human spirit demands a meaning. The meaning is developed by the use of rituals over the time span available. These are diagnostically discernible and creatively treatable by compassionate care from all those concerned.

THE SUFFERING OF BLACK AMERICA

And now we were given a sense of the prophetic witness among the black Americans by Dr. Henry James Young. His presentation, "Does Christianity Proclaim Redemption in and through or despite Suffering?," has special emphasis on the black experience. Exhibiting great poise, sensitivity, and strength, Dr. Young led us in reflecting upon suffering in the context of the black experience. Beginning with a recounting of the terrible sufferings of the black Americans during the time of slavery in America, he raised the question, "How have black Americans maintained integrity in the face of all forms of suffering?" He answered by saying that they have put these sufferings within a history and they have studied that history and beyond the history and have risen to an eschatological point. Joy and sorrow reflect this eschatological dialectic, he says, which has maintained that tension in their lives and has enabled them to survive. The black responses to slavery were, first, compensatory: being forced to capitulate, they went on believing that God would vindicate their suffering. This was an accommodation to the situation. Second, judgmental: slaves were taught that they were to be obedient and to avoid judgment of God. The third response, the protest element, emerged out of their growing edge of hope, an awareness of a moral aura in the world by which everyone lived. Referring to the contemporary scene, Dr. Young sees black Americans as involved in a vicarious suffering. He sees the redemptive possibilities within this vicarious suffering. The conviction for which Martin Luther King gave his life remains a powerful force. Nonviolent resistance, which is a method that is physically passive but spiritually active, has reconciliation as its end, says Dr. Young. It espouses hate the wrong, but not hate the one who does it. Dr. Young focused his discussion on agape—love: unconditional, without limitations, saying that the response to that love is faith that what is happening to you is redemptive. In the center of the universe, he said, there is a cosmic element of truth and it will prevail. The hope is in the realization that although we may not be able to understand the situation, we know that God continues to work redemptively through the situation.

SUFFERING IN THE THIRD WORLD

And what about the Third World and the sufferings of the people in the Third World? Dr. Joel Gajardo knows something of that suffering. He was in a concentration camp and released by Catholic intervention. Main concerns that he expressed in laying upon our hearts the needs of the Latin Americans began with the statement of the incursion of greed into Latin America by the Europeans. The Indians were plundered and forced into labor by Europeans. Some priests opposed the abuse of the Indians and one wrote against the practices. He was officially removed. That situation has continued until now and Latin Americans have not been able to extricate themselves. Social sciences have been throwing new light on the situation, but the leadership has been educated to ignore the conditions around them. Two areas where change is possible: politics and religion. The question of power is central to the political question to be solved. Politics, he said, makes the necessary possible, to change the world as well as to keep it as it is. There is no certainty, there are no maps, we must take risks, to make the models as a call of the future. This is an ideological battle, he says, and the Church cannot shrink from the struggle against suffering which is going on in

Latin America. The issue of violence is an inevitable one. Violence is not an option, he says; we are surrounded by it. One thousand children die in a year; who is responsible? I should raise that as an hypothetical question because he raised it as that kind of question. Institutional violence generates revolutionary violence, which generates reactionary violence, and so it escalates in Latin America. He then turns to collective and personal suffering. Life 's an open-ended process, he said, that includes recognition ' acceptance and rejection in the dialectic. There are two types in the suffering of the struggle against suffering: those who are part of the suffering masses—the movement is from suffering to sacrifice, like Latin American Indians are now organized to fight for their survival. The second type are people born in well-off situations, who are able to resign privilege, or as I said earlier, to be able to enter imaginatively into the sufferings of the masses, and who make common cause with the peasants. Those who would change the situation, he said, are labeled as Marxists. But the problem is not communism, it is suffering. Social reformers and religious leaders are moving from affluence to suffering and from suffering to sacrifice and that is an encouraging sign. Religious leaders are dying because of their commitment to lead the masses from their suffering in Latin America. The theology of liberation, he says, is wrapped up in the shift of the Church. God commands us to get committed to fight the oppression so that we can endow our suffering with sacrifice. Death without hope is death with escape from the sacrifice of suffering.

CONCLUSION

We have been richly blessed, I am sure you will agree, with these presentations of these people this week, and I would like to end my summary of what we have heard and what we have experienced with what I regard as the theme of my own presentation, and that is: surely, "He will bear our grief and carry our sorrows, by His stripes we are healed, and by His iniquities we are pardoned."

Part I

A PHILOSOPHICAL APPROACH TO THE PROBLEM OF HUMAN SUFFERING

Dealing with suffering from a religious viewpoint is often construed as avoiding a rational, real, existential confrontation with the subject; that it gets explained away with scriptural quotations and theological speculation.

For that reason, two outstanding scholars who have immersed themselves in the anthropology and the philosophical systems of various cultures were chosen to begin the Congress on a decidedly rational level. Dr. John Bowker, of England, carefully analyzes and refutes Marx and Freud, the two rationalists who have most influenced our century, and Dr. Stanislaus Breton, of France, gives a profound metaphysical treatment of suffering, and also an enlightening comparison between the Buddhist and Christian approaches to the same.

Chapter 1

SUFFERING AS A PROBLEM
OF RELIGIONS
Dr. John Bowker

On this occasion, we are engaged in a kind of operation, in which the Stauros movement is being transplanted from Europe to America. But like so many transplant operations, are there not great risks in the whole enterprise? Is there not a truly perverse absurdity in a group with specifically *religious* commitments exploring the reality of suffering? It is precisely at the point of suffering, death and their analysis that both Marx and Freud located the illusory and destructive nature of religion. Neither of them denied the power of religion in consoling us in our sorrow and in offering compensation for our present deprivation or grief. But both were unequivocally certain that religions blind us from a true engagement with reality, and that the time has come for the human race to strike camp and to march on from the religious illusion to an unevaded confrontation with the truth.

It is clear then that this issue must be faced by any conference which concerns itself with the religious or the Christian understanding of suffering. And therefore I want to approach what I believe to be the importance of Stauros along this route, by examining first the Marxist and the Freudian critiques, and by then asking where we go on the that criticism.

Suffering, then, as a *problem* for religions: as a title it seems both obvious and familiar. The extent of suffering and its unequal distribution seem to write an unanswerable question mark against the claims of religions to find purpose or providence in the universe, or to mark out a way whereby the reality of suffering may be transcended. Who causes the sharpness of the thorn? Who is the healer of the undeserved wound?

> O Lord, wilt thou not look upon our sore affliction
> Among these flames incessant labouring? Our hard masters laugh
> At all our sorrow. We are made to turn the wheel for water
> To carry the heavy basket on our scorched shoulders, to sift
> The sand and ashes, and to mix the clay with tears and repentance.
> The times are now return'd upon us; we have given ourselves
> To scorn, and now are scorned by the slaves of our enemies.
> Our beauty is cover'd over with clay and ashes, and our backs
> Furrow'd with whips, and our flesh bruised with the heavy basket,
> Forgive us, O thou piteous one whom we have offended! forgive
> The weak remaining shadow of Vala that returns in sorrow to thee.[1]

But *is* there a Lord to look upon our afflictions and forgive? Or, as the Buddhist might prefer to ask, is there any analysis which will provide a key to the apparently indecipherable code of suffering? That is the grim and searching edge of what at first sight seems to be so innocent a poem by James Stephens, a poem called "Bessie Bobtail":

> As down the road she wambled slow,
> She had not got a place to go:
> She had not got a place to fall
> And rest herself—no place at all:
> She stumped along, and wagged her pate;
> And said a thing was desperate.
>
> Her face was screwed and wrinkled tight

Just like a nut—and, left and right,
On either side, she wagged her head
And said a thing; and what she said
Was desperate as any word
That ever yet a person heard.

I walked behind her for a while,
And watched the people nudge and smile:
But ever, as she went, she said,
As left and right she swung her head,
—*Oh, God he knows! And God, He knows!*
And, surely God Almighty knows!

It is obvious, then, that the experience of suffering, whether in mind or body, or even outside one's own experience in the universe at large, is a fundamental challenge to many of the basic propositions of religion. The ways in which religions have responded to the problems posed by suffering and have described the nature of suffering are very varied indeed. They range from the Buddhist integration of *dukkha*, of transience, as the absolute and total truth of all appearance including ourselves, to the Muslim affirmation that suffering must necessarily be instrumental and can always be interpreted as an *ayat*, a sign of God, because there is nothing which can escape being a consequence of His creative will; they range from the Zoroastrian opposition between light and dark, between good and evil, to the Hindu unification of opposites as manifestations of *brahman*, of that which alone really *is* in its own nature; they range from the Chinese quest to restore the harmony which once obtained and for which the universe strives, to the Christian belief that a final victory over the reality of evil has already been won.

These—and many other responses—are not only different in themselves; they carry with them profound differences of anthropology—profound differences in their understanding of human nature and of what that nature is capable of being and becoming.[2] The general nature of these different accounts I have attempted, at a very elementary level, to describe in my book, *Problems of Suffering,* and there is no point in repeating the exercise here. What *is* important is to recognize how deeply religions are engaged with the reality of suffering—and how searchingly they are engaged *by* that reality as a challenge to the truth of what they claim to be the case.

And that at once makes the title of this paper, which seemed so obvious when we began, actually very strange. For what has become a commonplace in our time is not so much that suffering creates a problem for religions as that suffering creates the *opportunity* for religions; and the reason why that has become a commonplace is because it is derived from the pervasive analysis of religion, associated with Marx and Freud, but now almost an automatic reflex in popular accounts of religion. It is the analysis of religions which sees them as generating their power over human beings from the painful inequalities of existence and from the indifference of a hostile universe. To quote the *Great Soviet Encyclopedia,* from its entry under Hell: "Hell: According to the majority of religious teachings, the abode of the souls of sinners supposedly doomed to eternal suffering. . . . Theologians and clergymen use the concept of hell, which they contrast with paradise, to influence the conscience and feelings of believers."[3]

In fact, both Marx and Freud were capable of far greater subtlety than the crude, compensatory understanding of religion often attributed to them. But even so, there is no mistaking the thrust of the argument in both, that religions hold sway over human affections precisely because they offer an escape from the afflictions of this world, or a compensation for them. Even if we go back as far as the fragments of Marx's earliest work, this note is unmistakable. While he was still a student, he began a novel, *Scorpion and Felix,* which he never finished. What a different world it would now be if the novel had been better and Marx had remained a novelist for life! But in what he did complete, the ambiguity of perspective is already apparent which was later to culminate in his argument that the construction of heaven is a reflection of the real world. As Arend van Leeuwen summarizes it:

> In a passage which reads like an ironic comment on the New Testament parable of the Last Judgment (Matt. 25), the contrast between right and left is reduced to absurdity. Of course, if God's countenance sported a nose, it would be evident what is right and what is left. But they are completely relative concepts. If God were to turn over, after He had dreamt the previous night, then the goats would be standing at his right hand and the sheep at His left. If we could define what is right and what is left, therefore, the whole problem of creation would be solved. But as a matter of fact, we are all in the position of Faust: we don't know which side is right which is left: our life is a circus, we run in a circle, we look about us in all directions, until we bite the dust at last and are killed by the gladiator, life itself. We desperately need a new Saviour, because agonizing thought that keeps me awake, ruins my health, slays me!—we cannot distinguish the left from the right side, we cannot tell the location of either.[4]

If the criteria of judgment cannot be located in heaven, that is simply because they are a reflection in the imagination of the only real judgments of which we can be certain, those on earth. To quote the most familiar statement of this theme:

> Man, who looked for a superman in the fantastic reality of heaven and found nothing there but the reflexion of himself, will no longer be disposed to find but the semblance of himself, the non-human (*Unmensch*) where he seeks and must seek his true reality.
>
> The basis of irreligious criticism is: Man makes religion, religion does not make man. In other words, religion is the self-consciousness and self-feeling of man who has either not yet found himself or has already lost himself again. But man is no abstract being sitting outside the world. Man is the world of man, the state, society. This state, this society, produce religion, a reversed world-consciousness, because they are a

reversed world. Religion is the general theory of that world, its encyclopaedic compendium, its logic in a popular form, its spiritualistic *point d'honneur,* its enthusiasm, its moral sanction, its solemn completion, its universal ground for consolation and justification. It is the fantastic realization of the human essence because the human essence has no true reality. The struggle against religion is therefore mediately the fight against the other world, of which religion is the spiritual aroma.

Religious distress is at the same time the expression of real distress and the protest against real distress. Religion is the sigh of the oppressed creature, the heart of a heartless world, just as it is the spirit of a spiritless situation. It is the opium of the people.

The abolition of religion as the illusory happiness of the people is required for their real happiness. The demand to give up the illusions about its condition is the demand to give up a condition which needs illusions. The criticism of religion is therefore in embryo the criticism of the vale of woe, the halo of which is religion.

Criticism has plucked the imaginary flowers from the chain not so that man will wear the chain without any fantasy or consolation but so that he will shake off the chain and cull the living flower. The criticism of religion disillusions man to make him think and act and shape his reality like a man who has been disillusioned and has come to reason, so that he will revolve round himself and therefore round his true sun. Religion is only the illusory sun which revolves round man as long as he does not revolve round himself. The task of history, therefore, once the world beyond the truth has disappeared, is to establish the truth of this world. The immediate task of philosophy, which is at the service of history, once the saintly form of human self-alienation has been unmasked, is to unmask self-alienation in its unholy forms. Thus the criticism of heaven turns into the criticism of the earth, the criticism of religion into the criticism of right and the criticism of theology into the criticism of politics.[5]

That familiar passage is the clearest expression of Marx's understanding of the relation between religion and suffering; and when he wrote of the criticism of religion stripping away the illusion with which people have attempted to alleviate their distress, not in reality, but in the imagination, then the connection with Freud is obvious. Not that Freud had particular sympathy with Marx; but Freud also believed that when he was reflecting on the continuing function of religion in human life, he was reflecting on the future of an illusion. That particular work is one of the most implausible of all Freud's writings; indeed, one could go further and say that in its attitudes to what he called "the great mass of the uneducated and oppressed," in contrast to the "educated people and the brain-workers," few arguments more dangerous in their possible application were ever put forward while Freud was alive—except that *Die Zukunft einer Illusion* was written and first published in 1927, which happened also to be the year of the first Nuremburg rally.[6]

But Freud was not always so casual as he makes himself appear in *The Future of an Illusion*. If we retreat into his earlier life, as we did in the case of Marx, we find a much greater caution in his opinions. In the second year of World War I, Freud read a paper to the Bene Berith, the Jewish society to which he belonged in Vienna. It was called, "Our Attitude Towards Death." Together with another essay on "The Disillusionment of the War," it was published under the title, *Zeitgemässes über Krieg und Tod.*[7] In the second section on death, summarized his argument in *Totem and Taboo,* with its completely unverifiable and wholly improbable speculations about the primal horde and primal guilt; and he also anticipated a main argument in his later work, that man, confronting the reality of death, could not admit its finality, and therefore constructed imaginary ways in which its reality could be admitted and its finality denied:

What the attitude of prehistoric man was towards death is, of course, only known to us by inferences and constructions, but I believe that these methods have furnished us with fairly trustworthy conclusions.

Primaeval man took up a very remarkable attitude towards death. It was far from consistent: it was indeed most contradictory. On the one hand, he took death seriously, recognized it as the termination of life and made use of it in that sense; on the other hand, he also denied death and reduced it to nothing. This contradiction arose from the fact that he took up radically different attitudes towards the death of other people, of strangers, of enemies, and towards his own. He had no objection to someone else's death; it meant the annihilation of someone he hated, and primitive man had no scruples against bringing it about. He was no doubt a very passionate create and more cruel and more malignant than other animals. He liked to kill, and killed as a matter of course. The instinct which is said to restrain other animals from killing and devouring their own species need not be attributed to him.

Hence the primaeval history of mankind is filled with murder. Even to-day, the history of the world which our children learn at school is essentially a series of murders of peoples. The obscure sense of guilt to which mankind has been subject since prehistoric times, and which in some religions has been condensed into the doctrine of primal guilt, of original sin, is probably the outcome of a blood-guilt incurred by prehistoric man. In my book *Totem and Taboo* (1912-13) I have, following clues given by Robertson Smith, Atkinson and Charles Darwin, tried to guess the nature of this primal guilt, and I believe, too, that the Christian doctrine of to-day enables us to deduce it. If the Son of God was obliged to sacrifice his life to redeem mankind from original sin, then by the law of talion, the requital of like by like, that sin must have been a killing, a murder. Nothing else could call for the sacrifice of a life for its expiation. And if the original sin was an offence against God the Father, the primal crime of mankind must have been a parricide, the killing of the primal father of that primitive human horde, whose mnemic image was later transfigured into a deity.

His own death was certainly just as unimaginable and unreal for primaeval man as it is for any one of us to-day. But there was for him one case in which the two opposite attitudes towards death collided and came into conflict with each other; and this case became highly important and productive of far-reaching consequence. It occurred when primaeval man saw someone who belonged to him die—his wife, his child, his friend—whom he undoubtedly loved as we love ours, for love cannot be much younger than the lust to kill. Then, in his pain, he was forced to learn that one can die, too, oneself, and his whole being revolted against the admission; for each of these loved ones was, after all, a part of his own beloved self. But, on the other hand, deaths such as these pleased him as well, since in each of the loved persons there was also something of the stranger. The law of ambivalence of feeling, which to this day governs our emotional relations with those whom we love most, certainly had a very much wider validity in primaeval times. Thus these beloved dead had also been enemies and strangers who had aroused in him some degree of hostile feeling.

Philosophers have declared that the intellectual enigma presented to primaeval man by the picture of death forced him to reflection, and thus became the starting-point of all speculation. I believe that here the philosophers are thinking too philosophically, and giving too little consideration to the motives that were primarily operative. I should like therefore to limit and correct their assertion. In my view, primaeval man must have triumphed beside the body of his slain enemy, without being led to rack his brains about the enigma of life and death. What released the spirit of enquiry in man was not the intellectual enigma, and not every death, but the conflict of feeling at the death of loved yet alien and hated persons. Of this conflict of feeling psychology was the first offspring. Man could no longer keep death at a distance, for he had tasted it in his pain about the dead; but he was nevertheless unwilling to acknowledge it, for he could not conceive of himself as dead. So he devised a compromise: he conceded the fact of his own death as well, but denied it the significance of annihilation—a significance which he had had no motive for denying where the death of his enemy was concerned. It was beside the dead body of someone he loved that he invented spirits, and his sense of guilt at the satisfaction mingled with his sorrow turned these new-born spirits into evil demons that had to be dreaded. The (physical) changes brought about by death suggested to him the division of the individual into a body and a soul—originally several souls. In this way his train of thought ran parallel with the process of disintegration which sets in with death. His persisting memory of the dead became the basis for assuming other forms of existence and gave him the conception of a life continuing after apparent death.[8]

And on this basis also it is not difficult to see how the compensation and wish-fulfilment arguments of *The Future of an Illusion* came to be constructed:

> To assess the truth-value of religious doctrines does not lie within the scope of the present enquiry. It is enough for us that we have recognized them as being, in their psychological nature, illusions. . . . We know approximately at what periods and by what kind of men religious doctrines were created. If in addition we discover the motives which led to this, our attitude to the problem of religion will undergo a marked displacement. We shall tell ourselves that it would be very nice if there were a God who created the world and was a benevolent Providence, and if there were a moral order in the universe and an after-life; but it is a very striking fact that all this is exactly as we are bound to wish it to be. And it would be more remarkable still if our wretched, ignorant and downtrodden ancestors had succeeded in solving all these difficult riddles of the universe.[9]

But in his earlier essay, Freud was actually more sensitive to the complexity of the evidence. For what is undoubtedly remarkable about the earliest written evidence about beliefs in life after death is the extreme reticence of those speculations. I stress the phrase "written evidence," because burial customs unaccompanied by any reflection on their meaning can always be interpreted to support completely opposite inferences. This is a point made by Kurtz & Boardman on Greek burials,[10] and also by J. Z. Young, in much more general and open terms."[11] But when we get to the written reflections on the nature of death and of a possible existence beyond death, then what we know is that with one important category of exception, the earliest understanding of death and its aftermath was that death is something to be postponed as long as possible, and that life after death is emphatically not to be desired as a place of compensation or bliss. At the very most, a thin, insubstantial shadow of a person might continue, a kind of memory trace of a person without any power or form through which to enjoy a continuing life. In Greece, Mesopotamia, India, China, and perhaps most familiarly in Israel, the earliest beliefs in life after death were beliefs in the persistence, perhaps of some trace of the dead, but of no substantial continuity—except for heroic individuals (with heroism of course differently defined in different cultures) who are exempted from death and who are taken, often literally, to other outcome. To take the most familiar examples: far from there being in Tanach (in what Christians call the Old Testament) a compensation for suffering after death, there is *no* belief, until the very end of the Biblical period, in a continuity of life with God after death, except for the heroic figures of Enoch and Elijah who are literally taken (*ahad*) into the sky.

Freud actually recognized this as being factually the case, but he failed to understand the significance of what he had seen. Having argued at the end of the passage previously quoted, that man's "persisting memory of the dead became the basis for assuming other forms of existence and gave him the conception of life continuing after apparent death," he then went on:

> The subsequent existences were at first no more than appendages to the existence which death had brought to a close—shadowy, empty of content, and valued at little until later times; they still bore the character of wretched makeshifts. We may recall the answer to Odysseus by the soul of Achilles:
> "For of old, when thou wast alive, we Argives honored thee even as the gods, and now that thou art here, thou rulest mightily over the dead. Wherefore grieve not at all that thou are dead, Achilles."
> So I spoke, and he straightway made answer and said:
> "Nay, seek not to speak soothingly to me of death, glorious Odysseus. I should choose, so I might live on earth, to serve as the hireling of another, of some portionless man whose livelihood was but small, rather than to be Lord over all the dead that have perished."
> Or in Heine's powerful and bitter parody:
> Der kleinste lebendige Philister
> Zu Stuckert am Neckar

> Viel glücklicher ist er
> Als ich, der Pelide, der tote Held,
> Der Schattenfürst in der Unterwelt.
>
> It was only later that religions succeeded in representing
> this after-life as the more desirable, the truly valid one, and in
> reducing the life which is ended by death to a mere prepara-
> tion. After this, it was no more than consistent to extend life
> backwards into the past, to form the notion of earlier ex-
> istences, of the transmigration of souls and reincarnation, all
> with the purpose of depriving death of its meaning as the ter-
> mination of life. So early did the denial of death, which we
> have described as a "conventional and cultural attitude," have
> its origin.[12]

But what Freud missed in this argument is the cautious—one might well say austerely rigorous—realism in the human understanding of suffering, accident, and death. That in itself is curious when one reflects how preoccupied Freud was throughout his life with the reality of death, as Max Schur's classic and sombre study, *Freud, Living and Dying,* makes clear. On December 6, 1936, Freud wrote to Marie Bonaparte:

> If you, at the youthful age of 54 can't help thinking so often of
> death, are you surprised that at 80½ I keep brooding on
> whether I shall reach the age of my father and brother, or even
> that of my mother, tortured as I am by the conflict between the
> desire for rest, the dread of renewed suffering (which a pro-
> longation of life would bring with it) and the anticipation of
> sorrow at being separated from everything to which I am still
> attached? (Schur, p. 485).

But that letter has been written again and again, time after time, throughout the whole of human history—even in what Freud regarded as the age of childish credulity. Death was originally regarded as an invasion, a contingent "breaking-into" the natural continuity of life. Levy-Bruhl gleaned this from 19th century accounts of the first meetings with Australian aborigines;[13] but it is equally apparent in the fact that virtually all the myths gathered so extensively from all over the world relate the origin of death to trivial accidents or to seemingly unimportant choices: life *might* have continued undisturbed, but relatively simple accidents or choices have introduced the disruption of death. Here is an example from the Gilbert Islands, recorded before the arrival of the missionaries and therefore uninfluenced by them:

> Nakaa is the supreme ruler of both gods and humans. In his land of Matang he planted two pandannus palms, one in the north for men and the other in the south for women, and there they lived, neither growing old nor dying. But the time came when Nakaa had to go on a journey, so he summoned the people together to tell them this, and then he sent them back to their own trees. But the people were intrigued by the sight of each other, and before long the men had joined the women under their tree; and not long after, their hair turned grey. Nakaa, on his return, recognised this sign of disobedience and therefore expelled the people from Matang; but he did allow them to take one of the 2 trees with them.
>
> They chose the tree of the women, and Nakaa told them that they had chosen, not the tree of life, which would stay with him in Matang, but the tree of death. He then told them of a way of life and of a ritual for the dead, Te Kaetikawai, which would allow those who adhere to them to return to Matang; and then, as he finally drove them out, he stripped the leaves from the tree of death and used them to wrap up illness and plagues and threw them after the departing people.

It seems perhaps absurd that so much catastrophe could be derived from so slight an offence and so unlucky a choice—never has so much been owed by so many to so little. But the theme is repeated again and again in countless myths of the origin of suffering and death. As I argued in *The Sense of God,* there is no reason in principle why death must have seemed to early men and women the one wholly intransigent limitation which circumscribes the projection of a successful lifeway.[14] What, then, we find in general in the earliest accounts of suffering and death is a rigorous realism—a matter-of-factness which does not engage in wish-fulfillment, or in projection and compensation. Of the early records, the

Vedas come closest to that view, in the belief that admission
to the paradise of Yama and to the ultimate apotheosis may
be a reward for sacrifice and good works. But even this is
realistic in relation to the cosmological perspective of the
Vedas as a whole, in which both the gods and the cosmos
(particularly if the cosmos is a consequence of the gods) are
derived from a more fundamental principle; because in that
perspective all occurrence, whether of life or of death, is the
working out of a single frame of order and disorder.

But even if it were conceded that the Vedas come closest
to a wish-fulfillment theory, it is not so elsewhere, with one
major category of exception. There is certainly no evasion,
no compensation, in the account of the suitors in Hades in
Bk. XXIV of The Odyssey:

ὡς δ' ὅτε νυκτερίδες μυχῷ ἄντρου θεσπεσίοιο
τρίζουσαι ποτέονται, ἐπεί κέ τις ἀποπέσῃσιν
ὁρμαθοῦ ἐκ πέτρης, ἀνά τ' ἀλλήλῃσιν ἔχονται,
ὡς αἱ τετριγυῖαι ἅμ' ἤϊσαν.[15]

There is no evasion or compensation in the epic of
Gilgamesh; there is no evasion or compensation in Israel,
where the whole of Tanach, except at the very end, is written
without a belief that there will be a continuity of life with
God after death; there is no evasion or compensation in the
anatta of early Buddhism, although there will be continuity
of consequence; with the exception of the immortality cult,
there is no evasion or compensation in the earliest Chinese
understanding of the fate of the dead:

> Tzu-lu asked about serving the spiritual beings. Confucius
> said: "If we are not yet able to serve man, how can we serve
> spiritual beings?" Tzu-lu then said: "Then let me ask about
> death." Confucius said: "If we do not yet know about life,
> how can we know about death?"[16]

But some of his later followers were not even so agnostic

as that. Wang Ch'ung, an almost exact contemporary of Jesus, devoted one of his critical essays, "Lun Heng," to death and concluded:

> Human death is like the extinction of fire. When a fire is extinguished, its light does not shine any more, and when man dies, his intellect does not perceive any more. The nature of both is the same. If people nevertheless pretend that the dead have knowledge, they are mistaken. What is the difference between a sick man about to die and a light about to go out?[17]

Extensively, the most that our ancestors could realistically believe is that some faint trace of a person might continue, particularly if it is sustained in the memories of those who survive; and clearly the many rituals in relation to the dead reinforce memory very effectively. But there is a category of exception, of which Egypt is the most familiar example. As early as the Sixth Dynasty, around 2300 B.C., an inscription on the tomb of Herkhuf makes it clear that one's condition after death depends on one's behavior in life:

> I gave bread to the hungry, clothing to the naked, I ferried him who had no boat . . . Never did I say anything evil, to a powerful one against any people; I desired that it might be well with me in the Great God's presence.

But the Egyptians had discovered mummification long before that—probably, in origin, in as accidental a way as other peoples, for example in Peru or in Scandinavia, had discovered that in some circumstances—dried in the burning air, or in peat, or frozen in the ground—bodies do not necessarily decay and disintegrate. To quote the simplest summary of this:

> In Egypt in prehistoric times the dead were buried, sometimes loosely wrapped in mats or skins, in shallow graves, the body being placed in a flexed position. The hot dry desert sand came into direct contact with the skin and often so completely arrested the process of decay that the hair, skin and soft parts are entirely preserved. This phenomenon of natural preserva-

tion was probably made known to the Egyptians through the
ravages of grave robbers whose depredations exposed the
bodies to view. The discovery that the corpses of the dead did
not suffer corruption undoubtedly strengthened, perhaps
originated, the belief in the physical survival of the dead,
which underlies the practice of mummification throughout the
historic period, and prompted the ampler provision of food,
utensils and other objects necessary to physical life which
were buried with the dead . . . Mummification in various
forms has had a wide geographical distribution . . . In North,
Central and South America mummies have been found in
various localities, but the most numerous are those of the Inca
civilization . . . It was once believed that the preservation of
these Inca mummies was due to natural properties of the soil
and climate, and not to artificial measures. But, while the
natural conditions in many localities certainly favour preservation, the circumstances in which many of the mummies were
discovered, closely wrapped in dense coverings and tightly
corded, show that they must have been artifically desiccated
before burial.[19]

This is a very important clue, because it suggests that
our ancestors were nothing like so naive or so susceptible to
illusion as Marx and Freud supposed. What it suggests is that
they were capable of being as realistic about suffering and
death as any person in the 20th century contemplating the
possibility of his or her own oblivion. The analysis of Wang
Ch'ung is austere in its refusal of a continuing spirit:

People say that the dead become ghosts, are conscious, and
can hurt men. Let us examine this by comparing men with
other beings: The dead do not become ghosts, have no consciousness and cannot injure others. How do we know this?
We know it from other beings. Man is a being, and other
creatures are likewise beings. When a creature dies, it does not
become a ghost; for what reason then must man alone become
a ghost, when he expires? Man lives by the vital fluid. When he
dies, this vital fluid is exhausted. It resides in the arteries. At
death the pulse stops, and the vital fluid ceases to work; then
the body decays, and turns into earth and clay. By what could
it become a ghost? Anterior to man's death, his mental
faculties and vital spirit are all in order. When he falls sick, he

becomes giddy, and his vital spirit is affected. Death is the climax of sickness. If even during a sickness, which is only a small beginning of death, a man feels confused and giddy, how will it be, when the climax is reached? When the vital spirit is seriously affected, it loses its consciousness, and it is scattered altogether.[20]

Certainly the annihilationists in the classical world or in India or in China may have been a small minority. But they are a reminder that the human mind has been as capable of raising sceptical questions in the past as in the present; and capable also of questioning the other way round, whether an annihilationist analysis *does* in fact do justice to the evidence. For what *is* the ontological status of the impressions of there being a continuity beyond death of those who are known to have died? And what if the body does *not* decay? That at once suggests a plausible reason for supposing that the living aspect of a person is not wholly extinguished either. And it is by such cues of plausibility that the cautious exploration took place of the possible continuity of experience beyond death. But it was—and is—an exploration tied to the apparent data. And what are they? The most extensive are the most obvious, the observations of death and renewal in nature. If the seed falls to the ground and is born again into more abundant life, perhaps also the body will do the same; if the very same breath which returns finally to the air in death is the air which, when I have breathed it, you can inhale in your turn, perhaps also what I have been when alive can be breathed into another life; if the smoke of a fire can be carried beyond discernment into the sky, perhaps also the smoke of the burned body will carry the reality of that person beyond our discernment; if salt dissolved in water disappears and yet if the water is tasted is still undoubtedly present, perhaps also we will be dissolved in earth or fire and yet will still be discernibly present; if observably some of the features of parents and grandparents recur in offspring, perhaps also more than the color of the eyes and the shape of a nose is transmitted from life to life; if memory creates a strange but un-mistakable continuity in our own life, perhaps memory will sustain a continuity beyond our life; if the snake sloughs its skin and lives on with its dead and useless coverings left behind, perhaps also we will shed this body and live in a new realization.

All these, and many other, cues of plausibility underlie the myths and rituals of the human exploration of death. And because the cues occur in the natural order, just as death occurs in the natural order, so we find that the *same* cues are deployed in very different forms of expression. To take the last example, the snake and the skin: in Melanesia, the story goes that humans were first immortal, shedding their skins like snakes. But Quat the trickster one day laid Mate on a plank and covered him and said that if shell conches were loudly blown, death could not approach him. In the meantime he and the relatives divided up Mate's property. On the fifth day, the cover was removed and Mate was found to be nothing but a skeleton. At once Quat sent his brother Tagoro to Panoi, the dividing place of the roads that lead to the underworld and the skyworld, to ensure that Mate would take the upper road. But Quat had 11 brothers called Tagoro, including one who was known as Tagoro the Wise; however, Quat sent Tagoro the Foolish. Tagoro the foolish blocked the wrong road, so that Mate, death, descended to the under-world, where all people have been following him ever since. But elsewhere that same cue of plausibility, the snake and its skin, was more literally interpreted. In Middle America, human sacrifices had their skins sloughed forcibly from them—i. e. they were flayed, and the priests then stepped into the skins and wore them to symbolize the renewal of life.

So the point is this: there is no difficulty in the history of religions, in exemplifying what Marx and Freud said about compensation, projection, and wish-fulfillment. Again and again we can find exemplified exactly what they claimed to be the essence of religion or the reason why religious belief exercises such power in human imagination. But what we must emphatically resist is the conclusion that nothing else is exemplified, or that history is a simple evolutionary progression from wretched ignorance and superstition to enlightenment, from exploitation to liberation. Any analysis of that kind is too literally superficial: it confuses the surface picture through which people have expressed or explored their experience with the truth or falsity of that experience. We may doubt the actual existence of Prometheus and still understand and share the experience which Aeschylus explored. We may doubt whether the *Gita* records a literal and actual encounter between Krishna and Arjuna, and yet still understand very well what the *Gita* is talking about. The exploration of a continuity of life beyond death may well be motivated by wish-fulfillment and may often be deployed to perpetuate exploitation and alienation; but the development of what later became detailed pictures of heaven or of hell are parasitic on a much more cautious and prosaic interpretation of experience in this life. The point is simply this: human lives are set within parameters or boundaries of possibility: it is not possible (at least as yet) to be born without a parent; it is not possible to descend to the bottom of the Atlantic and live there without in some form taking your oxygen with you; it is not possible by an act of will to live to the age of Methuselah.

Not only do we live within the boundaries of possibility; we also live on the basis of programs in the brain, some of which are implicit as a consequence of the genetic code. What is clearly unusual about the human animal is that it monitors and interprets to itself the process and expression of its life within those very powerful constraints. As the poet W. S. Merwin once put it, "We are like dice, but dice somewhat in command of their own combinations." The experiences of men and women as they construct a lifestyle from birth to death are clearly not uniform, but they are consistent; or at least they are sufficiently consistent for us to sit down to lunch with Sophocles, to take tea with Nagarjuna, and to have supper with Lao Tzu. This does *not* mean that their experiences are *identical* with ours, but rather that their lives are constructed within the same boundaries of possibility so that one generation is not wholly alien from the next in its experiences of itself. This means that when human beings explore the reality of suffering and death, they may well identify those realities in different ways, and they may well project hopes and fears in terms and characterizations which we regard as mistaken—for example, in terms of what they propose to be literally the case. But they are mistaken about something which we can recognize as correspondent to ourselves, namely, the experience of constructing a lifestyle in the face of the major limitations which threaten its continuity. The issue of reality then remains an utterly serious one. *Are* the religious pictures—of, shall we say, a relatedness to God which may continue through death—constructed simply as a wish-fulfillment, or simply as a counteractive reflection of this unhappy world, or are they also constructed because there is a sufficient ontological demand for them in the human experience of itself?

It is not an issue of either-or, but one of both-and. And unless we combine the two, we will undoubtedly diminish humanity, because we will reduce the range of what this organism can legitimately—without pretense or self-deceit—be. Ironically, as I have pointed out before, Freud made that combination in the case of libido:[21] yes, certainly we approach the other in the case of sex with all sorts of base, abject, and neurotic motives, and yes, certainly we create the other in the image of our fantasy, both in dream and in the actual encounter; and some of us remain locked into that diminished and impoverished understanding forever. But the ontological reality of the other, the response of the other in the encounter, in his or her actuality—with all his or her neurotic history as well—the otherness of the other in response can create a disturbance like a rock in the midst of a river's flow, and can thus enable us by the matter-of-factness of its own reality to move far beyond the abject point of our departure, or of course to be drowned within the stream. May it not also be the case with God? Yes, certainly we approach the possibility of God for all sorts of abject, wish-fulfillment, exploitative motives, and yes, certainly we create God in the image of our fantasy; and some religious people remain locked into that impoverished understanding. But the apparent response of the other, in the modes of communication which are usually referred to as worship and prayer, the discovery of the other creating consequence in our experience has seemed to many to be a comparable disturbance—a comparable rock in the stream which is its own reality; and as a result of that engagement, in this area as in the other, we are able to be moved far beyond the abject point of our departure. "Blessed be God," as John Donne put it, "that He is God only and divinely like Himself"; and that line of thought leads inevitably to the conclusion of Aquinas, "Unde manifestum est quod Deus non est in genere sicut species."

Thus the issue of ontology will not go away simply by pointing to the absurdity of many of the characterizations of that claimed but unseen reality, or to the uses, in exploitation and wish-fulfillment, to which religious systems have been put. But characterization cannot be identified with ontology: the 18th century characterization of women is in as much need of revision as the 18th century characterization of God; but the need for that revision does not call into question the ontological reality of creatures known as women. Nor does it *necessarily* call into question the ontological reality of God, although in that case there may well be other reasons for the question.

But the issue of reality is exactly the issue which both Marx and Freud deliberately set on one side, Marx by his handling of Kant's Kroners,[22] and Freud by his argument in the passage already quoted, that even if some religious claims *are* well-grounded, the wish-fulfillment theory would be unaffected. But the issue of reality cannot be evaded. For what we share in common with our ancestors whom Freud derided is the exploration of the capacity of the human organism, which is still constructed within very similar boundaries and constraints.

And what I mean by the exploration of capacity is the exploration of what this strange architecture of matter or of energy is capable of being and becoming. We know that we are capable of walking, eating, talking, drinking; and when our ancestors talk of these things, although we cannot possibly know what exact attitudes and feelings they brought to such experiences or activities, we are not wholly disconnected from their language. We know that we are capable of experiencing feelings which we label (culturally) as beauty, truth, love, fear, hope. We know that we are capable of experiencing, and sometimes of inducing by appropriate practices, brain behavior's, the consequences of which are summarized as altered states of consciousness; and these altered states of consciousness are known about very extensively, both in space and time. It is equally widely and universally known that we are capable of God—capable, that is, of states of brain behavior in particular modes of attentiveness to their possibility, which have traditionally been described as God-related and God-derived.

All these are capacities of that strange accumulation of matter and energy which constitute you in human form. What we have to add here is that this strange architecture of energy is also capable of great destruction, of great violence, of great suffering, of great evil. The religious exploration of ourselves insists on taking seriously the whole range of our possibility, the evil as much as the good, the sense of God as much as the sense of the devil—the *whole* range, and not an impoverished and diminished fragment of it. There was once a French minister, Viviani, who rejoiced to say:

> We have said to the man weighed down by daily work and sorrow . . . that behind those clouds upon which his sad eyes are fixed are nothing but celestial chimeras. With a splendid

gesture we have put out the lights in the heavens and no one will ever light them.

On this Péguy commented:

> For the first time since the world began a romantic sees the gesture of putting out lights as splendid. . . . The municipal lamp lighter puts out the lamps as well as lighting them, yet until now lighting has been considered so much more honourable that we would have been ashamed to call him a lamp extinguisher.[23]

That is why I have spent so long examining whether suffering is a *problem* for religions or whether it is the *opportunity* which creates them and gives them their power. It is a falsely dichotomous question, and a dangerous one at that, because it traps us into a choice which is not only misleading but unnecessary.

Many instances of the fallacy of the false dichotomy are relatively innocent, particularly when they occur in such booktitles as *Plato: Totalitarian or Democrat; John D. Rockefeller: Robber Baron or Industrial Statesman; The New Deal: Revolution or Evolution.*[24] But the dichotomy created by the massively persuasive analyses of Marx and Freud is very dangerous indeed. For if we *do* allow ourselves to be trapped into that frame of argument, we will completely miss the point that while religions may well exemplify all that Marx and Freud suggest, they also preserve and sustain a rigorously cautious exploration of human capacity. They bring us to a seriousness about ourselves, about human complexity, about suffering, about evil—a seriousness which the simplified and inaccurate historicism of Marx and Freud makes completely impossible, because it always finds a justification, by way of explanation, for the extinction of the light. One has only to consider the justifications put forward for Stalin or for the Khmer Rouge to see the point. It is the religious exploration which alone continues to take us into the very heart of darkness. And unless we comprehend the seriousness of that religious engagement with the often unwilled disaster and tragedy in the enterprise of life, then of course the religious response to suffering will seem as superficial and unconvincingly palliative as Marx and Freud supposed.

"The heart of darkness": *that* is the territory which religions characteristically explore—not as a kind of intellectual curiosity, but because the very ground on which we stand trembles beneath our feet. The phrase "the heart of darkness" was of course chosen deliberately as a reminder of Conrad's novel, superficially a story of class and race exploitation and its nemesis, but in fact a study of human complexity and its capacity for disaster within the boundaries of the historically and geographically determined. For what was it that Marlowe saw playing through the face of Kurtz as he lay dying, as the moon struggles to reveal itself through a layer of ragged cloud? "Sombre pride?" "Ruthless power?" "Craven terror?"[25] Yes. But all three summarized as "an intense and hopeless despair."[26] And as Kurtz died, "he cried out twice, a cry that was no more than a breath: 'The horror! The horror!'"[27] The next spoken words in the book are of course the words which T. S. Eliot set at the head of "The Hollow Men," the words of the insolent manager's boy, "Mistah Kurtz—he dead."[28] Always the shadow falls:

> Between the conception
> And the creation
> Between the emotion
> And the response
> Falls the shadow.

We are the hollow men. The dried and shrunken heads, stuck on poles by Kurtz's house, were the first glimpse Marlow had into the heart of darkness, where the wilderness had whispered to Kurtz "things about himself which he did not know, things of which he had no conception till he took counsel with this great solitude—and the whisper had proved irresistibly fascinating. It echoed loudly within him because he was hollow at the core.''[29] We are the hollow men:

> Those who have crossed
> With direct eyes, to death's other Kingdom
> Remember us—if at all—not as lost
> Violent souls, but only
> As the hollow men.

And at the end, on his death bed, the voice of Kurtz was strong to the very last, hiding in the folds of eloquence the barren darkness of his heart:

> Oh, he struggled! he struggled! The wastes of his weary brain were haunted by shadowy images now . . . The shade of the original Kurtz frequented the bedside of the hollow sham, whose fat it was to be buried presently in the mould of primaeval earth.[30]

> Between the idea
> And the reality
> Between the notion
> And the act
> Falls the Shadow.

This too is a part of the boundary within which the construction of human life is set—within which the transaction of energy occurs in human form. The purpose and the importance of Stauros is to help us to understand the darkness, not to underestimate the shadow, and perhaps also, by this realism, to exorcise the devils which leap within our life. Stauros is rooted in the European experience of the 1930s and 1940s. It is not hard to recognize there the heart of darkness, which is a part of the human capacity of which I have spoken. But recognition of enormity is not enough. We have also to become more sensitive to the occurrence within ourselves of what a German woman during the war called *seelische Hornhaut*: the callousing—or even more literally the corneal blinding—of the emotional and mental self. The phrase comes from the diary of Ursula von Kardoff, later published as *Berliner Aufzeichnungen*, where she noted that her brother Jurgen grew visibly pale when he saw in the street an old Jewish woman and a young girl, both clearly distressed. "Jurgen," she wrote, "has as little as Father of that emotional callousing with which so many people try to get by."[31] And on March 3, 1943, she wrote:

> Frau Liebermann is dead [Frau Liebermann was the wife of the Jewish painter, Max Liebermann, and was a friend of the Kardoff family]. They came to fetch her with a stretcher to deport her to Poland—this 85 year old woman. She took poison at that moment, and she died a day later in the Jewish hospital without regaining consciousness. What ugly manifestation of evil shows itself here, and why does it show itself particularly among our people? By what transformation has a group of people who are basically good-natured and friendly been turned into such devils?[32]

It is onto that ground that Stauros is determined to take us, and it is in relation to that final question that it bids us to be realistic and unevasive in our awareness of ourselves. We have the capacity for great generosity, for self-sacrifice, for love; we also have the capacity for actions and for acquiescence which create great evil and suffering for others and for ourselves. Sometimes one wonders how any human being could ever be capable of the appalling things that are done. Yet they are not wholly other than ourselves; nor are they necessarily past all redemption. For one remembers also from that same Germany the final episode of von Trott's life. Adam von Trott was one of those involved in the July plot of 1944. Before the war, he had been an apologist for the necessity of the Nazi regime, as representing the only possible means to Germany's revival. But he changed because of his experience of Nazi rule; he joined the plot, and he received the news of the failure of the plot in his flat in Berlin. As he waited for the inevitable arrest and execution, he was visited by a friend, Melchers, who knew about the plot, but who was not himself arrested, and who therefore has left us this account of those last moments of freedom. Melchers himself flew into a rage at the thought of how the conspiracy had been bungled, but:

> Trott suddenly grew very gentle. "Are you angry?" he said. "Remember these people must pay for this thing with their lives!" There was a depressed silence between us . . . I asked if he had any hope for the future. "No," he answered, "there is no hope left now, or for the future. This is the end. The disaster must take its course—till there shall be left no stone upon another. Hitler will carry on this madman's war till everything is destroyed." "And yet," he added, "it is good all the same that there were people ready to break this reign of terror. It remains an historical fact, and more than that, a symptom."[33]

On this, Christopher Sykes, who wrote the life of von Trott, commented:

> The story of Adam von Trott's life is not that of a saint of anti-Nazism; it is something more human. To see it in hagiographic terms is to miss its significance, as though one were to see *Hamlet* solely as an edifying play on the subject of stainless filial duty. His story is of a man who met temptation and resisted it, sometimes with difficulty and sometimes without perfect success; of a man whose perception could be clouded, and who sought for moral truth with the stumbles of our human weakness. All the more wonderful is his ultimate moral triumph.[34]

This, then, is the point and the importance of the Stauros conference, that it bids us be serious about ourselves. Beyond the ultimately trivializing generalizations of Marx and Freud, exemplified though those generalizations often are, there lies more serious ground to be explored: the disposition of life within the boundaries of suffering and transcendence; the human capacity to gain the whole world and lose its own soul; the recognition that life yields to life, part to part, and that the attainment of the whole, whether it be the forms of life on a coral reef or in a modern city, seem to demand a sacrifice that few of the components of the scene are anxious to volunteer on their account. Sacrifice as the fundamental theme of all appearance and manifestation is most obvious in the Indian tradition; but it is deep within Christianity as well, in the figure held upon a cross—life yielding not simply *to* life giving place to other life but *for* life.

The meaning and the demand of *that* dimension of suffering are also a part of Stauros, as the name itself makes clear. Who causes the sharpness of the thorn? The Christian response has been, not so much to answer that question, as to say that the attainment of the whole, the reintegration of the divided parts into the realization of their true capacity in God, includes the sharpness of the thorn:[35] it is by that route, and not by evasion of it, that redemption is wrought, as in the ancient Latin hymn:

O spina mirabilis
Malorum solatium.

Wishful thinking? Compensatory reflection? Yes, both these have been exemplified in Christian life and history. But equally there has been exemplified a transaction in human life as a consequence of the cross which has given us, here on earth, "a means of grace and a hope of glory."[36] Whether that demonstration and that experience are wholly illusory is not an issue that can be resolved by rhetoric. It requires a serious and unfrightened exploration of what we really are. It is to that exploration that Stauros leads us, and to which we are invited to respond.

What, then, in brief, lies within a Christian response to that question? An absolute and unyielding realism about ourselves—a realism which should be deriving more insight than it is from the *whole* human exploration of its capacity, but which gains decisive insight and actual transformation from the person of Christ. One of the inhibiting paradoxes of

Christian history is that part of the realism about ourselves, about the shadow between the notion and the act which falls in every human life without exception, has been summarized in the concept of original sin; but because that concept has asserted the universality of failure, together with the fact that that failure is rooted genetically and contextually (in terms of the environment which forms us) in circumstances not of our own choice or control, the human exploration of itself has been able to be dismissed by *some* Christian interpretations as being of no saving value, or even as being a rebellion against God's own choice of the way of redemption. A true realism about ourselves needs a descriptive concept like original sin, and it is not difficult to see how that concept is to be translated into contemporary terms, but the concept and the reality to which it points need to be interpreted with a Thomist rather than Calvinist emphasis, or even more with an Eastern Christianity emphasis, rather than a Western. Realism, then, about the shadow within ourselves:

> Albion said: "O Lord, what can I do? my Selfhood cruel
> Marches against thee, deceitful, from Sinai and from Edom
> Into the Wilderness of Judah, to meet thee in his pride."[37]

We began with Blake and have returned in full circle to him; for Blake also asserts, through a blind and apparently uncaring universe, an equal realism about our strange capacity for good—an assertion of significance even in the apparent waste and blind alleys of the universe and its evolution. As Pascal once put it, "Nothwithstanding the sight of all our miseries which press upon us and take us by the throat, we have an instinct which we cannot repress and which lifts us up.[38] That is an assertion which is almost overwhelmingly difficult to maintain, particularly in our own time; and it is that assertion also which Freud regarded as the root cause of wishful thinking. But it is not wishful thinking in Blake's understanding, where the realization of that capacity for significance and good is itself "a little death":

> . . . Every kindness to another is a little Death
> In the Divine Image, nor can Man exist but by Brotherhood.[39]

This is at the heart of the Christian response, and it is not sentimental: this quality of engagement, in which we realize our nature and our capacity—in which, that is, we realize what we can be and perhaps are meant to be—*is* a little death, repeated again and again. It does not evade suffering but goes through it as the necessary condition of succession and relatedness; you cannot have a complicated, evolved universe without it; you cannot have human diversity and idiosyncrasy without it; in other words, you cannot have a soul without death. And in respect of relationship, what are for us the sexual overtones of "the little death" are by no means vulgar or inappropriate: sexual union in the circumstance of love has always been the furthest symbol of self-giving and self-loss, as mystics in virtually every religious tradition have well known. The Christian assertion remains that the loss of one's self, the dying to one's self, is the gain of one's relatedness to others and to God.

> Jesus replied: "Fear not Albion: unless I die thou cans't not live; But if I die I shall arise again and thou with me.
> This is Friendship and Brotherhood; without it Man Is Not."
> So Jesus spoke: the Covering Cherub coming on in darkness Overshadow'd them, and Jesus said: "Thus do Men in Eternity One for another to put off, by forgiveness, every sin." Albion reply'd: "Cannot Man exist without Mysterious Offering of Self for Another? Is this Friendship and Brotherhood? . . . " Jesus said: "Wouldest thou love one who never died for thee? And if God dieth not for Man and giveth not himself Eternally for Man, Man could not exist; for Man is love As God is love; every kindness to another is a little Death In the Divine Image, nor can Man exist but by Brotherhood."
> So saying the Cloud overshadowing divided them asunder. Albion stood in terror, not for himself but for his Friend Divine; and Self was lost in the contemplation of faith And wonder at the Divine Mercy and at Los's sublime honour.[40]

But is that significance, which undoubtedly and as a matter of fact can be realized within the human frame, *ultimate*? What trace, if any (to go back to the language of our ancestors), does that sacrificial realization of relatedness have beyond death? Here, it is essential to realize that although many of the older cues of plausibility, which were suggestive to our ancestors (snakes and skins, seeds and ground), are no longer suggestive to us (in general); there are now many other cues of plausibility but there may be a continuity through death. For example, books like R. A. Moody's *Lye after Lye* or Ian Currie's *You Cannot Die* (to quote only two out of many examples) articulate "out of the body" experiences which have long been known about but which suddenly confront at least some people with a plausible reinforcement of the belief that death may not be the end. But exactly as was the case with the earlier historical examples, so here: this "cue of plausibility" does not "prove" that there will be a life after death of a particular form, or that there will be life after death. Many different conclusions and rituals can be drawn from the same data.

To give another example of a novel cue of plausibility: in *The Religious Imagination* I have tried to indicate why, provided we are talking about the self created in conditions or networks of relatedness (and it is actually impossible to conceive of the human self in any other condition, as we experience that self here and now, even though in some religious practices we may be able to abstract our self from particular circumstances of relationship), then it is not in the least difficult to see that our relatedness to God could be realized beyond death. Many questions then remain about the nature of that realization, and about the self-consciousness which might obtain in it. As Festugière once put it, "L'immortalité n'a pas de sens que si c'est bien moi-même qui dure."[41] But maybe we have to lose even *that* attachment to the self, as the Buddha already realized in the actual moment of enlightenment. Even so, that there could be continuity of relatedness beyond death is not simply possible; it is actually highly probable in the universe as we happen to understand it at the present time. What the Christian has to say—*has* to say in response to the data which include the cross and the resurrection—is that death alone can decipher the code of death. It is therefore a fundamental responsibility for Christians at the present time not to lose confidence in the worth or the truth of what they propose about the human condition and its capacity. Surely these are not the times for an arrogant over-confidence at the opposite extreme, particularly when one bears in mind the contribution that Christian systems, jealous in their boundary maintenance, have made to human suffering in the past and continue to make. But we do have a reason for the hope that is in us.[42] And it is the greatest possible privilege of our growth and our maturity to express that gain-through-loss in action and in life, whereby we are enabled to stand amongst others as those who serve.[43] Therefore, as I concluded the recent article in *Concilium* (see footnote 2), let us regain our confidence in the resources which supply that quality of life; and let us be grateful to the Stauros Association for the encouragement it gives us in that endeavor.

> A Christian is rooted in the resources created by God in Christ, and they become the control and the inspiration of his life—in cybernetic language, they become the constant constraint[44] . . . What is urgently required is a new and restored confidence: confidence in the worth of what is discovered of God in Christ, . . . and the confidence to sit down with Paul and realise that there may be many different expressions of life derived from the same resource . . . The first and greatest thing is this, that we should have sufficient confidence in our fellow-Christians, which means a sufficient love for them, to regard the bewildering varieties of life which are likely to occur, not as a threat or as a disturbance, but as a consequence of the prolific exuberance of creation, which, in its apparent wastefulness, is the root of all our sorrow, but which, in its constant renewal and succession, is the ground of our hope and joy.

Discussion

QUESTION: The doctor spoke much about the different attitudes toward death, but I would like to know more about the attitudes regarding suffering, in particular the ones he indicated concerning the Greeks or Job lamenting the very day of his birth. If he had died, he would have gone down to Hades where everything is equal. The problem of suffering seems to be that some good suffer and die and why is this if all things are equal? The problem then is not so much in the human response, but why does God allow this. If God is intelligent and not capricious, if He is good, then how do we explain the suffering that is going on, especially among the good?

ANSWER: The immediate answer to that is that the Book of Job has been written in many languages. In the book, *The Religious Imagination* there is a long chapter on the death of God in the Greek and Jewish worlds. Sometimes we forget that the death of God is not a modern American invention; it has happened in many religions, in many generations. Indeed you may even say that it happens in every life in the occurrence of inexplicable suffering. It's only when you take the problem of the death of God seriously enough in the Jewish and Hellenistic world that you see what Jesus meant to those who became Christians out of the Greek and Jewish worlds because Jesus seemed to them to solve the problem of the death of God. In general, however, the death of God occurs exactly as you are describing. It occurs again and again at this knife edge that you have drawn out of its sheath, but the thing to remember is that although many characterizations of God go to extinction, they do not all go down the chute. Why do some characterizations of God reform themselves beyond the Job crisis or whatever? Freud and Marx say for compensation and wish-fulfillment, and I say yes, surely for that, but not for that alone. The history of religions gives us the sense of Edwin Muir's poem, "The Interceptor" where we do get rid of Him; we get rid of the childish picture and then we are confronted across the road and the recharacterization has to occur.

QUESTION: You stated that suffering creates opportunities for religions. How does that tie in with the present evolution of cults?

ANSWER: One would have to do a very careful and precise analysis of each particular cult. One generalization you can make about religions is that you can't generalize. There is a very wide range of ways in which the issue we are concerned with, suffering and significance, continuity and value or disintegration and waste, is going to be taken up by the cult, ranging from the Jones Church or the cults which deliberately espouse violence all the way through to abstraction into quietness and peace. One would have to study each one in terms of what it is actually doing. It is in this area of experience of ourselves, in Hardy's theory, that in much of our education we are forced to take a full look at the worst, and yet as Hardy said in one of his letters, "We nevertheless know that we are more than we are told we can be." It's in that kind of tension, of which suffering is a particular lens through which we see those two polarities, that clearly many of the new religions and cults are gaining their dynamic.

QUESTION: Dr. Bowker, my question pertains to the relationship between suffering and mysticism. We are saying that suffering is an intense experience of some kind; the general definition of mystical experience is that it is an intense experience of God. We know from history that many of the great mystics were also great suffers. Would you comment on the relationship between suffering and mysticism.

ANSWER: I'm not sure that everyone in this room would accept that general definition of mysticism. It's the same thing about not rushing too fast in concluding that all things are instances of the same thing simply because they are referred to by the same name. There are two levels on which to answer this. The first level is in terms of the straightforward attempt to understand the mechanisms of brain behavior. That would be a behavioral kind of approach that manifestly says that the induction of states of brain behavior which are subsequently labeled as mystical by those with experience, is enhanced by practices which involve suffering. So we can go all the way through from flagellants and those dancing on hot coals to asceticism, withdrawal of sensory stimuli, and so on. What we know on that level is that suffering and states of brain behavior that are labeled as mysticism have an extremely close relation. Another level on which to discuss this is that not all states which get this strange label, mysticism, are induced by those sorts of practices, but that there is a range beyond that is closely connected with specific suffering. This second level of discussion would be more transcendent in the sense that it will say that mysticism turns back on itself and enhances one's understanding of suffering as a necessary condition for the attainment of anything worthwhile in the condition of time. Two great exemplars of that, I think, obviously are Teilhard de Chardin and Carlo Caretto, the Little Brother, whose writings come completely to the point you make about the relationship between the mystical relatedness to God and the reality of suffering.

QUESTION: Would you please reflect further on the scriptural reference about "filling up what is lacking to the sufferings of Christ?"

ANSWER: I can't possibly do that; it's the exegesis of the whole of the New Testament and the whole of Christian history. I take the cry of dereliction to be absolute and serious because of the rather peculiar and idiosyncratic views I hold on what was going on in the so-called trial of Jesus in terms of the Jewish data. What does the Jewish data constrain us to think about the examination of Jesus and what was going on in the Jewish context of that time? Out of that background I take the cry of dereliction to be completely serious. Therefore, if in the Jewish context where Jesus, although He clearly opted for a continuity of God, did not know what form that continuity would take, then one sees an almost limitless extension of Jesus' own life commitment. If God were to be God, then He would have to be God. And you tie yourself to that wherever it goes. It is necessary for Jesus to go to Jerusalem. Whence that necessity? If he had stayed in Galilee, no trouble. Jesus recharacterized the nature of theistic reality, recharacterized the nature of God as Abba, Father—not that this was unknown, but He put the emphasis on it. So, if the whole thing for Jesus in an exploration of what that sense of the immediacy, the differentiating consequentiality of God is in His life, and then extending out—that takes Him to Jerusalem. Then the filling up of the suffering of Christ is the filling up of the exploration of exactly that same understanding of how we are related to that resource of our lives which we also refer to as Abba, Father. I might conclude by saying again that this is not an answer since I could not answer this question in a short time.

NOTES

[1] W. Blake, "Vala, Night the Second," G. Keynes, (ed.), *Blake, Complete Writings,* Oxford, 1972, p. 285.

[2] For a fuller account of the way in which religions create and sustain different (and in some respects competitive) anthropologies, see my article in *Concilium*, Feb., 1977, "Assimilation or Rejection? Christian Theology and the Understanding of Suffering in Eastern Religions."

[3] I, p. 623.

[4] *Critique of Heaven,* London, 1972, p. 47.

[5] "Contribution to the Critique of Hegel's Philosophy of Right," in *K. Marx and F. Engels, On Religion,* Moscow, n.d., p. 41f.

[6] *The Future of an Illusion,* in *The Standard Edition of the Complete Psychological Works,* XXI, London, 1971, p. 39.

[7] The English translation converts this into a direct statement, instead of the protasis of a conditional sentence (or possibly temporal clause), as in the original German, "Und wenn . . . , so . . . ": *Gesammelte Werke,* X, Frankfurt, 1969, p. 346.

[8] "Our Attitude Towards Death," in *The Standard Edition* of the Complete Psychological Works, XIV, London, 1964, pp. 292-4. Freud's views on death were extended later by the publication of *Beyond the Pleasure*

Principle (1920), when he introduced the idea of the death instinct.
⁹*The Future of an Illusion,* p. 33.
¹⁰Kurtz, D.C. and Boardman, J., *Greek Burial Customs,* London, 1971.
¹¹See *An Introduction to the Study of Man,* Oxford, 1971, p. 524.
¹²"Our Attitude Towards Death," p. 294f.
¹³L. Lévy-Brühl, *Primitive Mentality,* London, 1923. Although Lévy-Brühl gathered reports from Australia attributing death to the magical power of enemies, he concluded: "This attitude of mind is not peculiar to Australian tribes only. It is to be found occurring almost uniformly among uncivilized peoples who are widely removed from each other" (p. 40). The belief that death is unnatural persists into the present. For example, in August, 1972, the B.B.C. ran a series of short programs on TV, called "Times Remembered," in which people reminisced about their earlier life. In one of these, a boy, Michael Foster, who had been born in Ghana and who had subsequently come to live in England, was asked whether "the pagans," as the interviewer called them, performed their fire-dance in relation to death, even if the person had died an old and natural death. He replied, "No one dies naturally."
¹⁴"Death is a limitation which circumscribes the continuity of men's actions, even more than gravity or a hostile neighbour or the necessity of finding food. Consciousness can set itself against those limitations in ways which vastly transcend the possibilities of instinctually accumulated response, not least because it can begin to discern something of their nature by observing that different actions have different effects in relation to them. There is no reason in principle why . . . the limitation of death would have to be regarded as wholly impenetrable. In fact on the contrary, the care and variation in burials from at least as early as the Middle Palaeolithic period, suggest that men set themselves against this limitation, even though virtually no reconstruction of their actual beliefs is possible" (p. 69f.). See the whole chapter, "Death, Burial and Cremation," in *The Sense of God: Sociological, Anthropological and Psychological Approaches to the Origin of the Sense of God,* Oxford, 1973.
¹⁵*Odyssey* xxiv. 6-9. On Homer, Dietrich therefore concluded: "In Homer, then the chthonic figures of fate from popular belief are weakened; man is freed from the terror he might have felt at the workings of the gloomy subterranean agencies. The knowledge of imminent death is always in the foreground in an epic of war and adventure, but a hero's actions are untrammeled by a sense of fatalism, nor is his mind obsessed with a constant fear of his end, though once dead he might well say that he "would rather be a serf than a king of all these dead men that have done with life." Homer's audience sought fulfillment of their desires in this world and they rejected the belief of other people in a reward or penalty awaiting

them in the next, the *au-dela*. (B. C. Dietrich, *Death, Fate and the Gods,* London, 1967, p. 336 f.).

[16]*Analects* xi. 11.

[17]"On Death," in *Lun Heng,* translated by A. Forke, I, New York, 1962, p. 196.

[18]Examples of embalming in association with freezing occur in the Frozen Tombs of the Altai. Although the effects of "deep-freezing" may originally have been observed accidentally, the construction of the burial mounds was clearly a consequence of further observation of what enhanced those effects. This can be seen in the schematic representation taken from *Frozen Tombs: The Culture and Art of the Ancient Tribes of Siberia* (London/British Museum), 1978, p. 23. But in the case of the people of the High Altai, we do not know what beliefs accompanied their actions in embalming the dead and burying them in these circumstances, because, as M. P. Zavitukhina put it: "Little is known about the creators of the culture and art of the Southern Siberian tribes. They possessed neither writing nor coinage, and were far away from the ancient literate civilizations whose historians knew of them only as legendary tribes" (*op.cit.,* p. 11).

[19]W. R. Dawson, "Mummy," in *Encyclopedia Britannica,* 1973.

[20]Wang Ch'ung, *op.cit.,* p. 191.

[21]"On the one hand, love (*Liebe*), according to Freud, represents desire and frustration in the ego, as in this passage: 'Being in love is based on the simultaneous presence of directly sexual tendencies and of sexual tendencies that are inhibited in their aims, so that the object draws a part of the narcissistic ego-libido to itself. It is a condition in which there is only room for the ego and the object.' But there is in this case a responsive object which, *by* its response, enables the transcendence of the need, the point of departure: 'Love in itself, in the form of longing and deprivation, lowers the self-regard; whereas to be loved, to have love returned, and to possess the beloved object, exalts it again.'" (*The Sense of God,* p. 132; see the whole chapter, "Freudian Theory and the Projection of God"). It perhaps needs to be added that the condition of "being in love" does not escape the continuing needs and neuroses of the subject. To do *that* would be to die. Thus earlier in the essay "Zur Einführung des Narzissmus" he argued that "complete object-love of the attachment type . . . displays the marked sexual overvaluation (*Sexualüberschätzung*) which is doubtless derived from the child's original narcissism and thus corresponds to a transference of that narcissism to the sexual object." It is this, Freud claimed, which is the origin of the peculiar or characteristic state of being in love: "Diese Sexualüberschätzung gestattet die Entstehung des eigentümlichen, an neurotischen Zwang mahnenden Zustandes der Verliebtheit, der sich so auf eine Verarmung des Ichs an

Libido zugunsten des Objektes zurückführt" (*G. W.*, X, p. 154f.). On the other hand, some better resolutions are possible: "The return of the object-libido to the ego and its transformation into narcissism makes available [there is great uncertainty about the verb: the first German edition had *herstellt,* "establishes"; the English transl. in *Standard Works* read *darstellt,* "represents", the German text of *G.W.* has *stellt,* as translated here], as it were, a happy love (*eine glückliche Liebe*); and, on the other hand, it is also true that a real happy love (*eine reale glückliche Liebe*) corresponds to the primal condition (*Urzustand*) in which object-libido and ego-libido cannot be distinguished." (*S.W.,* XIV, p. 100; *G.W.,* X, p. 167).

²²This discussion occurs in the Appendix to his thesis on Democritus and Epicurus, "Critique of Plutarch's Polemic against Epicurus' Theology."

²³See M. Villiers, *Charles Péguy*, London, 1965, p. 208f.

²⁴On this point, see further D. H. Fischer, *Historians' Fallacies,,* London, 1971, pp. 9-12.

²⁵Edition cited, Joseph Conrad, *Three Great Tales*, New York, 1962, p. 297.

²⁶*Op. cit.,* p. 297.

²⁷*Ibid.,* p. 297.

²⁸*Ibid.,* p. 298.

²⁹*Ibid.,* p. 283.

³⁰*Ibid.* p. 296.

³¹*Berlineer Aufzeichnungen, 1942-1945*, Munich, 1962, p. 7.

³²*Op. cit.,* p. 36f.

³³Quoted from C. Sykes, *Troubled Loyalty,* London, 1969, p. 438.

³⁴*Op. cit.,* p. 455.

³⁵See especially Romans ch. viii.

³⁶*The Book of Common Prayer,* The General Thanksgiving.

³⁷W. Blake, "Jerusalem," IV, pl. 96, *Complete Works,* p. 743.

³⁸*Pensées,* 227.

³⁹Blake, *op. cit.*

⁴⁰Blake, *op. cit.*

⁴¹*Enfant d'Agrigente,* p. 120.

⁴²1 Pet. iii. i5.

⁴³Lk. xxii. 27.

⁴⁴The word "constraint" in this technical sense is often misunderstood as having only negative connotations; in fact it has extremely positive implications: see *The Sense of God,* p. 88.

Chapter 2

HUMAN SUFFERING AND TRANSCENDENCE
Dr. Stanislas Breton

It is "with fear and trembling" that I approach the subject of this lecture. The confession of this fear is not an oratorical device which is so often used as a modest beginning for an important conference. Let us admit that suffering and transcendence send us back to silence rather than to speech. We would readily apply to them Proposition #7 which closes Wittgenstein's *Tractatus Logico-Philosophicus*: "We must remain absolutely silent on what we cannot talk about." Indeed, as one Christian has expressed it, the "great sufferers" who have entered "into the density of the Gross" hesitate to say a word about what they have experienced and recommend to their friends the greatest discretion on this subject. Extreme "suffering," like death, leaves us *confounded*. Would suffering and transcendence then be a part of that reserved realm which has been designated by the name of "unspeakable?" An immediate objection would be made, it is true, that the "unspeakable" is still a manner of speaking and that the speaker is contradicting himself. But a contemporary logician has shown that the "theory of the unspeakable is not inconsistent." For a "certain object" could, without risk of incoherence, be inexpressible either in a definite language or in any kind of language.[1] Prescinding from all proof, I shall simply offer a twofold observation. The first concerns the relation, strange at first, which I am setting up between "suffering" and "transcendence." I shall suggest this relation by recalling with neoplatonism that there are two kinds of ineffable: the one, by excess, which religions and negative theologies have universally recognized, each in its own way. The other, by default, or privation, is on the side of "matter." *Excess* and *default* imply a certain indetermination by which they avoid the jurisdiction of *logos*. And it is because of this that the ancients saw in the quasi-nothingness of a "reality" which "was nothing by which a being is determined" the symbol of this "nothingness par excellence" or "uncreated nothingness"—that paradox handed on to us by the Latin John Scotus Erigena and the Upper German Henry Susso. My second observation is linked with the first. The obvious alliance between "suffering" and "negation" invites us—with all the prudence of a language also cautious because it is aware of its limits—to catch a glimpse of the depth of a negative whose miserable sounds scarcely offer any analogies with the gentle negations which appear in our learned or spontaneous speech.

These preliminary remarks can indicate the direction of our reflection. Without deceiving myself about the relevance of my procedure, I shall attempt first of all an approach to "suffering" which does not diminish the scandal of it. By avoiding the easy ways of a consoling piety, it will be possible then to perceive there a delicately definable direction toward transcendence, under the form which the shadow of Christ's cross has made familiar to us on our earth.

THE "TO SUFFER" AS EXPERIENCE AND AS PROBLEM

For the term "suffering" which I cannot dispense with, I shall usually substitute the verb "to suffer." The verb, it is true, denotes an action. And we can rightly ask in what measure does "what is imposed on us without us" depend upon an action which necessarily involves a spontaneous initiative—in a word, what is properly called "freedom." Is there not in this "trial" which we sometimes fear more than death itself, since death delivers us from it, the inevitable fate which we must *undergo*? And it is perhaps because there is nothing to be drawn from it, which would remotely or proximately be likened to a useful action and gain, that certain doctrines like Marxism in particular, have refused every reflection on "suffering" and "dying." They have done this, as if this inevitable "accident" could only be the individual and trifling complication whose revolutionary energy of a theory promises us, if not the disappearance, at least the progressive lessening by a continual improvement of social living conditions. This disparaging conception is easily understood if we reduce it, according to the famous thesis, to "the human essence in the totality of social relations."[2] In fact, social relations do not suffer, although they cause suffering. And the task of the scholar consists less in the hermeneutics of a "painful psychism" than in the analysis of conditions on which suffering depends and in the organization of means which guarantee its elimination as much as possible.

Plausible as they might be, because of the degree of truth they contain, these explanations are far from satisfying. Supposing with Bergson that we have arrived at the point an heroic ride one day turns "death itself" upside down, we shall not treat as an unimportant quantity the density of the past, the present and future which burdens with its harshness a long history which does not know a promised paradise and is sometimes nostalgic about paradise lost. Let us admit as genuine the ruling idea which activates the magnificent effort of scholarship—perhaps in an incompressible elan. Let us imagine a state of ''perfect'' nature, without constraint or threat, which would have warded off all the harmful forces of destiny. For all that, would this beatific vision of the new Eden have suppressed all discord, every question, however unsolvable it was thought to be, in such a glorious existence? An environmental adaptation which would not allow us to hear any gnashing of teeth or lamentation, no questioning, no torment—would it still be human life? And would it change our condition only to abandon us to the unconsciousness of the mineral? By these questions I do not intend to justify the necessity of suffering; nor to challenge the benefit of utopian dreams. But I think that it is useful to recall the bond, so difficult to break, between an activity, however successful it might be, and the ever humiliating obstacles it must overcome.

The horizon which these perspectives open reveals by contrast the terrible dailiness which the very phrase ''to suffer'' signifies to us, and which leads us ''where we do not wish to go'' toward ''this night when we can no longer work.'' I use these evangelical references purposely so as to indicate the paradox of an ''action which is not an action,'' or, more accurately, which is not a ''doing'' in the ordinary sense of an object's transforming energy. The very ''to act'' like its correlative ''to suffer'' is in fact intransitive. Both designate a ''state'' in some way consubstantial with the being which acts and which suffers. I shall return to these preliminary indications which are not mere lexicography. In passing I shall note that certain mystics, in order to translate their deepest experience have recourse to the expression ''naked suffering'' which translates the Latin *merum pati* and the German *reines Leiden*. In the present case, the main point is the reference to a ''nondoing,'' to an absence of transitive activity, or, if you prefer, to a nonaction, to a zero action whose profound meaning certain young people today find in the Far East. What is important consequently is to determine the relation between *acting* and *receiving* in the one same *suffering*.

When St. Thomas introduces the study of the passions of the soul in the *Summa Theologica* (I-II, 22 Art. 1), while specifying his terminology (which is never left to chance), he is careful to determine the different meanings of the essential word: *pati.* In its most generic meaning *"to be passive"* means to *receive*, prescinding from every loss of a previous determination: thus air, in receiving the light, far from losing anything, is enriched with a perfection. In a stricter sense "to be passive" means to receive but with the connotation of something taken away. But this happens either when that which is lost is unsuitable to the thing—it is the case of the sick person who recovers health—or it can happen when that which is taken away is suitable to it, as is the case of the healthy person who becomes sick. It is in this last very strict sense that we are speaking of "to be passive."[3]

These seemingly very ordinary observations are doubly precious to us. They clarify for us the complexity and ambivalence of "to suffer" from which, as we know, the spirituals have derived the most profit. But at an early age they cause us to hear, if I may say it, the depth of a negative deeply embedded in our flesh. The human experience of "to suffer" reflects this ambivalence and this rending. In that way it raises the inevitable human problem of its meaning and its "why."

THE EXPERIENCE OF SUFFERING

The human experience of suffering is both *passive* and *active.* It is in this coincidence of opposites that its enigma is concealed.

Since the negative is in the foreground, we shall give it the greatest attention. But whenever we try to name this negative, it seems, in our language, like the *other* and the *opposite* or the *opponent.* The other as other is more than the simple otherness which distinguishes a being from everything which is not. Certainly this otherness *defines* us, delimits us, and thus allows us to play the part in ourselves and for ourselves, while including in a certain way even what it excludes. But as long as we remain in this generality, we do not attain the true function of the *other* in the interior of *suffering*. The other verifies its full otherness only when it threatens our identity instead of supporting it. It is through this negative valence that it becomes for us the opposite and the opponent.

When we consider the opponent, the obstacle in its full extent, it has no face. It is faceless and nameless. It is experienced in the *sufferer* which we all are, as the unregulated and for us nonadjustable totality of hostile forces which can come at each moment and happen unexpectedly without informing us. In this sense we can define the "to suffer" in its receptive dimension, as the quasi-perceptive experience of the world, inasmuch as it is an indivisible power of destruction which permanently burdens our puny individuality, so as to remind us by way of concomitant awareness of its permanent frailty as well. The "contingency" so often discussed by the philosophers is experienced in us, at first, in this dramatic and rudimentary form. The world *is everything which can happen to us,* by falling upon us so as to make us fall from that state where we are standing in the calm serenity of a *vertical position* which was the first biological acquisition of the human animal. That is why common sense as well as the most rationalist philosophies, such as Spinozism, could believe in the purely external origin of suffering and of death.

Suffering, whatever be the specific modality which a form gives it, is the sign in us of that power of the world dispersed in an infinity of dangers. It is that which makes of the other and of the opponent the undesirable guest who makes himself at home with us. The "to suffer" then takes on a new inflection. It passes from the indetermination which anticipates the universal danger to the burdensome reality of an evil, a sickness, an "in spite of us" to which medical terminology gives a more or less precise name. It has often been said that there are sick people and not sicknesses. And this protest against the abstract has its validity. Each sufferer, we repeat, is a singular case which calls for a unique solution. Nevertheless, this dispute on the universals which the Middle Ages had not foreseen sometimes risks forgetting one essential element—that there be control over what a thing is called. It is important for man to give a name to the opponent or to the other who afflicts him. An evil which would be both "without name" and "yet have every name" would cause the harmful universe which we fear to weigh heavily upon us, not only potentially but also in act. By determining the threat, we limit it; by naming it in a precise way we acquire a certain power over it. But real as this power is, it always leaves open a margin of impotence. Not only because the remedy, like the *pharmakon* of the Greeks, is both remedy and poison, but also and chiefly because the universal connection which binds the parts of the human organism and the parts of the universe of things together, likewise regulates all the parts or all the forms of the nosologic world. Victory on a given point would be complete only if it were total by extending to all the real sicknesses, known and unknown. Consequently, to understand the depth of *suffering* well in this second stage of our analysis, we must add some new elements to it:

1. In its reality, which is no longer simple anticipation, it unquestionably calls for a certain negative object which we can name, at least theoretically. It is in this sense that "to suffer" implies an object, which renders it transitive.
2. However, helpful as this name might be, it does not eliminate the threat of other morbid determinations to which it is necessarily linked. In this sense the "to suffer" in its very intimacy is open to a "negative infinite."
3. This boundlessness is translated in the sufferer (when

he is not condemned to unconsciousness) by an impression of limitless frailty which affects the efficiency of our powers by an inevitable restraint. The victory should finally be a "victory over the world" which would be both definitive and total.

If the evil of our sicknesses is what we have said, it is because it appears, in its third dimension, as the division which pierces our being with a "contradiction." This term which recurs so often in dialectical conceptions has many usages. We can regret that we have no longer restricted it to the sphere of speech alone and of the proposition in particular. It would be presumptuous, however, to attack the dictionary. We shall uphold it but by including there different types of opposition. We have already indicated the "contrariety" which the forces of an inadequately controlled universe set against us. It remains to say a word about the "opposition of privation" of which the ancients spoke. "Privation" in the present case, touches our being rather than our having, although the frontier is rather unstable between these two instances. It touches it in a twofold way. First, by diminishing that interior richness which we call health. Health is in the organism what peace is in the city. It is not immediately orientated toward action, as our Medieval Master observed, who made of it an *"entitative habit."* This expressed well what it meant, namely, a balance in which all the parts correspond and master their own actions in a pleasing and serene wholeness like "the silence of the sea." When this balance is broken and *the body begins to speak* by those signs—symptoms which gather in syndromes—the charm of this beautiful infancy *infans* = one who does not yet speak) which we admire in healthy bodies disappears. The *suffering* echoes in this dissonance, thus reproaching in contrast to the disorder of "noise" the admirable silence where the word of the soul and body rested. I mean the substantial bond in which these very diverse elements *combine*, of which life makes a being, while sometimes adding the beauty of a lightning flash.

The loss of order and balance is accompanied, in the second place, by another feeling, apparently less precise but no less concrete. It is that the privation is not only the absence of the necessary which "befits the living." It sets up in us a kind of "counter-essence" which is perhaps the source of the satanic representation of evil and sickness. The sufferer feels himself invaded by a foreign power set up in him permanently. Popular language is very realistic in this respect. As regards cancer, for example, it speaks of "a beast which consumes you," which "gains ground," which pushes the living person "toward his last retrenchment"—terminology of struggle and of quasi-diabolical possession. This infernal machine which brings to naught, this foreign body becomes your body, henceforth is part of your being. In Hegelian jargon for which I apologize, I would say that *suffering* in its dull awareness is "the identity of the identical and the non-identical." The paradoxical identity which consumes the living person and which shortens his breathing draws the sufferer toward an ever increasingly accentuated solitude. In this sense, it is probably true that sickness sharpens "the knowledge of the singular." The medieval axiom according to which "every individual is ineffable" perhaps has its origin there. But we must complete it in the following way: at the extreme, the individual is the being who can no longer speak, who can no longer communicate. Privation cuts the ties with human or natural environment. Progressively destroying the system of our relations, it creates in us a marked substantiality. But this substantiality can no longer say: "I am who I am," because the presence of the foreign destroyer would rather breathe on it the word of the evil spirit: "I am no longer who I am." The weakened "I am" which the sufferer would murmur would then express the awareness of being too much in a world which rejects him in order to abandon him soon to the wind of the abyss and of death.

To these three aspects of *suffering* which I have retained in this rudimentary phenomenology—hostility of the world, specification of evil in a negative hierarchy, privation-contradiction—correspond as many aspects of a minimal activity. For it is impossible to identify the "to suffer" with a pure sensation which we would simply have to undergo. The medieval axiom, "everything which is received is received according to the mode of the receiver," finds here a very original confirmation. Each of us, in fact, has his own way of reacting. The universe which thwarts us is perceived differently in terms of our own approach and of the traditions which envelop us. Likewise we sustain our sickness as we bear our body—giving it a singular look, like to no other. And the same observation is applied to privation-contradiction. The importance which we give sometimes to the social and sometimes to the individual matters little here; the two are necessarily connected. The essential point is summed up in a simple statement: humanity, diverse as have been its cultural contexts, is never resigned to misfortune. If, without in any way inserting it into a catalogue of virtues, we are willing to give the word "patience" a generic meaning correlative to *suffering*, would gladly say that the "patience" constitutes in the "to suffer" the dynamic element which enables us to assume our capacity to suffer courageously. And this dynamism does not consist only in the capacity, sometimes extraordinary in certain persons, to take the blows of misfortune. This factor, no doubt of great importance, and more and more rare in our overmedicalized West, cannot be separated, simply by reason of temperament, from the overall picture. A Buddhist commentary sums it up very well. In English it would read:

> Just as the medical science is a system of four items, disease or sickness, causes of sickness, health (cessation of sickness) and the medicine to cure, this *sustra* is likewise a system of four: *samsara* (suffering in the form of repetitious rebirth), causes of

samsara, its cessation (freedom), and the means to achieve the
state of freedom.''[4]

The very localized accent of this text in no way
diminishes its universal scope. It seems to me that it defines
exactly this active patience which clearly confronts the evil by
the creation of a *medicine* (in the broadest sense of the word).
It is a medicine attentive to the "suffering" of men, but
which looks to disclose its causes, and to stop them by
appropriate means. It is not enough then to experience its
"evil" and indeed to think about it. We must also know it
through its causes, that is to say, to explain it, in view of suppressing it and of realizing, by an adequate apparatus, a
fragile freedom and one always threatened by the servitude of
suffering. We are wrong to forget that the religions
themselves are presented as *medicine,* as medical system
whose contents are very different. But on the basis of an
analogous structure and of a common finality—the idea of
"health," of wholeness to recover, and of *liberation,* as one
discovers it subsequently in the philosophical doctrines, is not
the private property of so-called religions "of salvation." It
represents a universal contrast. Thus we may ask whether
"medical science," prescinding from its concrete realiza-
tions, would not be thus understood as the "first science,"
the "first philosophy," the "first religion," and give birth to
the multiple disciplines which these names designate, by a
process of increasing specification. I propose an hypothesis
but I leave its possible verification to the more expert.

This "medical science" as expression of an active
"patience" prolongs, in a systematic form, the spontaneous
reaction which we necessarily associate with the apparent
passivity of suffering. As in every science, it is possible to
distinguish different levels. On the first level, we would give
considerable attention to classification. By way of example, I
refer to you to groupings worked out in certain Buddhist texts
which distinguish three kinds of "painful moments":

"the unpleasant things and unhappy mental states";
"every transitory object, even pleasant things and happy feelings, which change and decay";
"the essentially conditioned nature of our existence . . .
appears to be a self-perpetuating, imprisoned state dotted by
craving, driving for pleasure, the agony of search, dis-
satisfaction and further craving, happening in cyclic
order."[5]

The proposed classification is also a hierarchical
arrangement which proceeds from the more exterior and
more particularized to the deeper and more universal, by
passing through the middle term of "change" and of the
transitory. We would note some similar divisions in the West,
and especially the same final accent on the "extremely conditioned character" of our life. The phenomenological
analysis which I proposed previously would give place to a
different arrangement but it would follow the same progression from the more exterior to the more interior. In every case
we note the same desire to classify and to order, that is to say,
to reduce the "many to the one" whether by relations of
equivalence or by relations of a more or less strict order.

On the second level, reflection, without neglecting the
need for nomenclature, turns first of all to the causes of
"suffering." It is a matter then of explanation. And the need
to explain is much greater because, at first sight, the suffering
seems almost inexplicable because of its "absurdity,"
because of its evident opposition to the normal course of life.
We see that on this crucial point, ideas at best reveal their
differences.

The Problem of Suffering

The problem of suffering must arise for the simple
reason that man is man and cannot be content to consent to
the fatality of the inevitable without any further ado. He
awakens to the knowledge of misfortune only by transcend-

ing the statement, however universal it might be. He demands a principle of reason which sheds light on such an uncomfortable destiny. And on the other hand he asks for a solution which would unite the knowledge of a "way" with the knowledge of why. The efficacy of the "way" puts an end, as much as possible, to the harshness of its origin.

I do not intend to examine different theories on the origin of suffering one by one and according to their full scope, and on physical suffering in particular. It is important, however, to determine at least major thrusts. To be brief, I shall distinguish scientific or "naturalist" theories from the theories of a philosophical or religious nature, which arise from a totally different spirit.

The scientific conception of suffering is expressed in a context of evolution. In its pretheoretical presumptions, it is supported by the common opinion which sees in suffering "a useful evil" whose sign value informs us about a more or less threatening danger to the health of the organism. "Sign of an organic evil, it allows us to search for a remedy there: a simply affective evil which informs us of a more serious evil. It is then a defensive weapon . . . Selection would have developed this useful, although unpleasant sign of evil in the species; it will have determined this useful danger which constituted an embryonic painful awareness, of sub-painful irritability." The role of selection, if we deny it the inheritance of acquired characteristics "would have been to favor the action of natural causalities by eliminating all the individuals who had not undergone its adaptive influence."[6]

This explanation, as Maurice Pradines correctly notes, raises more questions than it answers. Not only does chance bring us back to the arbitrariness of "theological theories"; but the causality which it conceals by its name "violates the laws of conservation and of the development of living and conscious organisms." In the second place, they forget that suffering "is linked to singular conditions, and not to chance." "Almost unknown among the invertebrates; in man himself, rather dull when born and often enfeebled when old; very diminished in the case of senile dementia or general paralysis, it is developed with the brain-process of the races." Consequently, it seems probable that it keeps up with the intellectual development of definite relations." In the third place, the hypothesis of usefulness by which one is inspired is far from being demonstrated. In addition, if one accepted the hypothesis, one could not confuse "in the suffering-complex that at least relative finality, inherent in the defensive irritation and that which could belong to suffering as such (that is to say as affection) . . . What makes suffering a *natural mystery* is both the aversion it inspires for nature, the mediocrity of compensations which it can contribute to the living being for the addition of sensible evil which it adds to the organic disorder *and* for the diminution of life which it always brings, thus aggravating the evil which it indicates."[7]

If we do not understand that the living, in the course of its evolution, acquired some "painbearing organs," it is necessary to look for another solution. What Pradines proposes would merit a long study. I cannot delay on it here. As an indication for young researchers, I would point out that the Pradines hypothesis provides a certain justification of the principle "for the intellectualist theories of suffering." Suffering is the idea of an evil or a disorder; an idea which is not a concept, but an expression, a meaning. Suffering is thus linked to the intellectual life, in its broad sense, which embraces sensation and the perceptive life in its extension, under its highest forms, in particular those of sight and hearing. The meaning of the biological evolution is, in fact, clear enough. It indicates a sensory hierarchy in which the *impression-stimulus* leads more and more gradually, as one proceeds from odor and taste, passing through touch, towards the visual and audial representations, and turns into *expression*. By placing the stimulants at a distance, the "life movement" would then make possible a "reflective defense which anticipates and prevents irritation and consequently the suffering itself inherent to the irritation." But this good effect of evolution has as its price another effect "which inevitably accompanies it." For progress of the senses and of the intelligence "results in sharpening the awareness of the original, incipient irritation by raising it progressively above the threshold. Then the excitation which first indicated the threshold of a *justifiable conscious* aversion becomes the threshold of a more conscious aversion, that is to say, painful. Suffering is only this *increased awareness* of the original averse irritation." But instead of accentuating the moving or averse element of the original irritation, it makes this more sensitive by the very fact of the progress of awareness and understanding.

This second and unpleasant effect is the price, doubtlessly very high, for which an "incomparable good" is purchased. For "the intelligence has created the suffering, as an inevitable condition of its coming, only to furnish us both with the means to avoid it by the anticipation which it gives us and with the strength to sustain it by the remedies it gives."[8]

This thesis explains quite well how the progress of the intelligence through sensory development has spared us "this hell which physical suffering would be if the sensory diversion did not ordinarily cause its peace and light to descend there."[9] But this great improvement which has made us pass from a "reflex defensive to a well-thought out defensive"[10] would appear too superficial still and ultimately too reassuring to minds for whom suffering, *far from being a diverted phenomenon, is consubstantial with life itself.*

If, apart from their differences, we search out the common point which brings the theories of the "original suffering" together, it is perhaps, as Pradines himself suggests too quickly[11], the *stimulant* which we should examine thoroughly and which is semantically close to *irritation, danger,* and the *reflex of repulsion.* Indeed it does not necessarily provoke a reaction of rejection, since, as often as not, it offers the subject an object to possess. However, and it is here that the philosophical or religious sensibilities reveal their differences, the stimulant as such is originally double-faced and thus lays the foundation for the prejudice of options. This necessary ambivalence of the *stimulus* which can be positive or negative enables us to shift the accent from one pole to the other and to evaluate such a dominant rather than another. In a Thomist perspective, where affirmation necessarily precedes and establishes the negation, suffering has meaning only on the basis of a preliminary quest for the "good." It is in this way that the "irascible appetite" in its course of defense or of conquest is rooted in the "concupiscible appetite" which is under the sign of love, of desire, and of joy. The Indian conceptions would not easily adopt such a perspective. And it seems to me that the reason is this: the *stimulant* excites only by *irritating;* and it irritates only in virtue of its *aggressive exteriority.* Therefore its *nature* matters little; *its function will always be negative.* The world, in its becoming and in the infinity of its changing forms, can only impose on us the infinity of misfortune by this permanent excitation-aggression. Desire itself which promises us happiness through its quest is only a deceptive prolongation of this universal "pressure of exteriority." By thrusting us into this world game, it hands us over to that infernal cycle of which we have spoken. For all that, have we fully resolved the enigma of suffering? That would be unquestionably too optimistic. It remains for us to say why.

If we admitted this preceding explanation, it would not suffice. We can indeed ask ourselves why the world of things and of desire which determines our "imprisonment" in suffering appears to us such as it is. How is it then that it is what it is?

The monotheistic religions which admit the universality of the divine omnipotence from which nothing can escape, must ask the question, and with some anguish. The theologians, more subtle than the friends of Job, have multiplied distinctions, analyzed the different kinds of causality, in order to acquit from evil—moral evil in particular—the God of their faith and their love, Who, essentially good, can enter into the mystery of evil under all its forms only by the subterfuge of a "permission," respectful of the creatural condition in its finiteness, and particularly of human freedom. I do not insist on these well-known "justifications," which have transformed theology into "theodicy." The name of Leibniz, in our West, sums up rather well these heroic efforts of justification which took away all "responsibility" from the divinity, in order to put it back on an original transgression, angelic or human, based on the inevitable imperfection of created being. Evil, in its implacable evidence, was not then radical, to the extent that its intelligibility projected no shadow of malice or impotence on the Most High and required only a "deficient causality." This "deficient causality" in addition dispensed from all recourse to a Manichaean principle. Suffering, sorrow, sin, serious as they were, could henceforth be inscribed in a providential plan, and, far from seriously compromising the harmony of the universe, could, by virtue of grace and first love share with it in the glory of the redemptive mystery.

Buddhism has certainly the great advantage of being able to exclude these justifications of defense or struggle. And perhaps, but I say this "perhaps" only with reservation, it is atheistic only to avoid precisely these difficulties of theodicy, and so as not to sweeten the drama of universal suffering by compensations which it would judge too human. The negative here takes on such prominence that the positive of our traditional ontologies, such as the connection of the ancient transcendentals expressed it: being, one, true, good looks like a secondary and finally illusive accident. We understand that neither science nor religion are apt, in these conditions, to resolve the problem of "evil." Our Western thirst for existence, inseparable moreover from this will to conquer, which has thrust our knowledge, techniques, and Christianity itself on the roads of the world, is precisely that from which we must be delivered. For all our science, profane or sacred, inasmuch as it is *thirst for knowledge,* is only a way of turning us away from the "holy truth about the origin of suffering." It is not enough indeed, we repeat, to experience suffering. Suffering, as defensive reaction, preserves a will to conserve, a desire to be, which is that very thing from which we must be delivered. It is the suffering, *reflected on and known in its source,* which is important. Such is the essential knowledge, knowledge by causes also, which puts us on the way of salvation. And this origin is not far from us: we do not have the right to relieve ourselves of the burden for a reason other than ourselves. It consists finally in our ignorance of the cause of misfortune. Doubtlessly we will ask ourselves in what order must we rank the different causes appealed to: is it the thirst for existence? Is it ignorance? Is it their union? It seems to me that the logical connection of the "different causes" can be translated in a twofold series of implications: if there is birth, sickness, death, pleasure, etc., then there is suffering; if there is suffering, there is thirst for existence; if there is thirst for existence, then there is ignorance (of this thirst). If instead of proceeding from effects to their causes, we go from causes to effects, we get a reciprocal series of the first. But whatever might be the meaning of our reading, whether it be ascending or descending, it is the same principle, namely ignorance, which, as cause of the proximate cause (the thirst for existence) is, in the last resort, the true explanation. But we bear the full responsibility for this ignorance. The greatness of Buddhism is unquestionably in this proud claim which refuses every subterfuge, every transfer of culpability. But if suffering and death have entered into the world by fault of our ignorance; if original sin is our act itself of being, or our boldness to exist, the evil spirit, Eastern or Western—it matters little—which presses us toward new questions, would hardly be satisfied with an ultimate cause, even if this ultimate cause, whatever it might be, is of privileged excellence in the four holy truths. Why stop at some part in the explanation of suffering? The question mark, the firstborn, according to a Hindu legend of the *Prakriti*, would not leave us in peace. In the heart of Buddhism, as in each of us, this question mark always lying in wait, does not tolerate any rest which would appease it with a final word. Must we conclude that the explanation of suffering drives us into a corner in suffering a question which it is as impossible for us to refuse as to resolve? It would certainly be vain to respond in the abstract to this last concern. Religions and philosophies have proposed different ways. It is one of these ways which I would like to follow, mindful in my Christian faith, of this *other,* distant but always near, who does not dwell in our home.

SUFFERING AND TRANSCENDENCE

The term "transcendence," like all our human words, is laden with images and with a weight of history which has sometimes made it suspect. So as not to complicate my procedure and to determine clearly the fundamental directions of my thoughts, I shall limit myselt to two possible meanings. One, closer to the verb "transcend," puts the accent on the *act of surpassing;* the second, more in harmony with the noun "transcendent," envisions a *reality, irreducible to the act of transcending,* which is both the end and the principle itself of this act. These elementary explanations shall serve as a guide in this last stage of my inquiry.

Supporting ourselves on the "medical"analogy, we note that every medication for suffering requires reflection on suffering, on its causes, its cessation, and the means to obtain it. Each moment of this fourfold reflection is obviously linked to the other three. This formal structure is valid also for the "Sermon on the Mount" as well as for the "Sermon of Benares." But whereas in the first the cessation or liberations calls for the indispensable mediation of a transcendent, in the

the accomplishment of this task in a final state. The realization would then become *reality,* and there will be a certain qualification, however negative it might be, of this reality, if only to name it in a thought of "the living person who is freed."

There is more to be said. And it is on this point that Buddhism seems to me both so profound and so attractive. The heroic effort by which one proceeds to the "withdrawal of determinations" whatever they might be; the way of asceticism to which we are invited because it is not only possible but necessary; the abolition of suffering by the extinction of thirst and desire imply, in the living person who is freed, the *capacity to emerge beyond and above* the universal series which defines the world. This "I can" of emergence on the chain of becoming presupposes that a certain point in us, whatever might be the word which designates it does not appear among the elements of the world. Otherwise, as Schelling observed[15], since "what is part of a mechanism cannot be detached from it in order to ask: how has all that become possible," it would be impossible for one immersed without residue in the cosmic flux, to hold it in check. The Nirvana inserted again in the universal illusion would be no more than the last link of suffering and the last illusion. Let us go further. The mastery which we are granted so daringly over the becoming of births and rebirths is understood only if, by a first mistake, we are completely responsible for the world itself such as it is and such as it appears. For we can only *loose* what we have previously *bound* on earth as in heaven; we can only *undo* what was in our power to *do.* Would it not then ultimately be *the same power,* whatever its name be, which makes the world and which liberates us from it (such as formerly the god Shiva who danced in a rhythm of support and withdrawal over the progeny which he in turn begets and destroys)? The "nothingness" (or "emptiness") in these conditions would no longer be a vain word (*flatus vocis*), but the paradoxical way of signifying indirectly, or showing by a weak sign, this "X" which surmounts or "transcends" all the determinations and all the negations. In the interior of a language, whatever it might be, it indicates the inevitable limitation of it by liberating it also from the inexhaustible chain of "namings." In concluding these reflections which I entrust to my Japanese friends of Zen Buddhism, who paid me the honor of a meeting with them, I am aware of going beyond a limit. And I think that silence would be better.

THE SHADOW OF THE CROSS

The same silence would lead me to the foot of the cross and towards its shadow. For it also defies every word. The God whom it "nails to the tree" is an infinite power of detachment. He is nothing of what is in the world, as St. Paul so energetically reminded his faithful in the first chapter of the First Letter to Corinthians—neither human power, nor wisdom, nor even the power of miracles. "We preach," the apostle insists, 'a foolish and weak God, a scandal for religion, past, present and future. I would not want to be guilty of deceptive comparisons, or yield to some apologetic concern, but we must recognize that the expressions, which will appear afterwards, inspired moreover by a totally other context, of "nothingness par excellence," or "uncreated nothingness," find here a very new application. Transcendence in the second sense which I considered in my preliminary remarks, takes on a totally other direction. It is no longer the "most real being" of philosophies, plagiarized by religious traditions, which speaks to us from the height of the cross. By its presence alone, and in an image sensitive to the heart, the cross achieves a kind of radical critique of the most ordinary representations which we make of the divinity.

We think indeed that it is quite natural to offer the Most High our very rare talents as a gift. And the most sublime second the transcendence is exhausted in the human act of transcending. The duality of ways is then very clear. Each is enlightened by the very thing which it excludes, as if the "complementary" whole sustained the originality of its approach while opposing it. This is the reason why, as honestly as I can, I shall risk a personal approach to what was accessible to me of Buddhism as "royal way" of freedom.

The last two of the "holy truths" concern the suppression of suffering and the means of achieving it. In reality, if I read it correctly, and without useless subtlety, one can discern here the presence of two teleological microsystems. On the one hand, the trinomial *"suppression of suffering-extinction of thirst-annihilation of desire"* expresses very well the order of ends, but by insinuating there a hierarchy, since the close connection which unites suffering to thirst and thirst to desire is repeated in the strict and ordered implication of their respective suppressions. On the other hand, the fourth truth makes the order of means explicit, namely, the "sacred Eightfold Path." This way, simplified by certain Indian scholars who reduce it to *virtuous conduct* (or duties toward another; not to kill, not to lie, etc.), to *concentration,* and to *wisdom* (state of ultimate disposition for Nirvana), proposes the ordered whole of indispensable mediations to obtain the result or the cure.[12]

I shall not enlarge any further on the means. But it is impossible for a Christian not to cross the fatal Nirvana, on its way, however laterally it might be. Everything has been said on this enigmatic negative to which the last proposition of Wittgenstein's *Tractatus,* which I mentioned in the beginning, has been rightly applied. We would be tempted to compare it with the "meontology" of Neo-Platonism, which was the most radical form of negative theologies in the West. But the "ineffable," the "uncreated nothingness" or "nothingness par excellence" designate in their paradoxical keenness, a reality, transcending our act, which exceeds all determinations, and which is itself beyond affirmation as well as negation. In this regard Proclus had perfect discernment. We cannot say of the One (or of what protects this weak denomination and by which one is not duped) either that it is identical or that it is nonidentical. The principle of the excluded third has no application here. We do not deny it; we simply specify that there is jurisdiction only in a certain domain where determinations reign.[13] But this minimum speech which the negative theologies agree on would still be too much for Buddhism. For it would suspect in this language a "learned ignorance," still more or less a slave to a thirst to speak apropos a reality, and this would be its "ineffability" in a "cloud of unknowing." It remains no less true that *Nirvana* is an end, in the two fold sense of a cessation and of a goal to be realized and which, sometimes in certain privileged cases, seems to be realized well by some exceptional personalities. Consequently it is necessary that the language not of theology but at least of "teleology" flow back on this "ultimate." Contrary to what Matilal seems to insinuate, it is not at all necessary to think of Buddhism as a religion or religious tradition in order to reconcile it with a phenomenology of intentional act.[14] The intentional act, incontestably, does not always envisage a "real object"; a knowledge of the object can envisage this as pure intentional term of its act. We are correct to add, moreover, with Husserl that it would be vain—apropos this object *as such*—to pose the question of its real existence or nonexistence. In the present case, however, it is not a question of *any object of thought whatever* or of a simple absence of thought, but of a true *pro-ject*, of an end to realize, and consequently *as an end* to be realized. Whether we will it or not, the Buddhist language itself, unless we strip it of all meaning, implies certain teleological designations, relating to Nirvana, which it seems impossible to deny. In a certain way Buddha has spoken too much in order that we might not take it for the essential word of his doctrine and his way. A fortiori, if we no longer suppose it a simple, infinite task of realization, but ideas seem to us to express best and in an adequate correspondence what there is of God and of His Mystery in them. It is this naive confidence, sometimes sustained by impressive speculations which confuse this "question mark" planted on Calvary and which seems to say to us: *I am nothing of what you say.* The kenosis which is the issue in the Letter to the Philippians is something totally different from a beautiful metaphor. Lacking style, suppressing all pompous speech which we would think more worthy of the Lord, it turns us away from our ordinary way of speaking and thinking. It invites us not indeed to an abstract meditation on negation and negativity, but to a renunciation, to an operative negation which should change our hearts and spirits. The Greek term *"metanoia"* expresses the essence of this conversion very well; it is a transformation, a change of spirit which frees us, through a certain death, from a common sense shared by far too many.

There remains however the enigma of this God who manifests Himself to us through an unspeakable suffering. Would there not be there an exorbitant privilege granted to what causes spontaneous horror in us? Would there not be a morbid affection for "suffering" which would arise, according to certain psychologists, from pathology? Instead of encouraging us to struggle against "evil," do we not risk canonizing it as an expression of a divine will, against which we have no protest, because the Absolute has spoken in it and through it? It is true that we are promised its suppression in another life. But while awaiting it, we must be resigned, since, as Pascal wrote, suffering is "the natural condition of the christian." How, in the name of faith, could we, without sacrilege, combat this splinter in our flesh which is the sign of the elect?

These questions, more or less pertinent but not imaginary, compel us to ask ourselves about the Christian meaning of suffering. But before going into detail, it will be useful to delay a while onger on the image of the cross. That

God could reveal Himself through it is first of all what creates the problem. In what sense can we make it the image speaking of the true God?

In the beginning, I mentioned the Neo-Platonic theory of the two ineffables: the one by default, matter, and the other by excess, the transcendent. And I specified that the first "symbolized" the second in its own way. Transposing this doctrine, I shall make of the cross the functional equivalent of ancient matter, also ineffable because of its fundamental indetermination. In fact, it sums up very well the human universal passibility which Christ assumed in the limits of His condition. But this universal *passibility* is and remains under the sign of the negative. For "to suffer" in its component of *"to be passive"* reminds us of privation, that is to say, the *deprivation of all determinations* by which we can "be, live, and move." The cross, in this sense "sign of contradiction" and privation, awakens us to another knowledge of divinity. By representing it as the nothingness of our excellences and our "riches," through the mediation of "suffering," it obliges us to reform our understanding. The "spoliation" which suffering and death effect, in this paroxysm which the Crucified makes specific, means for us the necessity of passing to another realm of thought and conduct. It is only by this subterfuge that the cross has the value of symbol. It is a "sign" but a sign which contradicts a greedy spontaneity, proud of its riches or of its health, and very pleased to offer them to its God. Nothing less, nothing more. We shall not ask of a sign more than it can give. We shall particularly guard against confusing it with that of which it is a sign. The cross is a lesson. It is an image. The error would be to identify it with its "referent" as sometimes certain unquestionably well-intentioned attempts have done, especially in contemporary theology. They have tried to show at least partially that very subtle and very spiritual suffering could be found in God Himself and this would make Him more like unto us. We do not have to humanize the Transcendent to this point in order to be helpful to us. It is not by projecting our miseries onto Him, after having endowed Him with our perfections, that we shall love Him more. Every suffering, whatever it be, must be finally conquered. No way of eminence, even by proper analogy, would justify its sublimation in the Absolute.

But if the Cross does not canonize "suffering" by making it an unconditional value, it does take on a first-rate importance in the life of Christ. The "way of the Cross" was not a simple episode in His history. The essential point is to understand the exact place which it holds there. For this purpose I shall use the four-part schema which we have already used profitably.

The Letter to Hebrews (2, 17-18) says: "It was essential that He (Jesus) should in this way become completely like his brothers so that he could be a compassionate and trustworthy high priest of God's religion, able to atone for human sins. That is, because he has himself been through temptation he is able to help others who are tempted" (*Jerusalem Bible*). If we prescind from the reference to "atonement" which would today pose a rather delicate problem for theologians, the accent of these lines emphasizes above all a depth of experience, which makes Christ similar to us. He would not "know what is in man," if he had not passed through this density of night. The "sadness even unto death," the "sweat of blood" and the whole drama of the Passion express well that our model, in loving us even unto death, has known what the hour of darkness was. Unquestionably it would be improper to impose on Him the maximum of human suffering in extent, duration, and intensity in order to make Him an absolute exemplar. Genuine piety has no need of these pious exaggerations. But in His finiteness itself, which is our condition in everything, Christ has had His privileged role in universal *suffering.* First of all He has undergone the hostility of a physical and human world. However, as far as we can judge from the texts, we do not observe in His conduct an attitude so negative as that of Buddha. Perhaps a wave of poetic fancy would deny Him the sight of a universe inwardly dedicated to the desolation of the negative. Would the Biblical tradition on which He was nourished remind Him, as He contemplated the lilies of the field (more beautiful than "Solomon in all his glory") of the "look" of the last days of creation "when the Lord saw that all that was good?" We can hardly doubt it. Evident as suffering is, it always includes a terrible risk: that of spreading over the world the black ink which our misfortune releases. Our Crucified Lord has walked along our roads, but not clothed in black. In those "little ones whom He allowed to come to Him," did He not read the thrilling joy of those stars about which He had said that they would be happy "to shine in His presence?" It is true that at certain dark moments everything vacillates in despair and our language says no more than an immense anonymous "*il y a.*" But however deep the suffering be, it does not silence the voice of the original gift which inserted the irrepressible happiness of an epiphany in the heart of all things. I grant it: only a *superman disinterestedness* can prevent us from reducing, in our distress, the claim of these dead primroses which greet the spring, in order to engulf them in our night.

Did Christ know this weight of the world, which takes on in us the form of mortal sickness? In former times a perhaps too modest theology would have hesitated to weigh Him down with it. Be that as it may, He has at the very least fallen under the supreme torment which the punishment of the Cross represented. And it is through the Cross that He has experienced everything which the universe of things and of humans contained in adverse forces. As for the privation and intimate contradiction it sets up in us, He has experienced it in a twofold way. On the one hand, as conflict between our will to live and a higher urgency in us, which demands us to sacrifice it out of duty or submission to the divine will. On the other hand, as conflict between our "desire to be" and this "stranger" who affronts us even to the point of exhaustion. We can then prudently conclude that the three aspects of suffering which distinguished our phenomenology have been verified in Him according to an exceptional keenness. As we said, this is only half of the "suffering." Christ did not remain passive under the Cross which touched Him form his birth. Like all of us under the sting of suffering, He had to offer resistance to it—a resistance which would not be satisfied with a spontaneous or reflective reaction. He often had to combat it by means adapted to His times and to His mission. The miracles of Christ for the most part are miracles of healing or at the very least miracles of charity. This power which heals, and if such be the case, the power that commands winds and seas, has an eschatological meaning. It announces the time of the new heavens and the new earth, the time of the risen bodies. For if there should be a definitive victory over suffering and death, it *could not prescind from our poor flesh.* The doctrine of spiritual bodies which is integrated in St. Paul in a hierarchy of levels "corporeity" where we discern the "material," the "psychocosmic," and the " pneumatic" (a doctrine incidentally which is similar to the ideas of the same type in India as well as in Neo-Platonism) reveals in and behind our carnal materiality, a spiritual power capable of turning death upside down. But this "life-giving spirit" immanent to the body, "the temple of the Holy Spirit," inserts into the heart of the finite an active transcendence which in its own mode is the same as God's. It matters little moreover whether we give a "divine" name to this transcendence or whether by an extreme reserve we allow the shadow of a final "questionable" to hover over it. That by which a certain painful fatality of becoming would be overcome can only be of a nature other than that of a finite and imprisoned "I." Christianity could not save both "excess" and this matter which it animates. The victory of faith then must coincide with a Feast of Corpus Christi which would also be a feast of the universal transfiguration, human and cosmic, in the light of the Resurrection.

But can we trace the "untraceable" of suffering and death without an effective grasp of its origin? The New Testament does not separate suffering and death from the sin which gave them citizenship rights in the world. Jesus seems to have been very discreet about this causality. The episode of the cure of the man born blind (John 9, 11ff) is very precious in this regard. To the disciples who ask, "Who sinned, this man or his parents, for him to have been born blind?" the Master simply replies, "Neither he nor his parents sinned: he was born blind so that the works of God might be displayed in him" (*Jerusalem Bible*). This reply deters us from easy explanations of misfortune by the mere interplay of perverse wills. It suggests a discernment of causes which would not be placed at the same level. Without excluding the reference to an original rupture, which would be responsible for what happened afterwards, *it invites us to manifest actively* "the works of God." But this manifestation is not satisfied with good words. It has full meaning only in the clarity of the Last Judgment: "For I was hungry and you gave me food; I was thirsty and you gave me drink; I was a stranger and you made me welcome; naked and you clothed me, sick and you visited me, in prison and you came to see me" (Matthew 25, 35-36, *Jerusalem Bible*). The human and Christian experience of "suffering must integrate, in the depth of the negative, this dynamic and Christic dimension which brings God down to our earth through the generosity of a self-forgetfulness in which transcendence again *is affirmed in a patient transfiguration of misfortune.*

But whence do we draw the strength for this heroic self-forgetfulness? For our faith, there is no other source than those living waters of the Beatitudes which permit a joy no longer of this world to appear through their bitterness. This supreme joy illumines the end of a world only because it is the beginning of it: *In principio.* Christ has experienced it. He died for it. The cross unites this shadow and this light. But deserving speech about it surpasses our understanding. It is fitting then to conclude our discourse on this first Silence which would have to abolish it.

DISCUSSION

QUESTION: The clarity with which you spoke was certainly admirable, but if I understood your conclusion, the very last thing you said directly, you would say that suffering has as its goal or purpose the glorification of God. Do you mean by that suffering has some other cause than sin, i.e., the cause of suffering also somehow comes directly from God?

ANSWER: I thank you for that question. Exactly I thank you because it allows me to be more specific. I said with regard to the Gospel, with regard to the text of the blind man in the Gospel of John, I said that Jesus, Himself, did not recognize the exclusive cause of evil as being sin. It may be that suffering is linked up to the human condition as such. But even linked up to the human condition, it has a meaning and that meaning is not a usefulness, an efficient kind of meaning; it is the glorification, the manifestation of God in the glory of our bodies. And that's why I said that the Last Judgment in the Gospel will not be to know if we honored God in liturgy or in pious deeds; but the question is to find out if we have put clothes on the person who is naked; if we have given food to the person who is hungry. In other words, if we have made of this world the beautiful simple look of a child or the joy of the lily of the valley which, as we say, exists for the glory of God.

QUESTION: I'm trying to decide which question I want to ask. Let me stay with that one for the sake of clarity. If we say that suffering in part is in order, then, that God may be glorified, is that not saying, in effect, that God is an ogre who creates the world in which we must suffer in order that He be glorified?

ANSWER: I thank you again for your question, which is also as good as the other one. But I would like to say that when I say the glory of God, I'm not saying the glory *for* God. I recognize no definitive goal to suffering. I think that there is a joy of creating independently of any kind of usefulness, be it Western usefulness or non-Western usefulness. What struck me in my conversations with the Buddhists was that the master of the school of Kyoto made me understand that Christianity, as well as the Western world, is geared strictly to utilitarianism and to achieving an end product. He said to me: "If I read the *Bible,* it says, 'Go, conquer the world, dominate the fish, dominate the different creatures.' The Western world has a desire for total conquest and Christianity, science, and politics in the Western field are all geared to the same kind of productivity. You read the same in the Gospel of Matthew, once more: 'Go, make disciples of all the nations.' Christianity has a desire to conquer and a desire for power." But then this Buddhist master added, "But" (and there is a 'but' again), he said, "There is in the Gospel something that I will never forget. It is what Jesus said about the lilies of the valley, that they are there for the joy of being looked at, they don't exist for any particular purpose." No mentioning of conquest here, what counts is the glory of God which is the beauty of the world, as beautiful as is the lily of the valley, and as I said previously, as is the pure gaze of a child. And the question I'd like to ask Buddhism—because, unfortunately, in the Christian world we don't ask any questions anymore of the people who are Buddhists and I prefer to confront them with questions—and the question that I want to ask is: "Can you without anthropomorphism project on the world the black ink of total, of absolute suffering? Have you ever looked at the figure, at the face of a young child, of a young girl, and even at the Japanese gardens?" I say that there is something in the world that is deeper than suffering and pain; there is something in the world where the Beatitudes tell us that maybe that is what we have to look at, that is what we have to tie ourselves up with. We have to be close to the joy of the lilies, the joy of the beauty of a child's face, the joy of total and useless service, the joy of the glory *of* God but not the glory *for* God.

QUESTION: Can you step back for a moment from your ideas about Christianity and look at what Buddhism has to teach us about suffering and what it does to help those who are Buddhists deal with the problem of suffering? I have a problem with your comparing two different religions, with two different theological perspectives. So, if you could help me, could you take a step backward here with your good knowledge of Buddhism and tell me what are the positive aspects that Buddhism has to teach us about the meaning of suffering? And if I were a Buddhist, how does that religion help me deal with the meaning of suffering?

ANSWER: When I said I asked questions of the Buddhists, it is because I am loyal to them. As a Western person, I don't want only to hear stories from Buddhism. I think, and I said this at Kyoto, that the Western world, be it American or European, will only find its cures within itself. In other words, the Western world can be cured or healed only if it has the courage in maintaining its power to go beyond its power. And I think that's what Buddhism teaches us. But they are not telling us *how* to do it, because Buddhism did not go through mathematics, it did not go through geometry, it did not go through the question of the glory of power. And that is why it can't deal with it. I think that the Western world, as Christianity also, has to go through the testing of power. But it has also to face the problem of the "beyond of power" and the way in which we can go beyond power. That's what the Western world has to deal with, and I am not expecting this from Buddhism. But I must say, and I said it previously, that there is a glory within Buddhism, and I cannot do away with that glory; it exists. The fact is that Buddhism confronted with the world, which is the overall world of suffering, has the amazing capacity to say, "I can." It is called "I," the Self. There is something in us which is not the empirical "I," the anthropological "I," which allows us to face the world and say, "I am part of the world but I am not the world." That kind of glory I really recognize and that's why I like Buddhism.

QUESTION: I wonder if you would comment on the part that absurdity, chance, and accident have in suffering?

ANSWER: I have often meditated on the first proposition of Wittgenstein's treatise which is translated in the following way: the world is everything that happens, and I would say to a certain point, the world is the totality of cases or the totality of the possible accidents that can happen to us. Because we are in the world, we cannot dominate all these accidents. In this respect—and I'd like to highlight this—suffering or pain is not simply the fact that I am hurt and the hurt that I am carrying; it is the potential threat of a world which is a constant accident befalling us. I would say, therefore, that there is in suffering an element which is accidental, but accidental in the sense that we cannot dominate everything that threatens us. So I call accident the totality of all those things that happen to us upon which we have no control. Is that what you meant or wanted to ask?

ANSWER: Yes, it is. I would like to get the Wittgenstein reference. Dr. Breton: The first proposition of his Tractatus Logico-Philosophicus. It's the first one—you can't make a mistake on that. I ask my students to read at least the first one in German and in English.

QUESTION: Did I understand you to say that had there been no sin in the world, there would still be suffering? In other words, absolutely speaking, would there be suffering in the world had there been no sin? I recognize that the finality or purpose of suffering goes beyond retribution for or expiation of sin. Suffering can be sanctifying; but plausibly speaking, would there be any suffering in the world had there, absolutely speaking, been no sin?

ANSWER: Personally, I have learned that suffering in our theological manuals, as well as death in that respect, was only part of the whole question of original sin. It was a doctrine that was proposed by the manuals, by the important theologians. I think that today we would probably be a little bit more specific and more clear. I'm not saying that all suffering is based on sin or has sin as its root, but I can say that certain suffering might have as its cause a sin. In this respect I would argue that, first of all, suffering cannot be explained only by sin; but secondly, I would also say that it might happen, and this is a proposition of contingency I'm putting forth here: it might happen that suffering or certain degrees of suffering be linked up actually to what we call sin. I think that's the answer to your question—an answer which tries to distinguish and which is more in line with today's theology.

QUESTION: So that I may distinguish the word "explanation," do I hear you say that if we take explanation as cause, that sin is not the ultimate primordial cause of suffering?

ANSWER: I am saying that explanation through sin is an explanation through possible causes, proximate causes. What I'm saying is that today it does not seem that it is the only explanation and, therefore, it is not the ultimate explanation in this respect. But I think that human suffering is tied very closely to the human condition and that is a metaphysical view which is still quite valid today.

QUESTION: Within Buddhism suffering is not limited to just human beings and St. Paul speaks of the entire creation laboring in preparation of the glory. I'd like some of your comments on human suffering in relationship to that universal labor or suffering.

ANSWER: I think that there are two questions in the question that you are asking me. There is the question of suffering beyond man within Christianity and the question of suffering beyond man outside Christianity and the relationship—if one may say—between these two kinds of approaches to suffering that is beyond man in two different mindsets. First of all, with regard to Christianity, there is St. Paul's text on the groaning of creation waiting for the revelation of the sons of God. If you take St. Paul's text, as such, you could say that in a certain way and in a perspective like Teilhard de Chardin's, the total earth, the elements, the organisms, the animals are all growing towards the revelation of the sons of God. In other words, everything in the world is destined to the grace of glory, that is, to the praise of the glory of grace. It's something that is very beautiful. And in this respect I think that the groaning of the creature is the thirst for grace. But it is an analogical thirst because the scorpions, the centipedes, and even the elephants that I appreciate very much have a way of relating to grace that is not so gracious, and certainly not the kind of relationship to grace that I witnessed some days ago with a cancer patient.

Now, in Buddhism things are quite dif-

ferent. Suffering is universal and it calls for
some kind of compassion, some kind of pity.
Buddhism is a way through pity, implying
universal suffering, of refusing violence. In
other words, suffering of the world as
generating within us some kind of pity is an
invitation to nonviolence. This is totally different. To St. Paul, suffering is an invitation to
praise the glory of grace. But in Buddhism it
is an invitation to be nonviolent.

QUESTION: I don't want to pursue any further the line of
thought which I began and found hard to continue, but I think we got a clear answer on the
question, namely, if I understand you correctly, suffering has as its cause more than
just sin, but the human condition. It seems to
me that this leads to unavoidable consequences, namely that the glorified Christ who
is fully human must also suffer and that there
must be suffering in heaven, since we will not
lose our human condition but only have it
elevated. Those are problems that are unsolvable when we admit that suffering comes
in and out of sin.

ANSWER: I believe that the question that you have
raised was inspired to me previously by the
fact that after the Resurrection Christ keeps
his wounds. And I thought of certain paint-
ings of Jerome Bosch that I was able to comment upon at other occasions and where the
faces of the elected show a kind of inexpressible sadness. And I asked myself: is not
a certain glorified sadness necessary to our
supreme joy itself? To the extent that I was
able to give some kind of answer to this question in the book that I entitled, *The Word and*

the Cross, I would say that there will always be a certain suffering linked up to the greatest joy. And I think that's the suffering of the saints, of the mystics. That kind of suffering is tied to the human condition. It exists in that we are not God, that we are different and far from God. I would like to simply point out that there is something quite admirable in St. Thomas and in the medieval theologians when they comment on St. John's Gospel. In St. John's prologue, where it is said, "And without Him nothing was made," they read (because it is a question of punctuation), "What was made was life in Him." All things, before they existed, were life in God, were identical to God. Now, through creation, no matter how beautiful this creation is, things have become distinct from God, they are not in paradise anymore. Creation itself, in all its glory, is a first fall and from this fall there is no healing, no more than there would be healing for the wounds of Jesus. But it is a distance that is always glorified in love.

QUESTION: What role does Divine Providence play in suffering?

ANSWER: You know, that was the old problem of evil. We said, if God is all powerful and if He is good, how can evil exist? If there is evil, it is because God wants it or because He can't prevent it. If God wants it, then He is bad and if He can't do anything about it, then He is powerless. So, therefore, evil was a kind of refutation of God. Well, I think that is an image, an idea of Providence which is a bit human-like. We have a God who appears to be some kind of administrator, a president of the board, a prime minister who deals with this or that, who tries to adjust different things here and there. I think that such an image is probably deficient. I believe that the love of God is not a Leibnizian calculation of means and purpose, that the God of the Gospel is not a Providence in the sense of a teleological system. I think that the word *"agape"* is not meant to set up means in view of a purpose, but it means an overflowing without any particular reason, just for the joy that there is something that exists in the world, be it through suffering. And I would say, as Jesus said about the woman who is having a child, the woman is in labor and suffering, but she knows that through her somebody has come into the world. I think that is the final joy, which has nothing to do with a cosmic administration according to the regulation of purpose and means.

NOTES

[1]Cfr. J.J. Bochenski, *The Logic of Religion,* New York University Press, 1965, pp. 31-34.

[2]The sixth of the theses on Feuerbach: cfr. F. Engels, *Ludwig Feuerbach und der Ausgang der Klassischen deutchen Philosophie,* Dietz Verlag, Berlin, 1970, p. 77.

[3]Cfr. *Les Passions de l'ame,* traduction M. Corvez, Paris-Tournai, 1949, p. 11ff.

[4]The text is cited and translated by B.K. Matilal, *The Enigma of Buddhism: Dukha and Nirvana,* in Journal of Dharma, July 1977, Vol. II, n. 3, p. 302.

[5]Cfr. Matilal, art. cit., p. 303.

[6]M. Pradines, *Traite de Psychologie Generale,* I Le Psychisme elementaire, 3rd Edition, P.U.F., Paris, 1948, p. 371.

[7]*Ibid.,* p. 371, 372, 373.

[8]*Ibid.,* p. 382.

⁹*Ibid.*, p. 382.

¹⁰*Op. cit.*, p. 336.

¹¹*Op. cit.*, p. 281.

¹²Cfr. R. Le Senne, *Traite de Morale*, P.U.F., Paris, 3rd Edition, pp. 109-127. Despite a little outdated information, there is a suggestive study here on the "*Delivre vivant*" according to Buddhism.

¹³I disagree with Matilal on this point, *art. cit.*, p. 304. The polyvalent logic which he invokes has validity only in the domain of "any object whatever." It does not resolve the logical problem posed by Buddhism for the simple reason that this envisages an "X" which is not situated in any domain of object.

¹⁴*Art. Cit.*, p. 305.

¹⁵The complete text will be found in S.W. Beck-Oldenbourg, I, p. 666-668. The title of the work is *Ideen zu einer Philosophie der Natur*. Cfr. a translation of our text by S. Jankelevitch, *Schelling, Essais,* Paris, Aubier, 1946, pp. 50-51.

Part II

A SCRIPTURAL AND THEOLOGICAL APPROACH TO HUMAN SUFFERING

The Congress specifically intended to give a Christian perspective on the meaning of human suffering, hence enlisted two outstanding professors here in the United States to treat the subject from the basis of Divine Revelation. Dr. Carroll Stuhlmueller of the Catholic Tehological Union, Chicago, goes to the heart of the matter in the Old Testament, portraying the violence and suffering which gave birth to Israel and remained a continuing part of its history. Dr. Arthur McGill of Harvard, Cambridge, expertly interprets the New Testament teaching on suffering, particularly the meaning given to it by the passion and death of Christ. In doing this, he portrays this against our present day culture which is so antithetical to this meaning.

Chapter 3

VOICES OF SUFFERING IN BIBLICAL PROPHECY AND PRAYER
Dr. Caroll Stuhlmueller

The *Bible,* at least in many of its traditions and books, came to birth surrounded by voices of suffering. Such is the law of life, established by God (Gen. 3:16a) and recognized by Jesus (John 16:21) as well as by the early Church (Rev. 12:2), that a mother suffer birth pangs to bring forth new life. We expect the *Bible,* the word of life, to be obedient to this law.

The Scriptures[1] began their period of gestation when God responded to voices of suffering and said to Moses:

> I have witnessed the affliction of my people . . . and *have heard their cry of complaint* against their slave drivers. . . . Therefore I have come down to rescue them. . . . I will send you . . . to lead my people, the Israelites, out of [slavery and agony]. (Ex. 3:7-10)

Inarticulate groans, at times hopeless and meaningless for Israel, vibrated within God's loving concern, and in God they received a purpose, a future, a *word,* bringing them to birth and enabling them to live within His chosen people.[2] The words of the *Bible* preserve the memory of sorrow and its triumphs in new life.[3] Thus the *Bible* was able to provide a "word" for *new* mysterious moments of sorrow. What could have remained only jumbled and crashing noise was reassembled with script and interpretation, music and liturgical ceremony. Israel could then be sensitized to new voices of suffering, communicate with God, and praise Him for anticipated victory. The *Bible,* therefore, kept a continuous dialogue between Israel's voice of suffering and the Lord's response of redemptive action.

When, however, these sacred words lost contact with "the affliction of my people . . . and . . . their cry of complaint against their slave drivers," God decided to "rend the heavens and come down" again (Is. 63:19).[4] He would take action in the person of His servants, the prophets. The prophets drew upon traditions and transcribed these new scrambled voices of suffering into clear and intelligible sentences. Like Moses they bequeathed a humble confession or better a contemplative remembrance beyond words. In fact, the purpose of the sacred words was to communicate between a suffering people and an awesome, loving God and to be in touch with God's mysterious hopes for His people. We meet then in the Bible a mystical voice of prayer.

Some examples of contemplative interaction can be cited, to prepare ourselves for the investigation of this study.

> People trembled and said to Moses: "Surely this great fire will consume us. . . . For what mortal has heard . . . the voice of the living God speaking from the midst of fire, and survived?" (Deut. 5:25-26)
> As Moses "entered the tent (where) the column of cloud would come down[6] . . . all the people would rise and worship." (Ex. 33:9-10)
> The same Moses had to draw a veil over his face, which was radiant with splendor after he spoke with the Lord and received the sacred word. (Ex. 34:29-35)
> The prophets like Isaiah declared after a vision of the

Lord from the Holy of Holies, "Woe is me, I am doomed!"
(Is. 6:5), or cried out like Jeremiah, "You duped me, O Lord!
. . . you were too strong for me." (Jer. 20:7), or fell face
against the earth like Ezekiel upon seeing the glory of the
Lord. (Ex. 2:1)

The *Bible,* then as the Word of God, was born and
developed amid voices of suffering and prayer. We will investigate how these voices surrounded the origin of the *Bible*
in the Mosaic period and its transition at the crucial time of
the exile. This study will be divided into three sections:

1 . The secular violence of Egyptian slavery which
wrenched voices of suffering out of Israel; God
stepped forward with new violence against Egypt in
redeeming Israel; when Israel put this wondrous,
divine intervention into words and music, the *Bible*
was born and a glimpse was given of a future
shalom, a contemplative stance beyond words.
2. Groans and frustration were heard again, 600 to 700
years after Moses during the Babylonian exile. The
"Great Unknown," author of Is. 40-55, drew upon
the Mosaic traditions, in order to put these new
voices of suffering into words, words of vaulting
hopes and cosmic reach, a redemption beyond
human power, yet again making use of human
means, even the pagan Cyrus. At this point Israel
balked—as she once murmured in the desert against
Moses—and rejected the prophet who then wrote
the exquisite "Songs of the Suffering Servant."
3. The songs of the *'ebed yahweh* provide a rich synthesis of hope, suffering, and silent prayer.

Reassembling the material in this study in a slightly different way, we signal out three main elements: (1) *secular
violence and oppression* and God's determination to overcome it, even violently, out of compassion for the poor; (2)

prophetical determination to communicate with new acts of oppression, secular or religious, and to speak its voice of suffering; and (3) *contemplative prayer* which sustains a vision of *shalom* beyond the rational scope of words.

SECULAR VIOLENCE AND BIBLICAL VOICES OF SUFFERING AND PRAYERS

Biblical religion did not emerge out of a need for theological manuals, or for a code of morals, not even from the necessity to worship God with proper liturgy. In the *Bible* religion began from a *secular* situation of slavery and oppression which moved God to respond in turn with secular liberation. God sent Moses to deal with issues of military might and human indignity.

In this respect Israel's religion remained uniquely different from all other people's. Other ancient Near Eastern religions would not trace their genesis back to a humiliating moment of history but to the glorious establishment of a temple with its city, priesthood, and royalty.[7] While the literature of these peoples seemed to associate religious and secular origins with the creation of the heavens and the earth, the provincial purpose and narrow focus of this mythology quickly become evident. The *enuma elish* moves rapidly to the worship of Marduk at Babylon. Egyptian creation stories center around shrines. "Every important cult-center of Egypt asserted its primacy by the dogma that it was the site of creation."[8] Other signs of a limited setting can be detected in the myths. If in Mesopotamia the first days of planet earth were caught in a swirl of darkness and savage violence, the reason lies in the geography of the land of the Tigris and Euphrates Rivers. It was open to military invasion from all sides. In Egypt, on the contrary, the origin of life and society turned out to be peaceful and orderly, like the calculated rise and fall of the Nile River. The reason for this difference lies in

Egypt's almost impregnable borders of the Mediterranean or Red Sea to its north and east, the rapids and swamps of the Nile River to the south, and the mighty Sahara Desert on its western flank.[9] Even when the dawn of creation was tumultuous as in Mesopotamia, still the newly created temple-city became a model of peace, fruitfulness, and stability. All of these religions, therefore, looked *back* to their golden age. The purpose of religion was to regain as much as was humanly possible of this first, blissful age.

These religions seemed much more spiritual than Israel's, whose origins were not found in God's majestic creation of the universe but in freeing a couple of thousand people from forced labor. Not only in origin, but in all moments of history, other Near Eastern peoples saw a numinous or "supernatural" aura permeating life and culture far more seriously and extensively than Israel did.[10] Both Egypt and Mesopotamia, moreover, turned out to be far more advanced in legal structures, in the orderly arrangement of society, in wisdom and proverbs. Their kings were much more influential and manipulative than David or even Solomon. All this visible show of religion, however, could be judged a very rational or political attempt to control the mysteries of life and the destinies of people. When religion is compelled to manifest its divinity by every human means possible, religion becomes identifiable with politics in its compromise and intrigue, with military might and the latest weapons of war, with pageantry and its most awesome symbols and its mystifying language. Voices of suffering tend to be muffled; voices of prayer no longer rise from hopes beyond human experience and beyond rational control. The secular origins of Israel's religion, amid pain and humiliation, assured a more contemplative spirit at its heart and a continuous faith-compulsion toward the future.

In this first section we investigate voices of suffering and prayer: (1) in Israel's *secular origins* and *liturgical celebra-*

tion; and (2) in the divine order that Israel *wait* for 40 years in the desert and that the nonelect gentiles wait still longer.

Israel's religion, as we have already mentioned and now wish to explain more adequately, was born in suffering and for reasons very secular. Israel belonged to a group of Asiatic people—the Hyksos—who had migrated to Egypt, at first in small groups and scattered over a century or more. Eventually these Asiatics became strong enough, aided perhaps by "a new and well-organized wave of warriors,"[11] to seize power and set up the 15th and 16th dynasties of Egypt.[12] When they were overthrown and replaced by a native Egyptian dynasty, first in southern or upper Egypt, and then in the Delta region, Israelites suffered the consequences of this fall from power. Israel herself could once have been a part of the Asiatic or foreign masters of Egypt. Revenge, fear, and hatred were bound to dictate Egypt's later response to the Israelites, once the tables were turned round.

Violence breeds more violence. These words repeat a truism. Yet, they need to be said over again, lest we forget that the religion of Israel was born out of tumultuous voices of human suffering. And the violence which begot Yahwism, in its turn brought violence to Egypt. Such at least is the Biblical story of the 10 plagues and the account of the Red Sea. These important epic narratives contain a remembrance and spoke to a continuous reality of suffering which struck a whole group of people, the innocent along with the guilty.[13]

If conception and birth contain the genes, color, and character of a child's whole life, then Israel's religion must always remain a response to secular suffering and human oppression. It was more than that, as we shall see, but "that" it certainly was! And "that" it would remain ever afterwards: in the conquest and settlement of the promised land, in the wars and accomplishments of David and his dynasty, in the horrendous destruction of Jerusalem and the Babylonian exile, in the return from exile after the military victories of Cyrus the Great, and finally in the Maccabean wars of liberation and later the Roman occupation.[14]

Yahweh, the God of Israel, became forever associated with the liberation of Israel.[15] The Lord declared in the Ten Commandments:

> I, the Lord, am your God, who brought you out of the land of Egypt, that place of slavery. (Ex. 20:2; Deut. 5:6)

Among the most important titles or epithets of Israel's God was *yahweh sebā'ôt,* the Lord of hosts or armies. The root, *sāba',* indicates "service in war," "warfare," "fighting men."[16] Frank Moore Cross, in discussing "The Cultus of the Israelite League," begins with a section on "The Divine Warrior" and draws attention to Ps. 24:7-10.[17]

> Who is this king of glory?
>   The LORD, strong and mighty,
>   The LORD, mighty in battle. . . .
> Who is this king of glory?
>   The LORD of hosts. (Ps. 24:8,10)

Later we will pursue the epic or mythic proportions of Israel's religion, but for the moment we can remain with one of Cross' initial statements, that myth never dissolved the *historical* background of Israel's religion and its liturgical celebration.[18] Israel's history had begun with oppression and violence, and this situation dictated the major qualities of Israel's titles for God. At its birth, then, we can locate Israel in history and that history was secular and oppressive. *Essentially,* Israel's religion must echo within history its secular origins and must respond to new voices of suffering and oppression.

Israel's *secular* liberation sustained its momentum into the future *through religious celebration.*[19] The *Bible* recognizes the close connection between its secular origins and the cultic or liturgical renewal of these origins. Liturgy is one of the threads woven in and out of the warp and woof of the Scriptures.[20] In the exodus narrative, an episode will combine one account more sober and closer to earlier secular events, with another account far more exalted and closer to later religious experience. In the story of the first plague, the Yahwist ("J") narrative is already cast in epic form with strong influence from the prophetic stories or legends[21] (cf. 1 Kgs. 17; 2 Kgs. 6); it lacks, however, the characteristic cultic emphasis of the Priestly Tradition. "J" describes Moses' intervention before Pharaoh:

> The LORD now says: "This is how you shall know that I am the LORD. ([Moses] will strike the water of the river with the staff I hold, and the river shall be changed into blood. The fish in the river shall die, and the river itself shall become so polluted that the Egyptians will be unable to drink its water." As a result all the Egyptians had to dig in the neighborhood of the river for drinking water. (Ex. 7:17-18, 24)

Along with the Yahwist, we meet another tradition folded into the Biblical account of Ex. 7:14-24. This Priestly Tradition enhanced the role of the *priest* Aaron and the *religious-liturgical* significance of the plague-epic. The variations from "J" are significant:

> The LORD said to Moses, "Say to *Aaron;* Take *your* staff and stretch out your hand over the waters of Egypt—*their streams and canals and pools, all their supplies of water*—that everything may become blood. Throughout the land of Egypt there shall be blood, even in the wooden pails and stone jars." (Ex. 7:19)

Clearly enough not only is the role of the priest superseding that of Moses but a religious-liturgical application is stressed, as the plagues find their ultimate solution in the cultic celebration of the Passover. The catechetical message here in the first plague teaches that everything a sinner touches will turn to blood—that is, turn against him or her and become destructive of life.

Another example by which we can observe the transfer from secular events to religious celebration is located in Num.

10:35 and Ps. 68. The passage in Numbers recalls the phenomenon of the "Holy War," in which the ark of the covenant was "the visible sign" of the Lord's presence.[22] A long tradition associated the ark with Israel's wars, and this historical background governs the setting in Num. 10:35:

> Whenever the ark set out, Moses would say,
> "Arise, O LORD, that your enemies may be scattered,
> and those who hate you may flee before you."

This same verse, however, with slight modifications becomes the introductory lines of Ps. 68. This psalm, admittedly one of the most difficult in the entire psalter from a textual and redactional viewpoint, clearly enough combines several liturgical forms: vision (v. 2-3); oracle (v. 12-14); narrative of salvation events (v. 8-11, 15); cultic acts of procession (v. 25-28), and prayer (v. 28-32).[23] Ps. 68 then has thoroughly transferred the war cry into a liturgical summons, the secular dependence upon the family or clan into a moral command to care for the orphan and widow (v. 6), the warriors' gathering at a central sanctuary like Shiloh before battle, into a religious assembly at Shechem or Jerusalem.

The story of earlier incidents, moreover, is told in such a way that the Lord's mysterious presence and hopes were accentuated. Thus voices of prayer were made to accompany a remembrance of secular oppression and deliverance. This goal was achieved by incorporating elements of Canaanite myths. These mythological features never falsified memories but served to bring out the hidden potential of God's presence. Myths spoke to the residual faith of a people. They set up a relationship between the narrow world of Israel and the cosmic sweep of the universe.[24] Israel's wars were associated with titanic battles of good and evil across the universe; and these mythological struggles heightened Israel's awareness of the overwhelming consequences of its own moral decisions.

By forcing Israel to look beyond the horizons of their Promised Land, at least momentarily, a seed was sown for their religion to become worldwide. This hope was to remain hidden and almost totally unnoticed; it would burst into bloom only in the "Songs of the Suffering Sevant." For that we must wait, but it is helpful to see that voices of contemplative or mystical prayers will come to new life amid new voices of heroic suffering.

Such liturgical celebrations, as we have already mentioned, transformed the early episodes of Israel's existence into "history." When Israel came out of Egypt, nothing of historical significance happened. The exodus made no dent upon Egyptian economy, politics, or international relations; there is no allusion to it in the many historical documents from the land of the Nile.[25] It seems quite likely that kindred tribes or related people had slipped out of Egypt before Moses and found their way into Canaan where Joshua encountered them and made treaties with them. Yet, it was only the exodus led by Moses that qualified as history—because that by Moses was to be liturgically celebrated and so to impart its religious meaning and interpretation to the others.[26] Without liturgy and the extraordinary faith of Moses in Yahweh, Israel would be no more remembered today than are the Moabites or Ammonites. In fact, not even the great historical Pharaohs of ancient Egypt rank in importance with Moses in world history today.

Liturgy then—and the same must be said for the Church—not only derived its existence from God's merciful concern for the poor and the oppressed, but liturgy gave hope to each new generation of the poor and the oppressed. Moreover, as we will point out in studying the prophets, only when liturgy maintained its continuous contact with the poor in the secular world and endeavored to express their voice of suffering, did it have a right to exist.

Up to now, we have attuned ourselves to hear voices of suffering and prayer in the *physical and moral* violence within Israel's origins as a people and within the liturgical reliving of those first days. We turn now to another type of violence, already alluded to in this study, the *psychological* violence of *waiting*. God sentenced Israel to 40 years of wandering in the desert (Num. 14:20-35,) a penitential period with profound effects upon biblical religion. All other nations, moreover, had to wait even longer than Israel and according to the Hebrew Scriptures to remain in the category of the nonchosen or the nonelect. We hear new voices of suffering, each of which will resound through the long history of the *Bible*. The motif of *waiting*, moreover, nurtures that type of faith essential for contemplative prayer.

Waiting can be as joyful as a child's expectation of birthday gifts, or it can drive a person or an entire people to desperation. When, for instance, King Ahaz faced military invasion and a serious threat to his dynasty, the prophet Isaiah advised waiting upon the Lord:

> Take care and be calm!
> Do not fear and do not let your heart be frightened. (Is. 7:4)

The King and all the people refused to "wait." Instead, they panicked. The prophet was later to comment on the situation:[27]

> For thus said the Lord God, the Holy One of Israel:
> By waiting and by calm you shall be saved, in quiet and in trust
> your strength lies. But this you did not wish.
> "No," you said, "Upon horses we will flee."—Very well,
> flee!
> "Upon swift steeds we will ride,"—Not so swift as your pursuers. (Is. 30:15-16)

Such a response on Israel's part is normal; all of us easily lose heart and then overreact either with excessive fear or with a stampede of hysteria. It will help to look at the Biblical background of such psychological tension and to learn its potential as well for contemplative prayer.

Biblically, we trace the sources of such tension to a double-track religious system, whose two lines seldom met but rather were generally placing one another in jeopardy. The strain and stress of this difference were well expressed by Walter Brueggemann under the rubric of Israel as "God's *homeless* people" and as "God's *landed* people"[25]—a people of the exodus and desert as well as a people of the promised land and holy city.

Even to this day Israel remains God's homeless people in search of its land. We find this image already in Abraham, summoned by the Lord to "Go forth from the land of your kinsfolk and from your father's house to a land that I will show you" (Gen. 12:1). In this new land, however, Abraham waited as a *gēr* or resident alien. Roland de vaux compares the *gēr* to "the refugee or lone man who came seeking the protection of a tribe other than his own."[29] Once Israel acquired possession of Canaan, Israel became the *'am ha'ares* (the people of the land) and the former owners were reduced to the status of *gēr*! Yet, the levitical tribe of priests, symbolic of Israel and particularly of the firstborn who inherited a double share of family property (Num. 8:16-18; Deut. 21:15-17), themselves owned no property (Judg. 17:7-9; 19:1; Deut. 18:1-5) and therefore were legally grouped with the *gēr* (Deut. 12:12; 14:29; 26:12). The tension between the *gēr* or "homeless people" and the *'am hā'àres* or "landed people" is very evident: Abraham the *gēr* longed for the promised land; the landed people, recipients of that promise, were typified by Levites, deprived of that land! Religion somehow was always drawing the people away from where they were rooted and offering a vision of things "unseen" (1 Cor. 4:16-18).[30]

The tension shows up in another basic, religious motif of the *Bible:* the exodus out of Egypt and the wandering through the Sinai Desert. God could have chosen another group of refugees who took a northern route out of Egypt and acquired their territory quickly and "peacefully."[31] Instead, however, the basic theme and structure of Biblical religion were to be drawn from the experience of Moses' followers who had been condemned to desert wandering. Yet, the entire exodus would make no sense, if it were to lead nowhere, and the sentence of 40 years of desert wandering for rebelling against the Lord would have been no punishment at all, simply the normal way of life for a nomad, if Israel's hopes and theology did not include the promised land.

Wandering in the desert drew cries of pain and unrest from Israel. These were "not disgruntled complaints (but) . . . open rebellion."[32] As George W. Coats established in his monograph, *Rebellion in the Wilderness,* Israel's murmuring, which began in the desert against Moses on the part of a few families (Num. 16), was seen as a pattern by which to explain Israel's continuous history in the promised land. This history of revolts and jealousy continued in the conflicts between the northern and southern Kingdoms—as reflected in the Yahwist Tradition—and in Israel's tragic lack of faith and God's anger in the fall of the North—as reflected in the Deuteronomic Tradition.[33] All of this history was accompanied with tension and voices of suffering, as well as a contemplative vision and its voice of anguish and desire.

The promised land, consequently, became at different times a sign of the Lord's generosity, a temptation, a task, a threat, a sign of destruction as well as of new hope. Some texts, as in Jer. 2:2-3, reflect the idyllic joy of a honeymoon; others, like Is. 5:1-7, announce "ruin" and "bloodshed." Because Israel's religion combined two motifs, exodus wandering and promised land, each equally essential and yet each at odds with the other, there lay at its heart a tragic tension, "tragic" in the classical sense of heroic proportions beyond human control. Walter Brueggemann wrote it: "The *Bible* is the story of God's people with God's land. It is the agony of trying to be in history [theme of the "promised land"] but without standing ground in history [theme of continuous exodus or wandering]."[34] The former is a "secular" call, the ground of biblical religion; the latter, a "contemplative" call, the flowering of seeds hidden in that ground.

Earlier in discussing voices of suffering in Israel's origins, we delayed over the pain and contemplation which accompanied *physical* or *military* violence. More proximately we investigated the *psychological* violence inherent in a religion which relied upon such conflicting motifs as a "homeless people" with their exodus through the desert and a "landed people" with their rural countryside and urban affluence. Such violence, physical and psychological, disrupted God's peace; and as in the case of Adam and Eve, it wrung voices of suffering from Israel and her neighbors, but it also led continuously to a vision beyond human comprehension, deserving the name of contemplative prayer.

To summarize this first part, we find that the initial and formative period of Old Testament religion can be drawn only with deep lines of physical violence. It resulted in voices of suffering and in contemplative prayer beyond normal human hope. It found innocent people, like Israelites enslaved in Egypt and crying out for relief, or like Egyptians, hurt and destroyed in God's deliverance of Israel. Not all Egyptians were evil,[35] and the Bible is clear enough that not all Israelites were saintly. Egypt, moreover, typifies all the gōyîm or gentile nations, the nonelect people of the world; this group "groans (silently) and is in agony even until now" (Rom. 8:22).

Both Israel and the nations were required to "wait." Faith to wait for a future beyond human understanding and beyond one's lifetime engenders an attitude or voice of contemplative prayer.

PROPHETIC HOPES AND NEW VOICES OF SUFFERING AND PRAYER

The pointer of Israelite history reacted in shock and

charged forward a full 180 degrees. Nebuchadnezzar had destroyed Jerusalem, looted and demolished the temple, and marched the people into exile. The "landed people" were reduced to a "homeless people," the sacred people were once again "on unclean soil" (Am. 7:17), a victim trampled down within the world of secular politics. Although Babylon, the oppressor, was no longer Egypt, but a country far away in the opposite direction, nonetheless, a "desert, [even more] vast and fearful" than Sinai (Deut. 1:19) separated Israel from their homeland. Once again the Lord says: "I have witnessed the affliction of my people . . . and have heard their cry of complaint." Because of these new voices of suffering God must appear again as at Sinai (Ex. 3:19) and summon Israel on a new exodus. Such a message rings out in the golden poetry of Deutero-Isaiah, the "Great Unknown" author of chapters 40-55 in the scroll of Isaiah.

Within Is. 40-55 we focus our investigation upon prophetic voices of suffering and prayer. We will listen to these voices (1) as Deutero-Isaiah sang of the *new exodus* theme and (2) argued the fulfillment of prophecy in poems about *first and last*. While these two themes are found principally in chapters 41-48, we will turn (3) to chapters 49:1 and 55:11 for its reflection on suffering and prayer as the prophet became isolated from the people and even from himself.

Only a remnant of tired and hopeless people remained (Is. 40:27-31). Secular forces had swept in and seemingly destroyed their theology! Yet, by remembering the words and theology of temple ritual, mediated through Deuteronomy and the prophets Hosea and Jeremiah,[36] Deutero-Isaiah was able to enunciate what was happening and to interpret the dreadful events. Mute groans and hidden suffering were given a voice with which to cry out and be heard by God, so that a new and even more glorious exodus would begin (cf., Is. 43:16-21).

Particularly in chapters 40-55, Deutero-Isaiah drew upon the exodus symbolism, updated it with later prophetic themes and Babylonian mythology, and finally integrated it all into a new systematic theology of redemption. Within the synthesis we hear different voices of suffering. We could, however, fail to perceive these expressions of pain because the dominant note of the prophetic preaching reached high with hymnic praise over God's victory and Israel's redemption.

The basic motif is that of the exodus. This new exodus will be undertaken not only with world attention but even at the command of God's heavenly court. The Book of Consolation opens with the well-known scene of the divine throneroom where God is in dialogue with the celestial assembly.[37] The scenario seems to combine earlier prophetic scenes from the prophet Macaiah (1 Kgs. 22:19), the call of First Isaiah (Is. 6:1-3), and possibly the divine *kebôd yhwh* (the glory of the Lord) in Ezekiel (Ez. 1 & 10). Important features are incorporated from the Babylonian New Year's festival, when at *akitu* Marduk was enthroned within the Ziggurat, surrounded by tutelary gods which had been borne here in solemn procession from neighboring city-states.[38] The opening words of the Lord combine pathos and regret as they announce a new exodus, to be carried out amid cosmic upheavals of collapsing mountains and rising valleys. "Comfort! Oh, Comfort my people. . . . Speak to the heart of Jerusalem."[39] These words occur in the plural imperative form and therefore were addressed to several lesser gods or angels within the assembly. These members of the divine court obediently cried out, one after another in v. 3-5, v. 6a', v. 8, and v. 9-10.

God's own sorrow or regret is clearly registered in the divine confession: "Indeed, she Jerusalem has received from the hand of the Lord *double* for all her sins." Did God feel that Israel had been punished too harshly? The double command, moreover, to "Comfort! Oh, Comfort!" plus the grammatical (*piel*) form of comfort, *nahămû nahămû,* and speak, *dabbĕrû,* emphasize the forceful reaction of God. The response of the prophet in v. 6b-7, "I answer, 'What shall I cry out? All flesh is grass!'" well up from a desperate, almost hopeless person.

In another poem on the new exodus (43:1-7) we can perceive still more poignantly God's sense of pain—or in the language of Abraham Heschel, the divine pathos.[40] God is speaking to an Israel, destitute and miserable, scattered like orphans to "the ends of the earth." We are impressed by the terms of endearment, spoken by the mighty Creator to this helpless, forlorn people, his very own children:

> Fear not! I am your blood relative, I call you by *your* name.
> Your are mine. As you pass through the waters, I am with you.
> . . . Because you are precious in my eyes, and glorious. I, yes I
> love you. I give all other peoples in exchange for you! . . . All
> are to be called by *my* name. . . .[41]

Deutero-Isaiah formed an "inclusion," signifying the start and especially the end of a literary piece, by repeating "called by name."[42] In the beginning God is said to call Israel "by *your* name," but after Israel experienced the transforming and creative love of the Lord, she is "called by *my* name." God must have been in pain and agony—just as at other times he was angered or made jealous by Israel—when he addressed such tender, caring words to a people, his very own children, in such desperate distress.

This voice of divine suffering, can be heard still more distinctly in 43:22-28. Here the prophet applied both to Yahweh and to Israel the Hebrew word *'ābad*, which means "to serve as a slave." It is employed twice, according to the Hebrew *hiphil* or causative form of the verb: "to force someone to bear the burdens of slavery." The passage takes on a special significance, when we recall that this same prophet wrote the *'ebed Yahwe* or servant of the Lord poems. In 43:22-28 God himself is the "suffering servant," affected by Israel's sins and disloyalty:

You were not worshiping me, O Jacob, that you should become weary of me, O Israel. You were not bringing me sheep for your holocausts, nor honoring me with your sacrifices. *I did not burden you (he'ĕbadtîkā)* with grain offerings nor weary you about frankincense. . . . Instead, *you burdened me (he'ebadtanî)* with your sins, and wearied me with your crimes.[43]

Deutero-Isaiah wove a double *Schüsselwort* in and out of this passage, to be burdened (*'ābad*) and to be weary (*yāqa'*). Perhaps, no one is more overburdened with useless pain than that person who silently groans: "'I am tired and weary.'" Such a one is close to despair and suicide. Here that one is God who says: "You have made a slave of me; I am wearied with your crimes. I am tired and almost giving up." Yet, God has not given up, and the very next verse begins with the repeated, "'ānōkî 'ānōkî hû'—I, yes I am that one, wiping out your crimes for my own sake.'"[45] Such tender love had been taken advantage of and almost destroyed by its all-consuming goodness. Yet now it becomes the all-powerful force—for its own sake and for no other human reason—why sins are forgiven and wiped away.

In Deutero-Isaiah's poems about the new exodus, we heard voices of suffering. While in earlier texts of the *Bible* these voices were wrung from Israel and the foreign nations, now in the Book of Consolation we perceive them to issue also from the heart of the Lord God.[46] If Israel sensed this blending of voices in suffering, her own and God's, then a mystic aura must have pervaded the suffering. Voices of contemplative prayer are merging with voices of suffering.

This perception of divine pathos brings the sublimity of the Godhead immanently present within the human heart. Such majestic grandeur must have accentuated the people's suffering. How could the exiles in their misery listen to the magnificent poetry of Is. 40:1-11, where God is surrounded by his heavenly court and these command mountains to collapse and valleys to rise? Or in 43:1-7 God's children are seen in divine oracle, streaming towards him from the four corners of the universe. We meet a rich ensemble of Biblical and Mesopotamian motifs like exodus, covenant, New Year's festival, miraculous water in the desert, opening of the sea, and gō'ēl relationship. Liturgical styles intermingle like hymns, praise, oracles, homiletic disputation, and credal confessions.[47] Visions of such grandeur make the miserable reality of life unbearable. It is all the more difficult to disentangle the voices of suffering, God's and Israel's, from one another and from the voices of prayer.

To appreciate the prophetic voices of prayer in Deutero-Isaiah, we turn to another series of poems, dedicated to Yahweh as "First and Last." The prophet here put together one of the first extended theological discourses in the *Bible*.[48] He consistently develops his topic by means of sacred traditions and contemporary problems; he argues his case in the literary form of a disputation or judgment speech.[49]

The main theme or question is placed clearly enough in 41:21-23, where Deutero-Isaiah editorially addresses the pagan gods:[50]

> Present your case, says the Lord; bring forward your reasons.
> . . . Let them come near and foretell to us what it is that shall happen! What are the things of long ago? [predicted by you and fulfilled?] Tell us, that we may reflect on them And know their outcome; or declare to us the things to come! Foretell the things that shall come forward, that we may know that you are gods!

Because Yahweh alone has fulfilled the words of the earlier prophets, who were persecuted and rejected by the people of Israel, he can be counted on right now. The prophet wrote:

> See, the earlier things have come to pass, new ones I now foretell; Before they spring into being, I announce them to you. (42:9)

This "new thing" is Israel's return from exile.[51] The fact that the prophet had to argue his case over and over again reinforces the impression left with us in chapters 40-55, that Israel was afflicted with malaise. Voices or sighs of suffering rose from the Israelites as they listened to the prophet.

To realize the depths of prophetic prayer in these poems, Deutero-Isaiah stressed a fulfillment of prophecy that is *surprising, imminent,* and *personal to Yahweh.* We meet the Hebrew word *pit'om,*[52] which means "suddenly" or "by surprise" in 48:3:

> First things ahead of time I announced; they issued from my mouth and I made sure you heard them; Suddenly I took action, and they came to be.

According to these lines, even the most carefully articulated prophecy, announced ahead of time and effectively communicated, never provided such a clear blueprint of the future that Israel knew exactly *what* would happen, *when* and *where.* Fulfillment could and did come *pit'om,* suddenly and by surprise.[53] Israel must await the future with faith and a sense of wonder, most important qualities for prayer.

Later in the same poem, Deutero-Isaiah introduced another significant factor for prayer. We read:

> From *now* ('*attâ*) I announce new things to you, hidden things which you had not known. *Now* ('*attâ*) they stand created.
> (48:6b-7a)

The repetition of "now" ('*attâ*) shows that fulfillment can happen almost at the moment of prophecy, so powerful and effective is God's word. Prayer, in which we remain very close to God and God to us, prayer which impresses us with wondrous hopes, such an experience is *immediately* transforming and sets us at once towards a future beyond our control. Already in the depths of ourselves, we are what we hope to be. *"Now"* they stand "created."[54]

For Deutero-Isaiah, moreover, fulfillment involved people of international stature: Cyrus and his victory over Babylon, his edict of liberation for Israel, the return of Yahweh's elect people. Yet, no matter how momentous be any single one of these details, the focus returned to the person of Yahweh.

> I am that one, yes I, the first. Indeed, I am [also] the last.[55]
> Yes, my left hand laid the foundations of the earth my right hand spread out the skies. When I call out to them they stand forth at once. (Is. 48:12b-13)

These lines abound with ecstatic wonder as the entire cosmos becomes a temple of liturgical action, each part of it responding majestically to God's command, and everything caught up in the presence of the Lord. "I am all of this, the first and the last, and I order all of it to fulfill my promises to Israel."

Prayer has reached such an intense degree of mystical contemplation that even the most engrossing of world events do not distract from the presence of Yahweh. This profound recollection did not result from cutting oneself off from international politics and national tragedies; rather, one must listen to these secular events in such a way as to hear God's voice within them. We are back again with the founding of Israel in Mosaic times. At that time God heard the voice of His suffering or murmuring people.[56] Deutero-Isaiah added that God not only listened, He also suffered with His people and carried their burden, even their sin (43:24). When, therefore, the voice of oppression and sorrow was heard, God's presence was perceived. "I am there, yes I, the first in the fulfillment of every prophecy. Indeed I am the last now in the new creation, appearing suddenly by surprise."

Another voice of suffering can be heard in the poems about "First and Last," in fact throughout chapters 40-55, were we to center attention on the foreign nations. These gentile peoples are roundly rejected and severely punished in a whole series of passages (40:15-20; 41:14-16, 25; 42:13-17; 43:3, 6; 45:24; chapter 47); this number of texts rises significantly if we include the pronouncements against foreign gods and idolaters (40:18-20; 41:6-7; 40:26-27; 41:21-29; 42:8-9; 43:9-12; 44:9-20; 45:14-16; 45:20-25; chapter 46; 48:1-11). At best the nations are granted neutral status; or perhaps a better way of describing it, they are permitted the role of stage props or literary embellishment, as when they stand at attention, astonished at what the Lord Yahweh is doing for Israel (40:5, 28; 41:1, 5; 42:10-12; 43:23; 45:20-25).

In any discussion of the nations, we must recall what is obviously true yet overlooked in reading the *Bible:* (1) their basic pattern of life had to be wholesome, otherwise their culture could never have survived as long as it did; (2) whatever were their faults, personally or nationally, their numbers included many sincere, good people; (3) they were human enough to possess hope for themselves and their children, and to suffer at its loss and destruction. Therefore, Deutero-Isaiah's polemics against the nations and anticipation of their military destruction must be read with an ear for their voices of suffering. From Adam, Noah, and Abraham, gentiles belonged in the *Bible!* Prophetic enthusiasm for Israel's future tended to block out any concern for the nations, even for their nonelection and destruction. Yet, in the midst of international turmoil, the gentiles endured physical harm and psychological distress. We will soon be asking how their voices of suffering contributed to Biblical history.

In following the voices of suffering and prayer in Deutero-Isaiah's poetry, we come to the crucial transition from chapters 41-48 to chapters 49-55.[57] This step draws us towards the "Suffering Servant Songs." The details here will further enrich our double thesis: (1) voices of suffering on the secular scene of life effect notable changes in theology; and

(2) beneath these secular voices are God's inspired hopes which reach beyond the secular with voices of contemplative prayer.

Within the prophecy of Deutero-Isaiah, we define three major periods of ministry, leading to the "Servant Songs," which are perhaps the most mystical voices of suffering and prayer in the *Bible.* The title "Great Unknown" indicates not only the mystic overtones in the prophet's preaching but also the lack of scholarly consensus in clarifying the career of the prophet and the editing of the book. I suggest this hypothesis:

> Chapter 40: An orchestration of major themes, composed last (but from pre-existing poems) as a grand overture to the book.
> Chapters 41-48: Poems composed after the initial victories of Cyrus the Great, at least after 550 B.C. and the conquest of the Median capital, but before the capture of Babylon in 539. Deutero-Isaiah foresaw not only this defeat but also the return of his people and possibly the conversion of Cyrus.
> 49:1-55:11: Poems reflecting the somber heaviness of a disappointed people and prophet. Cyrus has taken Babylon, but without converting to Yahweh and without any world enthusiasm centering on Israel.
> "Servant Songs": A prophetic ministry of silence, rejection, and possibly martyrdom. In the initial fragmentary attemps at the "Servant Songs," the prophet announced the salvation of the gentiles. The four major songs develop the two motifs of personal persecution and the salvation of the foreigners.
> 55:12-13: Redactional conclusion to the Book of Consolation, composed earlier by Deutero-Isaiah but placed here by the general editor.

Here we study the transitional period of the prophet's life from chapters 41-48 into chapters 49-55, we hear the voices of suffering and prayer increasingly more painful and psychologically more intense and mystical. Compared to chapters 49-55, chapters 41-48 strike even a casual reader as much more expansive and elevated, with a greater uplift and a more continuous hymnic style, with a surer sense of prophecy-fulfillment and with a more integral synthesis of major theological themes. Turning to chapters 49-55, we find that an important theme like prophecy-fulfillment has been abandoned; Cyrus is no longer mentioned, perhaps because he failed to convert to Yahweh and establish a world kingdom for Israel (cf., 45:1-7). The pervasive hymnic style in the first chapters has given place to an almost continuous sense of discouragement. Israel's depression, more *sotto voce* in chapters 41-48, now comes repeatedly and explicitly to the surface. Creation vocabulary, so frequent in chapters 41-48 to announce the Lord's total transformation of Israel and the cosmos, almost drops from sight. Israel as Yahweh's elect people, oft-repeated in chapters 41-48, is reduced to a fragmentary verse (49:7).

It seems that the new exodus anticipated joyfully in chapters 41-48, turned out to be just a trickle of people, with only a few of the industrious ones, who had established themselves in Babylon. Although the exodus motif is still woven into chapters 49-55, nonetheless, the prophet's attention has shifted for the first time to Zion-Jerusalem. Even these references to Zion are generally melancholic and subdued, or else they envisage Zion's children collapsed on the street corner (51:20) and in need of a rousing call to stand up! The people of Zion seem as spiritless in chapters 49-55 as in the later prophecy of Haggai.

In another publication I had summarized Deutero-Isaiah's attitude in chapters 49-55 and the community response to him:

> Second Isaiah struggled between his *faith* which called for God's hand in directing world events, as in the many, earlier discourses on "First and Last," and his disenchantment over those same events as they actually took place. Feelings of ambiguity began to emerge. It is likely that he was already rejected, but not yet persecuted, by the majority of the people; or perhaps, he was simply ignored. He himself remained in Babylon; such at least is the general tenor of the texts which still speak of a new exodus. His earlier poetry might have been too eloquent, his hopes too exalted, and, therefore, the present letdown too discouraging, for the people to give him any more attention.[58]

I agree with P.E. Bonnard that Deutero-Isaiah's audience is no longer the large assembly, excited by his vision and carried forward by his poetic brilliance. Only a "remnant" remained with him, and even these were drifting away, for the future no longer belonged to this prophet.[59] Ezekiel and his followers, who included the former Zadokite priests of Jerusalem, were in control of the *'am yiśrā'ēl* (the people Israel) and would direct the future. The Priestly Tradition of the Pentateuch, redacted by this latter group during the exile, would dominate later history.

As we gather together these observations on chapters 49-55, we can relate our conclusions about prophetic suffering and prayer with directions for pastoral theology.

In chapters 41-48, Deutero-Isaiah drew upon an exodus and wilderness tradition, as these had been transformed and idealized. He had declared that Israel must brave the desert wilderness and believe that its hardships will be overcome by a divine power, exercised through their own courage, faith, and energy (40:5-31). The desert will be turned into paradise with its abundant rivers and mythical trees (41:17-20).[60] Yet, Israel must not stop to savor the delicious taste but plunge forward into more desert waste. Israel could not deal with such ideals. If we transfer this image to people, it is far easier to live with mediocre persons than with geniuses who expect a consistently above-average response. No one, moreover, suffers more that those gifted people who are called upon to maintain ideals and yet to remain tolerant towards mediocre or overly cautious people.[61] Just as the exodus had become a symbol, gifted or saintly people tend to live on, more as a symbol or a wonderful memory than as achievers of lasting results. The poetry in chapters 49-55 allow us to hear the interior groans of a disappointed genius like Deutero-Isaiah. These chapters also raise a serious question for pastoral theology: is it good to maintain ideals and symbols, so transcendent and seemingly so unearthly, that suffering always ensues? The presence of Deutero-Isaiah in the Bible answers that question affirmatively.

There is still another way to relate chapters 49-55 with the theme of this investigation. People could not say "why" or "why not," yet *instinctively* they could not accept this transfiguration of historical events into idyllic, religious symbols. First, they wanted something more precise, more detailed, more regulatory of their daily life, than the gigantic hopes of this prophet. They could get their hands around the exodus pattern as employed by Ezekiel[62] and make definite application to their immediate needs as Israelites. Deutero-Isaiah's symbols charged across the universe and left the people uneasy, and with good reason. Deutero-Isaiah was forcing Israel to keep their exodus in continual contact with the secular world. It was no longer a retreat from the nations, even though exodus technically means just that; it was an act of salvation in which the nations were increasingly involved. It would be a single but gigantic step—and Deutero-Isaiah would show himself capable of accepting it—for the nations to leave their position of admiring bystanders and join the chosen people.

Deutero-Isaiah, moreover, like any great poet, saint, or idealist, was driven more by the implicit inspirations of the heart than by any carefully planned theological or political position. What was a source of excitement for the prophet turned into a warning signal for most others. And in the midst of such excitement, geniuses tend to become impatient. Deutero-Isaiah became impetuous in commanding Israel, "Awake! Awake!" (51:17; 52:1). When the people were annoyed and turned a cold shoulder, we can hear, in the silent, retreating footsteps of the "Great Unknown," another prophetic voice of suffering. The prophet pays the costly price of sustaining high ideals in a mediocre society. Then small-minded or jealous people can pride themselves in belonging to a religion of prophetic ideals, all the while killing their prophets. Jesus described it as building sepulchre-monuments for the martyred prophets (Luke 11:47). We still hear a voice of groaning not so much from the prophets, for they are dead, but from oppressed people forced to erect ostentatious monuments to other people's complicity.

Finally, prophetic voices of suffering and prayer are detected in chapters 49-55 in still another way, as wails of isolation closed in upon Deutero-Isaiah. So profoundly was the prophet perceiving God's intense but delicate presence within the circumstances of his daily secular life, that he was becoming a mystery, even to himself.

An example from Deutero-Isaiah will assist our discussion. Throughout chapters 49-55,[63] the prophet maintained the *leitmotif* of the new exodus: 49:9b-12; 50:2, 9b-11; 51:9-10; 52:11-12. Consistent with the proclamation of Israel's separation from the gentile nations, another thread was woven into the tapestry of these chapters: the angry rejection of the nations: 49:23-26; 51:22-23; 52:10. All the while, as we have already shown, there is still another line of thought, of dark and somber color, appearing within the scene: an Israel, tired, melancholy, and indifferent towards the prophet, and it is possible that this isolation of the prophet from his kin and neighbors was putting him in touch with still another, deeper and truer part of himself. This latter theme was favorable to the nations, at least implicitly and incipiently, and here indeed is the source of future orientation.

The nations stand on the outer edge and admire what the Lord is doing for his people. The important (and for the *Bible,* very rare) references to Abraham (51:1-3) and the Noachic covenant (54:9-10), plus the unique handling of the Davidic covenant (55:3-5), all insist that the nations must have a favorable and dignified part within Israel's religion. Abraham and Sarah were originally gentiles; by God's call, they became the ancestors of the chosen people. The question is: can God call the nations again? Noah's covenant, like the symbol of the rainbow, joined the Lord with *all* humankind; it made no distinction among earth's inhabitants (Gen. 9:8-17). David and Solomon had established an international empire with trade agreements between Jerusalem and far-reaching kingdoms (2 Sam. 7-8; 1 Kgs. 3:1-15; 5:1-14; 9:10, 10:29).

This movement in the preaching of Deutero-Isaiah ostensibly in opposite directions, away from the nations in a new exodus yet embracing the nations in a new universalism, was recognized by the later editor of the book. This individual inserted 51:4-6[65] which evinces a favorable, even a generous attitude by inviting the nations to share in Israel's light, hope, and salvation. The other passage, also added by the general editor, 51:12—16,[66] introduces the cosmic dimension, frequently met in chapters 40-48 but almost nonexistent in chapters 49-55. Israel's redemption, based on Yahweh's creation of the world, cannot be properly separated from this world. These editorial insertions then mirror the tensions within the conscious and subconscious of Deutero-Isaiah's soul.

Whenever we observe such a contrasting series of human reactions, we must determine the relationship between them. It is our conclusion that God was inspiring in Deutero-Isaiah a pro-Gentile, universal vision at the deepest level, too profound for a conscious evaluation even by the prophet. As the prophet surrendered to this vague but imperative vision, he was plunging into a psychological/spiritual depth beyond concepts, even those of theology! Here he was experiencing an all-absorbing prayer of faith in the truest mystical sense.

One last observation reminds us that this phenomenon of prophetic suffering and prayer grew out of a gripping challenge from the secular world. The setting of Mesopotamia, with its cosmic liturgies in the sacred *ziggurat* and its whirlwind companions of Cyrus in the military arena, forced forced a rethinking or the exodus tradition. It blew open what originally was a separation from the nations into a vision of one world. As yet, the vision remained so vague as to be imperceptible. We turn to the final stage of Deutero-Isaiah's career for the manifestation of this vision. It will be a stage of severe suffering and absorbing contemplation.

Voices of Suffering and
Prayer in the "Servant Songs"

As mentioned earlier in this study, we divide Deutero-Isaiah's career into three major periods. The *first* preaching of the prophet, represented by chapters 41-48, qualifies as a true theological synthesis. Major themes have been drawn from Israel's sacred tradition and enriched or updated by features of Babylonian religion and by contemporary questions from the secular situation. Here hope and jubilation prevail. The *second* part of the prophet's ministry (chapters 49-55) was characterized by disappointment, increasing isolation, and spurts of opposition from his own people. The rush of events, like Cyrus' conquest of Babylon and the edict of emancipation for Israel, as well as the collapse of hopes for Yahweh's world empire through the conversion of Cyrus and a magnificent new exodus—all this left Deutero-Isaiah no time to develop a theological synthesis. The final stage of the prophet's career is represented by the "Suffering Servant Songs." We now turn to these passages for their contribution to a theology of prophetical suffering and prayer. We present (1) our own conclusions how the servant songs relate to the Book of Consolation; (2) the voices of suffering and prayer in the initial, fragmentary attempts at writing the Songs; and (3) those voices within the four major songs.

The *Servant Songs,* in our opinion, were composed by Deutero-Isaiah when his mission to Israel had collapsed and he had to begin all over again.[67] Although mostly in the style of lamentation, the first two songs (particularly 42:1-4) include important features of a "call narrative."[68] Like any deeply personal, intensely contemplative piece of literature, those songs developed almost subconsciously within the memory of the prophet. It is very understandable too that initial attempts were partial, unfinished, and fragmentary.

We can identify these fragments, by noting (1) that the Book of Consolation reads more smoothly if the Servant

Songs are removed; 69 (2) that the insertion of the Servant
Songs frayed the edges in the texture of the Book and occa-
sioned serious redactional problems; (3) that fragmentary attempts at Servant Songs, like isolated verses, were added
almost like appendices at the end of the first three Songs.[70]
The following outline may clarify this complicated question:[71]

Book of Consolation	Servant Songs	Fragments
41:21-29 First and Last v. 29 speaks of idols		
	42:1-4 First Song	
		42:5-7 Fragment about the servant
42:8-9 First and Last v. 8 speaks of idols		
48:20-21 Conclusion to Part One (chapters 41-48 about the new exodus		
		48:22 Misplace here: occurs also in 57:21
	49:1-4 + 5c Second Song	
		49:5ab, 6, 8, 9a Fragments about the servant 49:7 Fragment from the Book of Consolation
49:9b-12 New Exodus		
50:1-3 Consolation for Israel. V. 3 speaks of sackcloth		
	50:4-9a Third Song	
50:9b Continues image of sackcloth in 50:3; phrases here all borrowed from 51:6b, 8d		
		50:10-11 Comment by the editor, admonishing us to heed the servants message
	52:13-53:12 Fourth Song	

The fragments were crucial for the development of Deutero-Isaiah's theology of suffering and prayer. yet all commentators experienced awkwardness and difficulty in dealing with them. We can recognize enough unity and genuineness about these fragments to admit a real contact between them and the servant songs plus the larger Book of Consolation. Yet, there are also notable differences. Ernst Vogt, S. J., summarized the points of meeting and distance:

> The [the fragments] do not have the dramatic character of the [Servant] Songs, where the speaker [-Servant] proceeds immediately in his own name rather than mediating the word of Yahweh with the introductory formula, "Thus says Yahweh" (42:5; 49:5a, 7, 8). In the [Fragments] hymnic participles occur (42:5; 49:5a, 7a); these are entirely missing in the Servant Songs, but are found very often in the Book of Consolation. Moreover, in both [the two latter] collections the infinitive of purpose is met frequently, while it is entirely missing in the Servant Songs (except 50:4). In both Fragments [42:5-7, 49:5ab, 6, 8, 9a] the servant is called a "covenant of the people" and a "light for the nations." In the Fragments the role of the Servant towards Israel is described in time-related forms, while in the Servant Songs no traces of this form are present. In the original setting of the Songs, the Servant in no way has a political role . . . but only a purely religious-spiritual activity. Action vanishes in the particular timelessness of the future vision, which the prophet is experiencing.[72]

The Fragments reveal a mystic reach towards the timeless visions of the Servant Songs. Ideas which were relegated to a peripheral role in the Book of Consolation have moved to the center. Such themes include the Lord as Creator *of the Universe* and the call of the gentiles to share in Israel's election.[73] It is this latter revelation which after a long struggle in Deutero-Isaiah breaks open. We read the startling announcement in the Fragment of 49:8-9a, 5ab, 6:

> The Lord *had said* to me: In a favorable time I answered you and on the day of salvation I helped you. I formed you as a

> covenant of the people [Israel] to restore the [ir] land and to
> allot the desolate heritage, Saying to those in prison: "Come
> out!" and to those in darkness, "Show yourselves!"
>   *But now* thus *says* the Lord, the one calling me from the
> womb to be his servant, to bring back Jacob to him and to see
> that Israel is gathered together. It is too small a thing for you
> to be my servant [simply] to raise up the tribe of Jacob and to
> restore the survivors of Israel. I make you a light to the
> nations, the mediator of my salvation to the ends of the earth.

Simply and quietly spoken, these words issued from a broken heart, which lacked the strength to be dramatic, Deutero-Isaiah is confessing: I have exhausted myself for the sake of Israel, and only now at the end when my strength is spent, do I see a world to save! How did I forget the forest and see only a few trees?

We for our part might want to reverse the judgment. It was *no* small thing to have worked for Israel in such a tireless way and to have produced some of the most mystical poetry of the *Bible.* Yet, like another extraordinary theologian with monumental work to his credit, Deutero-Isaiah must have considered it all "just straw" (cf., 49:4a).

If the fragments are just that—no more than isolated pieces, without order or synthesis—we might ask if they could have been otherwise. A heart that is breaking cannot control the fallout. These bursts of desperation, outrage, hope and radical change, all at once, cannot be regulated. Yet, for all these very reasons they reveal what later Christian mystics called the dark night of the soul and the total surrender of love.[74] At the end of his career, Deutero-Isaiah truly became the Servant of the Lord.

Deutero-Isaiah lived long enough to reflect upon these initial fragmentary bursts of the Spirit. Quietly he composed what we call the four "Songs of the Suffering Servant." We turn to these Songs in order to draw out some of *the major qualities of prophetical suffering and prayer.* In no way do we propose a full, exegetical study.

The First Song (42:1-4), a solemn investiture of the Servant in his new vocation, seems to take place in the same heavenly court as chapter 40. This may be one of the reasons why the Song was placed within chapters 40-48; other reasons consist in the contrast of the Servant with Cyrus the military conqueror (41:1-5), with Israel the blind servant (42:18-20), and with the nations summoned to trial (41:1). It reads in part:

> Here is my servant. . . .
> Upon whom I have put my spirit. . . .
> Not crying out, not shouting. . . .
> A bruised reed he shall not break and a smoldering wick he shall not quench,
> Until he establishes justice on the earth; the coastlands wait for his teaching.

The Servant possesses those *qualities essential for contemplative recollection* as well as *for affective leadership:* the pervading presence of the Spirit; quiet perseverance and personal composure; a sense of good judgment; a contact with sacred traditions about royalty, prophecy, and priesthood, yet a tolerance towards others allowing them to pursue this wisdom at their own pace; a respectful realization that others, even the gentiles, already possess *in germine*[75] what was being proposed to them. Because of his wisdom and meekness the Servant was able to communicate with others in their hopes and ideals. What a new way to conquer nations! The Servant repudiated all violence, an element which we found consistently present in earlier voices of suffering in the *Bible*. Yet the Servant's actions would eventually make him the object of violent persecution! In this reach outward beyond Israel and her traditions, there is a combined voice of prophetic suffering and of prophetic prayer. The Servant must have *suffered* for what was being lost or transformed of Israel's ancient traditions about priesthood and prophecy. Yet, there must also have been a sense of *mystic recollection* as the Servant's eyes peered beyond clear concepts and rational order, to what God had placed deeply at the heart of all peoples. "The coastlands wait for his teaching."

The Second Song (*49:1-4, 5c*) is an autobiographical account of the Servant's call, addressed to distant nations yet actually heard by Israel. This second song begins majestically, not in the divine assembly like 42:1-4 but in the expansive arena of the ancient Near East. "Listen, O coastlands! Be attentive, O distant peoples!" Yet, we sense at once the irony of it all; it almost seems ridiculous. No foreigner close at hand, much less any nations afar off, took any notice of this prophet. Such is the lonely agony of the bearer of prophetic dreams. Yet, the anguish intensified when not even Israel would take seriously this prophetic call to world mission.[76] The prophet considered himself "a polished arrow hidden within the quiver, held captive within the Lord's hand." He was ready with the answer yet unable to go anywhere with it. A lifetime of preparation, with its total expenditure of energy in preaching to the exiles and composing the *Bible's* golden poetry, with its dramatic changes and adaptations—and now this life just stops!

This abrupt ending to a life's work brings the prophet Jeremiah to our mind. There are other literary contacts as well. The Suffering Servant must have found in Jeremiah not so much an explanation as simply a stark and simple way of remaining in God's presence in the midst of this mystery. To live with the arational and the divine paradoxes of human life, both Jeremiah and Deutero-Isaiah took refuge in the faith-conviction that God had arranged it that way from their mother's womb (Jer. 1:5; Is. 49:1). If the position is correct that Jeremiah composed the account of his vocation only towards the end of his life, then we find that these two prophets sighted clearly the call of the gentiles only after a lifetime of unsuccessfully struggling for Israel's redemption, only when it was too late to act upon the inspiration.[77]

The Servant, moreover, was like Jeremiah in that each

experienced the tired uselessness of their life (cf., Jer. 12:1-5; 15:10-21). His words are pathetic in that the prophet confessed the sin for which he had once faulted the people, their weariness and weakness of faith (40:26-31): nor could the servant accept the Lord's attempt to console him.

> He [the Lord] said to me: You are my servant, Israel through whom I show my glory. But [in reply] I said: I have wearied myself uselessly, I have spent my strength for empty breath.

The word for "weary" "*yāga'*" had appeared three times in 40:27-31 for the people of Israel in their sinful lethargy. Another three times in 43:22-24 not only for the sinful people but also for God who as suffering servant was wearied with carrying their sins, and now for the prophet-servant in his dejection. Again, in a way similar to the Lord's treatment of Jeremiah, the prophet's load of worry and depression is only made heavier, not lighter. He could only say: "My case rested with the Lord" (49:4a)[78] Perhaps, this line can be paraphrased with a play on words: I can do nothing else but rest in the Lord. Here is the ultimate disposition of *mystic prayer,* of death to all human ambition, perception, and hope. Purest hopes demand this high a cost. Their reward is not the right to circle one's arms around accomplishments but to be embraced by the arms of the Lord.

The Third Song (50:4-9a) is still more personal and autobiographical than the second: it mingles various literary forms like a protestation of prophetic call (v. 4-5a), a psalm of lament (v. 5b-6), and a psalm of confidence (v. 7-9a).[79] Once again the closest biblical model is found in the confession of Jeremiah,[80] in which God leads the prophet into a ministry of failure, which then becomes the occasion for glimpsing the mysterious purpose of the call. A literal translation of several key lines lacks the succinct strength of the original but hopefully communicates the meaning more fully:

> The Lord God gave me the tongue of one who has been

schooled [taught] to know [through this experience] how to
sustain those who are exhausted [with] a quickening word. . . .
My back I gave to be flogged the beard on my chin to be
pulled. My face I did not hide from shameful spit. Yet the
Lord Yahweh was assisting me, and so I felt no shame.

Key words here enable us to penetrate to the strong,
broken heart of the servant and to hear his voice of suffering
and prayer. These words also form a concatenation of
passages from the prophecy of Jeremiah into the Book of
Consolation. One of these words—to be exhausted or fainting, "yā'ēp"—can be joined with the synonym, "to be
weary" "yāga"[81] These expressions had been used to
describe the depression of all the people;[82] now as they are
used of the Servant, we see that the weariness of the people
has penetrated his heart and bones. Through his own aching
tiredness, the Servant has been schooled in the way of the
Lord with the weary. The Servant has been instructed by the
spirit and message of Jeremiah, and through that prophet's
compassion to experience the rising hopes but most of all the
blanketing disappointment of hopes collapsed. Another key
word—to learn by experience, "yada'"—occurs twine in this
third Song (50:4b, 7b). Passivity to the sacred word heard in
the preaching of Jeremiah as well as helpless humiliation
before persecutors indicate how totally the Servant was
schooled by the Lord. From this passivity there derived an exceptional, interior strength.

Another play on words heightens the paradox. According to v. 6b the Servant lamented: "My face I did not hide
from *shameful* spit"; but in the very next verse he intoned a
prayer of confidence: "Yet the Lord Yahweh was assisting
me so that I felt *no shame.*" The same Hebrew word, *k-l-m*,
occurs twice. Shamed by others, he was not ashamed. The
most shameful abuse of pulling the beard and spitting on the
face only braced and envigorated the Servant's personal
dignity. As a result, we meet the Servant, alone in a law
court, looking straight into the eyes of judge, witnesses,

prosecutor, and opponents, to exclaim: "Stand up, come on! Who can impeach me?" In these lines (v. 7-9a), replete with technical, legal language,[83] an inclusion or repetition of identical words envelops the section so that its power is not dissipated. Those words are: "The Lord Yahweh was assisting me." The Lord was granting exceptional strength to withstand all opposition in the moment of total surrender and passivity. We witness here an unusual combination of passivity and energy. In this third song prophetic voices of suffering and prayer reach beyond the rational into the realm of contemplative silence.

The Fourth Song (52:13-53:12) is as complex as it is masterful. The central section (53:1-11a) consists of a collective lament, which the author placed on the lips of gentile kings and people.[84] The introduction (52:13-15) and the concluding oracle (53:11b-12) are best attributed to God himself. Yet, no one speaks to any one else. We quote at length from Professor Clines, for he sets forth quite well the· contemplative silence of this song:

> Throughout, silence is kept, speech is avoided. The kings are speechless before the servant (52:15). The servant is not addressed by God, withdraws from the society of men . . . (53:3), and at the moment when some word of protest may have been expected to be uttered—the moment of the unjust judgment passed upon him—silence again rises to the surface of the poem: "who complained or mused aloud on, spoke of . . . his fate?" (53:8). Likewise no other *persona* speaks to or is addressed by any other. The only "hearing" has gone on outside the dimension of the poem: the "we" *do* hear *about* something (presumably the servant), but from whom or what is not clear. What is clear is that what goes on in the poem is a matter of "seeing". . . What has *not* been "told" . . . and of "considering" . . . what has *not* been "heard". . . . The poem is about seeing, not hearing; so it is about vision rather than verbal communication.[85]

The contemplative quality can be appreciated still more if we attend to the continuous use of contrast. This literary characteristic follows from the inability of language to plummet any single idea to its depth and to communicate that insight adequately. As a result, the idea must be reversed and then explored from a very different viewpoint. Such is the way of contemplation—to pursue a quality or epithet *about* God until we are lost either in the mystery of God or in the negation of our thoughts.[86] So, we must begin all over again in a very different way, or simply rest in the mystery.

We cite some of the intriguing contrasts. The Servant is intensely present, yet in the central stanzas of the song (53:1-11a) he is never mentioned by name. Again, the Servant turns out to be a very public figure, attracting world attention, yet he is portrayed as lonely, silent, and maybe dead.[87] The Servant is despised yet triumphant, lamented yet glorified. The Servant seems hidden beneath desert wilderness, yet from this dead rocky earth he springs up like a sapling, fresh and new. The Hebrew text shifts back and forth between "he" and "we" as in 53:4-5:

> Indeed, it was *our* infirmities that *he* bore *our* suffering that *he* endured. While *we ourselves* regarded *him* stricken. Indeed *he* was wounded for *our* offenses. . . .

Or again the juxtaposition of speaking/hearing/seeing in 52:13b-53:1 reveals a mystery reaching beyond stylistic features:

> For what was never *told,* they see, and what was never *heard,* they *contemplate.* Who could have *believed* what we have *heard,* and the [powerful] arm of the Lord, to whom has it been revealed?

Within these mysterious lines, we meet a voice of prophetic suffering, choked and muffled, yet shouting so loudly that nations and their kings declare: "Who could have believed what we have heard?" When these nations recognize that "it was our infirmities he bore . . . " they reclaim what was truly theirs but heaped upon the Servant. They find their sins with him or upon him. Yet once borne by the Servant the sins no longer exist, for how can we ever call the Servant a sinner? The problem of sin ceases to be a problem, once servant and sinner are united. Yet there is the serious problem of the Servant's destruction by sin, and the sinner's solitary amazement at such a death.

That rich phrase, "the discipline of our peace," occurs in 53:5b. Discipline (*mûsār*) carries the force of suffering that simultaneously chastises, restrains, regulates, and prepares for life's decision making.[88] While the Servant because of his suffering, "surrendered himself to death" (53:12), still because of these same sufferings, "he shall see his descendants in a long life" (53:10). Suffering became purifying and transforming, not simply because the Servant took the blame of others upon himself, but rather because the Servant and Israel, in fact the Servant and all the world, were united as one *'ebbed Yahweh.* If the lines separating life and death, servant and king, Israel and the nations, and innocence and guilt, seem to blur and merge—that is exactly where the Songs have brought suffering to the outer edge of our understanding, and beyond. Prophetic suffering is thus caught up in contemplative silence.

Just as the voice of suffering seems to be silenced, the voice of prophetic prayer gives way to overwhelming vision where every sound is hushed. "The Poem," writes Professor Clines, "is rich in the language of seeing."[89] Perhaps this contemplative gaze is expressed best of all in the opening stanza:

> Look! My servant shall *prosper wisely,* lifted up, elevated and raised on high. Even as many are *appalled at you.* . . .
> (52:13-14a)

What is translated "prosper wisely" comes from a Hebrew word, *s-k-l,* which means "to give attention to," "to have insight," or "to act with insight," as in other passages of Deutero-Isaiah (Is. 41:20; 44:18).[90] It describes the Servant as a person who has not only absorbed a lifetime of wise experiences but who is also an object of a prolonged and admiring gaze "lifted up, . . . raised on high." The next verb, "appalled," usually refers to "desolate wastes" (Is. 49:8, 19), and forms the first and most unexpected contrast, here with *s-k-l*—to prosper wisely. Another abrupt transition occurs. While the Hebrew text has been speaking *about* the Servant, suddenly the Servant becomes the subject of address: "many are appalled *at you.*"[91]

"Many nations . . . and kings are silenced." Here, as elsewhere, silence grips the onlookers, and their eyes center upon *a person*. This Servant unites all peoples, in their sins and hopes, in their sacred traditions and secular surroundings, in their most intense union with God's will. This Servant, who is the people, is the Servant *of the Lord.* Contemplation is caught up in the mystery of *God the Redeemer.* Contemplation focuses upon God, not as divinity but as redeemer who unites Himself with Israel and the nations, in the person of the Servant.

As we look back on the Servant Songs, we see that peripheral ideas in the Book of Consolation have suddenly come to the center and there exploded beyond words with suffering unto martyrdom. These ideas were present earlier in the preaching of Deutero-Isaiah, embellishing his poems, as nations stood in admiration (40:5) and the pagan Cyrus took on the role of a new Moses (45:1). Through a quick succession of events, however, these ideas claimed a central place. At this point the prophet was rejected by his own people (45:9-13). To maintain the strenuous momentum, which was let loose within him by secular events and divine inspiration amid clashing voices of unrest and suffering, Deutero-Isaiah scribbled down *fragmentary* statements, like: "It is too small a thing for you to be my servant, simply to raise up the tribe of Jacob. I make you a light to the nations" (49:6).

The *four major Servant Songs* were now composed. In

the last three of them amid excruciating suffering and personal shame, the prophet still mustered the strength and dignity to exclude all shame and to rest in the overwhelming insight that all nations shared the privileged role of Israel. As the nations and Israel heaped their crimes on the Servant, they could identify themselves with one who was most innocent. The mystery became so massive that all was lost in a prophetic prayer of contemplative silence. "Who could have believed?"

CONCLUSION

Biblical voices of suffering and prayer in their deepest origins are to be traced to the "groans" and "longings" of the "secular" or non-Biblical world, to which Paul alludes in Romans:

> The whole created world eagerly awaits the revelation of the children of God. . . . [Yet, all the while it] groans and is in agony even until now. (Rom. 8:19, 22)

The *Bible* provides a script and a liturgy for these profound movements of the human spirit, where God's image was created from the beginning (Gen. 1:27). The Scriptures enable first the elect people Israel and eventually all men and women to share their mystery of life harmoniously with one another as God's gō'ēl—family.

The secular or non-Biblical world provided the substance or raw material; the *Bible* supplied the insight to identify and the organization to celebrate. The secular situation—like Israel in Egypt or in the Sinai desert—could never survive as history without the liturgical renewals of the *Bible*; the *Bible* was not worthy of survival without substantial input from the secular and its ongoing challenge. What Israel sang in sorrowful lament about Jerusalem during the Babylonian exile could be addressed to Moses, Egypt, and Sinai:

If I forget you, Jerusalem, may my right hand be forgotten.
May my tongue cleave to my palate if I remember you notl (Ps.
137:5-6a)

Only by Israel's remembering the *secular* city or event
religiously was there any hope of survival for the secular; and
with the secular, Israel itself would have been swept away.

Unable to articulate its hopes and ideals, the secular
world would explode from misguided energy and bias, unless
its desires and potential could be more clearly understood,
balanced and purified by a proper relationship among men
and women and unless they be directed towards a future not
only determined by God but in a very true sense also identified with God. The Lord declared through the prophet
Deutero-Isaiah: "I am the one, yes I, *the first.* Indeed, I am
the last" (Is. 48:12b).

The *Bible* had a vital role in offering a script to the hidden hopes of the secular and in directing its struggle. Both the
script and the direction had to be sustained over the centuries
and so were purified, transformed, and revised at decisive
crossroads in history. The *Bible* developed from these inspired voices of struggle, suffering, and wonder and absorbed
the finest and the most genuine within its pages.

In this investigation we delayed over the Mosaic period
for its creative energy and over the period of the exile for its
work of re-creation. Each of these two historical ages had
much in common. At both times Israel groaned under a
secular oppression, enslaved by a foreign power. Suffering,
provoked by secular powers, became intolerable because of
God-given hopes (inarticulate voices of prayer) and because
of God-inspired leaders like Moses and Deutero-Isaiah.
These religious giants articulated those hopes into community
prayers, songs, and tradition. Israel then glimpsed a future
promised land at the end of its slavery. The traditions from
the Mosaic age and the exquisite poetry of Deutero-Isaiah,
however, never dwelt over installation in the land but, instead, they wrestled with the desert and its murmuring and

miracles. They waited upon the Lord.

"Waiting" played an important part, as it accentuated the voice of suffering and deepened the sense of contemplative prayer. During the Mosaic age it provoked the people to murmur against the Lord; in Is. 40-55 "weariness" and "tiredness" led inevitably to the Suffering Servant Songs. Deutero-Isaiah added a whole, new aspect to waiting and weariness. God himself, he stated, has been wearied and burdened like a slave because of Israel's sins and frustrations (43:22-24). A mystery, so profound as to violate correct theology (we ask: can God be enslaved?), crushed Deutero-Isaiah. It forced upon him a new call and vocation, which heaped shame upon his person. Yet he emerged with appalling dignity. The response of kings and nations leaped beyond words (for who could believe what we heard?); and the image of the Servant, beyond innocence and life (surrendered to death and counted among the wicked). He became "a light to the nations" and transformed election into universal salvation. When voices of suffering become so strident and so fierce, as in these songs, they destroy their speaker and we are left with a vision, a contemplative prayer, with the most immanent, personal presence of God.

In the Old Testament then we are a "homeless people" in a secular world, always on an exodus, enduring the demands of our hopes and uttering our voice of suffering. We are a "landed people" resting in the presence of the Lord and glimpsing a vision which becomes so overwhelming that voices of prayer eventually are hushed in contemplative ecstasy. We are a sinful people, who betray our landed presence in the Lord and allow our contemplative prayer to be seduced into lazy affluence and cold indifference to the new cries of the oppressed. This degeneration happens when we no longer hear new secular voices of suffering from our brothers and sisters in exile. So, the secular claims its own and reduces all of us to new slavery. In such darkness, God is a suffering servant with us and because of us, and we are plunged anew into true contemplation. He chooses a servant from our midst, to speak our voice of suffering. As we see our sins on this servant, we are reunited with the blessed pure of heart "with whom I [the Lord] am pleased" (Is. 42:1).

DISCUSSION

QUESTION: You said that the Church cannot proclaim what is or is not oppressive apart from the experience of the world and perhaps you are alluding there to the Che Guevara. Could you expatiate on that a little?

ANSWER: The Church does have in her tradition, as Deutero-Isaiah had in his, the language, the models, the sequence of how God is acting with his people through the centuries. But the Church cannot determine ahead of time simply from her tradition what will be oppression and liberation today. Often the response to oppression, as in Africa, or South America, or in the United States regarding the equal rights of women in employment and salary, originated with forces areligious and at times antireligious! The abolition of slavery did not owe its *origin* to an ecclesiastical *proclamation!* Secular movements of liberation, moreover, evolve quickly. Again, the Church must attend to these sudden leaps. For instance, the struggle of the blacks for equal rights has advanced beyond the positions and methods of Dr. Martin Luther King, Jr., and with Rev. Jesse Jackson it is being tied in with other liberation movements throughout the world. The American dream which welcomed many ethnic groups to its shores can degenerate into a strong, aggressive movement against the black, the Hispanic, and the native Americans who are migrating into our large cities.

The Church does possess from her sacred traditions the language, the models, the hopes, and the wide variety of choices from which to speak and act, but the immediate context and the alignment of forces come from the secular world of the contemporary moment. The world rather than the Church determines the agenda. Secondly, the Church can strengthen the worthy aspects of the secular movement, purify it of harmful ingredients, sustain it in its weakness, and keep its goal or purpose pure and visible. The Church cannot excuse herself of cooperative action with secular movements because these latter contain sinful or false values. The Church should never underestimate her ability to purify and redirect.

QUESTION: As a continuation of the previous remarks, what would happen to prophecy in the Church were it reduced to a position of *reacting* to secular movements rather than to a creative stance of new *action*? Are we depriving the Church of its own prophets?

ANSWER: Part of the difficulty in this question is located in still another question: what do we mean by Church? Exclusively the Pope, bishops, priests, theologians, and other designated leaders? Or its members, ordained or not, with the ability to identify the problem, the wisdom to mount a program of response, the strength to persevere in the new movement, the charism to gather a following? Taking this question back into Biblical times, the prophets were certainly part of Israel, the people of God, even though, like Amos, they were expelled by the legitimate high priest Amaziah (Am. 7:12), or like Jeremiah they were repudiated by their own family (Jer. 12:6) and imprisoned by priests and official prophets (Jer. 26:8). Eventually it was the Jerusalem priests who incorporated the message of Amos and Jeremiah into the Bible. It is quite likely that nonordained members of the Church will be the front-line prophets in most social movements. They will find themselves on the periphery of normal Church life. In their passion for righteousness they will be guilty at times of theological excess. Perhaps like John Courtney Murray on the question of religious liberty and the separation of Church and state they will experience serious opposition from many official quarters of the Church. Yet they are the Church, initiating a position that will become official ecclesiastical doctrine.

QUESTION: My question relates to some comments at the beginning of your presentation, particularly in connection with your use of the word "violence." You commented that violence is a part of life. I am asking for a definition of violence and how you are using it in your presentation. I see in your first major point you have the term "secular violence" and then a little later, "secular liberation." What strikes me about the biblical clebration of the deliverance from Egypt is the emphasis on God as the one who initiates the deliverance and the role of the people in standing still and receiving His salvation. That theme of the exodus is then carried forward in liturgical celebration. Then you have the violence of waiting. I am not sure what that means. I am asking for a definition of violence vis-à-vis God, the concept of the secular and also vis-à-vis the role that God's people are to play in this human drama.

ANSWER: It is always difficult to define a negative concept like violence; we can more easily say what is meant by peace! Violence is a situation of conflict in which great possibilities, great hopes, and extraordinary energy are exploding in a serious opposition to evil. The human body likewise responds violently to poison in its system by vomiting, diarrhea, fever, chills, boils, rashes, etc. Violence results from a mighty effort to achieve a goal seemingly beyond normal ability and the natural turn of events. If we integrate some of these ideas in a Biblical context, we find that God has placed extraordinary possibilities and "supernatural" hopes within us, individually and as a society, beyond our normal physical and psychological ability, yet to be fulfilled through the human process of earthly existence. In the *Bible* there is a mystery of faith hidden within each major event: the liberation of Israelite slaves from Egyptian taskmasters was to become a type of freedom from sin to grace, as in Ps. 95 or Hosea, chapter 11, even a model of Jesus' resurrection from the dead and ascension to glory. Luke 9:31 refers to these mysteries in the life of Jesus, involving His heroic martyrdom and miraculous resurrection, as His "exodus" (the *New American Bible* translates the word as His "passage"). God, therefore, has placed the seeds of a violent explosion within human

existence. Furthermore, the Bible is very conscious of world sin, mammoth forces of evil
amassed against God's people, as in Is. 51:9-10
or Ps. 48. The supernatural struggle to express
a form of goodness and glory beyond our
normal ability must now war against supernatural evil; only by violence will this poison
be ejected from the system.

"Violence" reappears Biblically in still
another way. Almost all of God's servants in
the *Bible* died, clinging to hopes, not enjoying
their fulfillment. Moses' last hour is described
in a sense of heroic tragedy. God brings him up
a high mountain, allows him to scan the entire
promised land from the far side of the Jordan
River, and then tells him: "I have let you feast
your eyes upon it, but you shall not cross
over." In one of the saddest yet most glorious
sentences in the Hebrew Scriptures, we then
read: "So there, in the land of Moab, Moses
the servant of the Lord, died" (Deut. 34:4-5).
In this passive obedience God's servants suffer
more violence than if they were to exercise ag-
gressively every human faculty.

Violence then is the result of a divine call
to strain every human faculty to seek a super-
human goal, at times against the super-human
opposition of sin and demons. Out of such
martyrdom we rise a new creature in Christ
Jesus.

QUESTION: I would be very grateful for your comments on
a possible Church policy towards oppression.
It is not so simple as to say that the oppressor
is totally evil and that the oppressed is totally
good. The Church should be saying to the oppressed with the voice of Christ, "Anger is one

of the seven deadly sins and is never a constructive response to anything whatsoever.'' After saying this to the oppressed poor person, the Church ought to turn to the wealthy oppressor and respond with every kind of whip, scorpion, excommunication, whatever you like. What sort of policy would that be, Christlike or un-Christlike?

ANSWER: I find the direction towards an answer already within your question. You carefully presume different pastoral moments, one that encourages peace and patience, and another that reacts sternly and angrily with excommunication. Allow me to expand upon this statement. Within Israel, within the Church, and within ourselves there are many different kinds of gifts. Some have the gift of patience, others the gift of clarity, still others the gift of sensitivity to social evils, others again the ability of administration. Each is to be encouraged in his own proper gift for the enrichment of the total body. It is not proper to tell the person with the gift of clarity always to be silent, or to command the person gifted with contemplative qualities of silent prayer to be the spokesperson, or to command the person exceptionally sensitive to oppression never to shout their anger and frustration, or to prevent the good administrator from organizing a strong movement against oppression.

It is also important to point out that there are certain moments in Biblical history necessarily dominated by one salient gift: the age of Moses with law and organization, the age of the Judges with military operations against aggressors, the age of David and Solomon with wars of liberation and with a glorious revival of national life.

Therefore, it is the role of good pastoral judgment to determine the proper response, at a given moment of time, by each individual person. I submit that the *Bible* offers firm support that among the gifts to be put to the service of God's people—by special individuals in certain situations—is the gift of godly violence, the instrument of divine wrath.

QUESTION: I was very intrigued with your historical development of the tribes of Israel and with the viewpoint that their suffering often resulted from their inability to understand God's word. I was also intrigued that you introduced the Old Testament concept of God's *weariness.* It implies imperfection in God. It seems to me that if there is a problem of communication, so that Israel misunderstands God's word, then it is as much God's problem as ours! I challenge God's capacity to communicate!

ANSWER: A question can be put to your question: "Is weariness necessarily an imperfection?" The prophet who made that statement—like Second Isaiah in 43:34—spoke deliberately. He could call upon a long tradition of God's weariness as expressed in Deuteronomy, Hosea, and Jeremiah. He did not speak off the cuff but carefully balanced his words, as is the case in 43:24-25. He did not consider it necessarily an imperfection to be weary. Out of such a human reaction extraordinary examples of patience and wisdom emerge. Secondly, the communication of truth is not the primary goal of divine revelation. God never intends to confuse us but neither is He simply a teacher communicating accurate information. In all of His interaction with us—in our minds with truth, in our hearts with love, in our hopes with mysterious goals, in our bowels with groanings of compassion—God is leading us to struggle heroically, to die to ourselves, and to obediently rise to life beyond any truth known on this earth.

Again, as in anwering the preceding question, I ought to repeat that the charism of pastoral ministry gives a person the ability to determine how God is interacting in the Church at large and in an individual's life. James Alvin Sanders, a respected Old Testament scholar, once wrote in an article about true and false prophecy: "A false prophet is one who speaks a decently good theology at the wrong time." In other words, the ministry of God in the *Bible* and of the Church today is not to be limited simply to speaking or communicating the truth. There are times when we ought to be prudent and sensitive enough to leave aside the quest for truth and simply to weep with the sorrowful or, may I add, to cry out in rage with the oppressed.

QUESTION: In your response to Christopher Dering did you mean to imply that there is a God-given charism of leading people to violent bloodshed.

ANSWER: God never leads people simply and exlusively to bloodshed. God is guiding His people to peace, but never to peace at any cost, and certainly not to peace at the price of human indignity. For the heavenly vision of peace we must struggle against evil, and not simply evil.

in the abstract but evil as incarnated in people, ourselves, or others. A good Biblical example occurs in the symbol of Jerusalem as the city of peace, where all nations are streaming in joyful procession and where they will beat swords into plowshares and spears into pruning hooks (Is. 2:2-4). The prophet Joel reversed the image and wrote: "Beat your plowshares into swords, and your pruning hooks into spears; let the weak man say, 'I am a warrior!' " (Joel 4:10). Goodness or evil, I contend, is not to be measured in terms of greater or lesser peace, but rather in the total expenditures of one's energy and gifts for the supernatural goal imbedded within us by God.

NOTES

[1]Scriptures or *Bible* are understood here as the sacred, normative tradition, interpreting and applying God's will for His people within an organized way of life and worship. Scripture, therefore, presumes "religion," which began only with Moses. Abraham did not develop a religion with separate priesthood, ritual, and shrines. Yet, as the ancestor of Biblical religion, Abraham too was called amidst trials and difficulties (cf., Gen. 15:2-3).

[2]This sentence has important implications for a theology of revelation. This transition from "inarticulate groans" to word and sentence that are part of the Scriptures or *Bible* (cf., footnote 1) is well-described by Avery Dulles in "The Meaning of Revelation," *The Dynamic in Christian Thought,* Villanova University Symposium, Vol. 1 (Villanova, Pa.: 1970) p. 56, " . . . revelation is an extraordinary transforming event, which, without ceasing to be mysterious and beyond human comprehension, illuminates the human situation and opens up the meaning of history and of the universe. Such an event comes upon man without his being able to control or master it; it is a gift, and from the ultimacy of its significance, confirmed by the united testimony of those who have witnessed and experienced it most closely, it may be reasonably regarded, in faith, as the self-giving of God himself."

[3]We hope to establish this ambient of suffering for the origin of most Biblical books and traditions. Yet, we recognize at once that praise and life rather than lament and suffering/death turn out to be the basic attitude of prayer and worship in the Old Testament. The earliest psalms are hymns of praise like Ps. 19A, 29, 89:6-15, Ex. 15:1-16: Judg. 5; or blessings like Gen. 49 and Deut. 33; these speak of life and victory so that death and suffering are present only as overcome by the victorious army of Israel. Israel's profound theological ritual difficulties with sickness and death are apparent in a text like Lev. 21. [cf., Frank Moore Cross, Jr. & David Noel Freedman, *Studies in Ancient Yahwistic Poetry*. SBL Dissertation Series, 21 (Scholars Press: 1975).]

[4]A footnote in the *New American Bible* for Ex. 3:8 points out: "*I have come down* [is] a figure of speech signifying an extraordinary divine intervention." The Hebrew word *yārad* is frequently associated with a theophany: Gen. 11:5, Ex. 3:8; 19:11, 18, 20; Num. 11:17, 25; 2 Sam. 22:10; Is. 31:4; 93:19; Ps. 18:10.

[5]Cf., R. V. Bergren, *The Prophets and the Law* (Hebrew Union College, 1974); Joseph Blenkinsopp, *Prophecy and Canon* (University of Notre Dame Press, 1977); R. E. Clements, *Prophecy and Tradition* (John Knox Press, 1975).

[6]See footnote 4.

[7]Cf., Walter Harrelson, "The Significance of Cosmology in the Ancient Near East," *Translating and Understanding the Old Testament*, ed. by H. T. Frank & W. L. Reed (Abingdon: 1970), pp. 237-252; L. R. Fisher, "Creation at Ugarit and in the Old Testament," *Vetus Testamentum*, 15 (1965), pp. 313-324; W. G. Lambert, "Destiny and Divine Intervention in Babylon and Israel," *The Witness of Tradition* (Oudt. Studien, XVII; Brill: 1972), pp. 65-72.

[8]John A. Wilson, "Egyptian Myths, Tales and Mortuary Texts," *Ancient Near Eastern Texts, Relating to the Old Testament,* ed. by James B. Pritchard, 3 ed. (Princeton University Press, 1969), p. 8.

[9]For a comparison of Egyptian and Mesopotamian mythology, dependent upon geography, see: H. and H. A. Frankfort, John A. Wilson, & Thorkild Jacobsen, *The Intellectual Adventure of Ancient Man* (University of Chicago Press: 1946), also reprinted as *Before Philosophy* (Penguin Books: 1949); R. A. F. MacKenzie, *Faith and History in the Old Testament* (University of Minnesota Press, 1963).

[10]The wisdom movement especially represented a process of secularization away from the pansacralism of the earlier days of Israel before the monarchy. G. von Rad, *Wisdom in Israel* (Abingdon: 1972) entitles Part Two "The Liberation of Reason and the Resultant Problems" (p. 53-112). This knowledge of a secular kind is most evident in Prov. 10-29. Later a process of "religionization" took place, to use the phrase of

James L. Crenshaw, *Studies in Ancient Israelite Wisdom* (Ktav: 1976), pp. 24-25. Wisdom in Egypt and Mesopotamia turned out to be much more religious, with emphasis upon magic: cf., Hans H. Schmid, *Wesen und Geschichte der Weisheit* (Berlin: Topelmann, 1966). Even a cursory reading of sapiential literature from non-Israelite countries will detect the more religious-cultic character compared with Prov. 10-31: cf., Walter Beyerlin (ed.), *Near Eastern Religious Texts Relating to the Old Testament* (Westminster Press: 1978), pp. 44-62, 133-145.

¹¹John Bright, *A History of Israel,* 2 ed. (Westminster Press: 1972), p. 61.

¹²Roland de Vaux, *The Early History of Israel* (Westminster Press: 1978), pp. 318-320, recognizes the difficulties of identifying the descent of Israel's ancestors into Egypt with the Hyksos penetration. He states that the "movements [of Semitic groups] into Egypt may have been spread over several centuries. . . . The first entry . . . took place just before or at the beginning of the period of Hyksos rule." While various groups came out of Egypt at different times, "the experiences of the group led by Moses during the exodus from Egypt and in Sinai became decisive in the formation of the people of Israel and the establishment of their religion" (p. 320).

¹³We call attention to the attitude of "collective personality in biblical culture": see H. Wheeler Robinson, *Corporate Personality in Ancient Israel,* Facet Books, Biblical Series, 11 (Fortress Press: 1964), with informative introduction and bibliography by John Reumann; H. W. Wolff, *Anthropology of the Old Testament* (Fortress Press: 1974), chap. XXIV, "The Individual and the Community"; Roland de Vaux, *Ancient Israel* (McGraw-Hill: 1961; paperback 1965), I, pp. 1-61.

¹⁴An honest yet indecisive struggle with *The Problem of War in the Old Testament* (Eerdmans: 1978) is undertaken by Peter C. Craigie; while this book is informative and in some ways conclusive, still in other ways it shows the theological impossibility of settling the question of war. M. C. Lind, "Paradigm of Holy War," *Biblical Research,* 16 (Chicago: 1971), pp. 16-31, surveys the positions of F. Schwally, J. Pedersen, and G. von Rad; Lind concludes to a "faith in the immediacy of Yahweh's political leadership to which Israel was called back again and again by the great prophets." Holy War thus led to holy "waiting" and "trust" with the prophets (see footnote 27).

¹⁵A very balanced, comprehensive study on "liberation through the Bible" (book's subtitle) is given by L. John Topel, S. J., *The Way to Peace* (Orbis Press: 1979). A vigorous critique of liberation theologians is done by Alfredo Fierro, *The Militant Gospel* (Orbis Books: 1977). A helpful bibliography of books in this area is provided by Robert McAfee Brown, "To Orbis, With Thanks," *The Ecumenist* (July-August, 1978).

[16]L. Koehler and W. Baumgartner, *Lexicon in Veteris Testamenti Libros* (Brill: 1958), p. 790. R. de Vaux, *Ancient Israel* (McGraw-Hill: 1961; paperback 1965), I, p. 259 and II, p. 304 is less certain about the relation of this epithet with war. Yet "the word certainly includes the idea of power." James L. Crenshaw, *Hymnic Affirmation of Divine Justice*. SBL Dissertation Series 24 (Scholars Press: 1965), pp. 18-20 summarizes various views and concludes with Victor Maag that *ṣebā'ôt* indicates that "various powers previously attributed to Canaanite mythological beings were absorbed by Yahweh through a process of identification, elimination and integration." I would use a stronger word than "elimination" as the battles between Yahweh and the gods were portrayed fiercely (cf., Ps. 74:13-14; 89:11; Is. 51:9).

[17]Frank Moore Cross, *Canaanite Myth and Hebrew Epic* (Harvard University Press: 1973), p. 91.

[18]*Op. cit.,* p. 90.

[19]Cf., Carroll Stuhlmueller, "History as the Revelation of God in the Pentateuch," *Chicago Studies,* 17 (Spring 1978), pp. 29-44, where an attempt is made to wrestle with the process by which insignificant events become historical landmarks through liturgical celebrations.

[20]Cf., Carroll Stuhlmueller, "The Interdependence of the Old Testament Liturgy and the Bible," *The Church Year* (The 19th North American Liturgical Week Proceedings: 1958), pp. 139-155.

[21]Cf., B. S. Childs, *The Book of Exodus* (Westminster Press: 1974), pp. 144-9, who reasons behind the stylistic features in common with the prophetic stories of legends to "the mystery of Pharaoh's resistance." This problem is "profoundly theological . . . the mystery of God's power over human pride" (p. 149). The plague narratives of the "J" tradition recognize a constant cycle of such a mystery in the secular politics of royal courts.

[22]R. de Vaux, *Ancient Israel*, I, p. 259.

[23]Cf., Hans-Joachim Kraus, *Psalmen* (Neukirchener Verlag: 1960), I, p. 469.

[24]See footnotes 17 and 18 and accompanying text.

[25]The first mention of Israel in Egyptian texts is found in the "Hymn of Victory of Mer-ne-Ptah," dated "about 1230 B.C.," according to John A. Wilson, who notes that "Israel is the only one of the names in this context which is written with the determinative of people rather than land," showing that Israel is "not yet a settled people." The reference to Israel is hardly central to this commemorative hymn. Cf., *Ancient Near Eastern Texts,* ed. by J. B. Pritchard (see footnote 8), pp. 376-8. Also Roland de Vaux, *The Early History of Israel* (see footnote 12), pp. 390-1 who corroborates Wilson's statement, and p. 156, "this first allusion to Israel . . .

is ambiguous because it contains no explicit reference to the Hebrew patriarchs, the period spent in Egypt, or the conquest of Canaan.''

[26]Cf., footnote 12. I am aware of the challenge to place the Pentateuchal traditions at the beginning of the exile and later. See the discussion of this question in the *Journal for the Study of the Old Testament*, No. 3 (July 1977); for methodology, see S. M. Warner, ''The Patriarchs Extra-Biblical Sources,'' *Journal for the Study of the Old Testament*, No. 2 (Apr. 1977), pp. 50-56.

[27]Cf., Friedrich Huber, *Jahwe, Juda und die anderen Völker beim Propheten Jesaja* (de Gruyter: 1976), pp. 148-160, investigates the Hebrew words *bithä* (calmness, unconcern, quiet, like *šóqẽṭ* in Judg. 18:7) and *šûbâ* (here, ''lifting oneself up'' towards Yahweh, perhaps like flowers towards the sun). Isaiah condemned Israel/Judah for seeking help from foreign nations, and stated at the time of the Syro-Ephraimite invasion (Is. 7) that Judah had no other option but to believe that the Lord alone would save the country and dynasty.

[28]Walter Brueggemann, *The Land* (Fortress Press: 1977), Chap. 1, ''Land as Promise and as Problem.'' He writes: ''Israel experienced the bitterness of landlessness, being totally exposed and helpless, victimized by anything that happened to be threatening'' (p. 8). And on p. 9, ''Of course Israel's history is not all of landlessness. It had its moments of being in the land, of controlling and celebrating and exploiting the land. Having land turned out to be nearly as great a problem and temptation as not having land.''

[29]Roland de Vaux, *Ancient Israel*, I, p. 74. W. Baumgartner, *Hebraisches und Aramaisches Lexikon zum Alten Testament*, 3, Aufl. (Brill: 1967), I, p. 193, ''*gēr* is a man, who alone or with family on account of war (2 Sam. 4:3; Is. 16:4), famine (Judg. 1:1), troubles, blood-guilt, etc., has been constrained to leave his original place or tribe and seeks shelter and dwelling at another place, where he is restricted in the civic rights of property-ownership, marriage and partaking in worship and war.''

[30]Cf., 1 Cor. 4:16-18.

[31]Roland de Vaux, *The Early History of Israel*, p. 540. George E. Mendenhall, *The Tenth Generation* (Johns Hopkins Press: 1973) has questioned whether Israel ''conquered'' the land. He opts for peasant revolts against petty Palestinian kings and the acceptance of new patterns of Israelite trans-tribal peace on the part of existing population groups in Palestine. See especially pp. 19-31. The question is discussed in the *Journal for the Study of the Old Testament*, No. 7 (May 1978), particularly by Alan J. Hauser and Thomas L. Thompson. I myself find that a combination of internal revolt and external violence best explains all the data.

[32]George A. Coats, *Rebellion in the Wilderness* (Abingdon: 1968), p. 249.

[33]Cf., Coats, *op. cit.,* chap. 6.

[34]Brueggemann, *The Land,* p. 13.

[35]Even when Egypt was an ally of Israel's, as in the days of King Jeroboam II (786-746 B.C.), "Egypt" remained a symbol of bondage and sin (cf., Hos. 8:13; 9:3, 6).

[36]For the dependence or relationship of Deutero-Isaiah and the other books of Deut., Hos., & Jer., see Carroll Stuhlmueller, *Creative Redemption in Deutero-Isaiah* (Biblical Institute Press, 1970), pp. 60-64; p. 118 footnote 415; p. 175. J. Vermeylen, "Les prophètes de la conversion face aux traditions sacrales de l'Israël ancien," *Revue théologique de Louvain,* 9 (1978), pp. 5-32 holds that the classical prophets contradicted, relativized or reinterpreted its constituent traditions. At least Amos presented the election tradition in a way that was unacceptable to Israel's religious authorities (Am. 3:1-2; 3:12; 9:7; 7:12-15) and Jeremiah was imprisoned for announcing the destruction of Jerusalem (Jer. 7; 26).

[37]Cf., F. M. Cross, "The Council of Yahweh in Second Isaiah," *Journal of Near Eastern Studies,* 12 (1953), pp. 274-8; Stuhlmueller, *Creative Redemption,* pp. 179-180.

[38]Cf., *Creative Redemption,* pp. 74-82.

[39]H. van Dyke Parunak, "A Semantic Survey of *NHM,*" *Biblica,* 56 (1975), p. 532, writes: "The basic meaning of the Hebrew root *nhm,* attested both etymologically and in every form of the Hebrew, is 'comfort, console.' By metonymy, nominal derivatives of *nhm* may take the meaning 'compassion' as well, denoting the emotional pain or sorrow felt by a comforter through sympathy with the mourner. The *Piel* and *Pual* stems . . . suggest the sense 'compassion' through frequent parallels with *nud.*"

[40]Abraham Heschel, *The Prophets* (Harper: 1962; Torchbook, 1971), II, p. 4.

[41]The Hebrew *geʾaltîkâ* is usually translated "I have redeemed you." Because Deutero-Isaiah generally and 43:1-7 specifically stress the blood bond between Yahweh and Israel as the reason why Yahweh intervenes to bring his enslaved children back, I translate the word "I am your blood relative" and as parent, "I call you by your name" and therefore "you are [obviously] mine." See my *Creative Redemption,* chap. 5, "Yahweh-gōʾēl."

[42]Other elements in the inclusion are the words create *(bārā)* and form *(yāsar).*

[43]"Grain offerings" in the Hebrew minhâ can also mean "tribute to an overlord" (Judg. 3:15, 17-18; 2 Sam. 8:2).

[44]Is. 43:24 is theologically impossible! C. Westermann, *Isaiah 40-66*

(Westminster Press: 1969), pp. 131, writes that "the words . . . are offensive to, if not indeed impossible for, the Old Testament concept of God. . . . If God is made into a *'ebed*, if he is made to serve, he has his divinity taken from him." God makes himself into the "suffering servant," "the clearest proof that the latter [songs] come from Deutero-Isaiah" (Westermann, p. 132).

⁴⁵The Hebrew is exceptionally emphatic here. Four consecutive lines begin with *lō'* (not), the fifth with the intensive particle *'ak* (indeed), and then the repetition of *'ānōkî 'ānōkî hû'*.

⁴⁶Some prophetic precedent can be found in Hos. 11:8-9, about which we read in H. W. Wolff, *Hosea* (Fortress Press: 1974), p. 201, "Again and again we see the God of Hosea in conflict with himself over Israel." Cf., Am. 7:3,6; Jer. 26:3,13,19; 31:20.

⁴⁷Stuhlmueller, *Creative Redemption,* p. 16, "Dt-Is, however, composed his poems with masterly freedom . . . we see a fusion of literary types, one merging into another, several combined in a single poem."

⁴⁸Cf., E. Vogt, "Einige hebräische Wortbedeutungen. I. 'Voraussagen" in Is. 40-48," *Biblica*, 48 (1967), pp. 57-63.

⁴⁹For a list of these poems and of their literary form, see my *Creative Redemption*, p. 286; also pp. 135-162.

⁵⁰Because Deutero-Isaiah considered the pagan gods just empty wind (41:29), he quickly stopped addressing them and proceeded to speak about them—for gods are unable to hear anything anyway!

⁵¹The identification of "first" and "last" is seriously debated, and the question becomes all the more complicated when "last" is associated with one's concept of eschatology. See *Creative Redemption*, p. 136, footnote 458; pp. 162-7.

⁵²Cf., Is. 29:5; 47:11; Mal. 3:1.

⁵³Westermann, *Isaiah 40-66*, p. 197, "Then God would act all of a sudden, and the thing proclaimed would come to pass. That is to say, the matter of fulfillment rested entirely with God; as well as the proclamation there was a separate and independent event which could not possibly be deduced from the proclamation."

⁵⁴The word *bārā* (create) stresses that what happens is due solely to God's initiative and activity. The verb occurs in the completed tense: *i.e.,* now, at once, it stands completely accomplished.

⁵⁵Other examples, directing the fulfillment of prophecy not to events but to the person of Yahweh, would be: Is. 41:4; 43:13; 44:6.

⁵⁶Is. 48:1-11 contains a double set of messages for Israel: one is more consoling, the other is threatening and condemnatory. The unity of the poem is disputed; see my *Creative Redemption*, pp. 266-7, footnote 6. In one of the latest stylistic studies of Deutero-Isaiah, Anton Schoors, *I Am God*

Your Saviour (Brill: 1973), pp. 283-292 argues convincingly that Deutero-Isaiah's poem of a disputation has been expanded with verses from Trito-Isaiah. Even without the emendations, Israel remains in a doubtful, argumentative mood towards the Lord.

[57]As the outline of chap. 40-55, later in the text of this study, will show, we are using the terms chap. 41-48 and 49-55 for the sake of simplicity. Actually, we are excluding the Servant Songs from these chapters, and we consider 55:12-13 to be a redactional conclusion to the Book of Consolation.

[58]Carroll Stuhlmueller, "Self-Determination as a Biblical Theme: Prophetic Vision on Particularism Versus Universalism," *Christian Spirituality in the United States: Independence and Interdependence,* Proceedings of the Theology Institute of Villanova University, ed. by Francis A. Eigo, O. S. A. (Villanova University Press: 1978), p. 119.

[59]P.-E. Bonnard, *Le Second Isaë* (Gabalda: 1972), pp. 19-28.

[60]The trees in 41:17-20 are associated with liturgy, divine wonders or the divine dwelling: Is. 55:13; Ez. 31:3, 8-9; Zech. 1:8; Neh. 8:15.

[61]In this way we can explain the "sin" of Moses in Num. 20:6-13; the incident is recast in Deuteronomy so that Moses, "the [suffering] servant of the Lord" (34:5), bore the sins and punishment of Israel (1:37; 4:21). We see here another point of contact between Deutero-Isaiah and Deuteronomy.

[62]Ez. 16:6-14; chap. 20; 23:8, 19-21 present the exodus as a past event with which to compare the present moment, not as a symbol challenging the present and demanding to be relived. Only in 20:32-44 did Ez. describe his contemporary age in terms of the exodus, yet as a threat, not a consolation, and so differs from Deutero-Isaiah and Deuteronomy. Dieter Baltzer, *Ezechiel und Deutero-jesaja* (W. de Gruyter: 1971), tends to gloss over these differences and overemphasize the likeness between the two prophets.

[63]As mentioned in footnote 57, we are excluding the Servant Songs from the phrase, chap. 49-55.

[64]D. E. Hollenberg, "Nationalism and 'The Nations' in Isaiah XL-LV," *Vetus Testamentum,* 19 (1969), pp. 23-36, writes convincingly that at times Deutero-Isaiah addresses himself to crypto-Israelites who hide their identity and pass themselves off as gentiles (44:5; 45:20-25). Hollenberg places other passages in this category, which in my judgment refer to gentiles *simpliciter.*

[65]Anton Schoors, *I Am God Your Saviour,* p. 156, writes about 51:4-5, "From a literary standpoint, the most plausible solution is, that we have a composite interpolation, combining proto- and dt.-Isaian elements with the proper flavour of the Servant prophecies."

⁶⁶Schoors, *op. cit.*, p. 124, recognizes a textual disorder here, but confines the interpolation to v. 15-16. For authors who admit their doubts about v. 12-16, see *Creative Redemption,* p. 14, footnote 44.

⁶⁷The dramatic shift from preaching excitedly to his own people, Israel (chap. 41-48), to a growing isolation from them (chap. 49-55) and then to persecution (Servant Songs) is mirrored in 44:24-45:7 and in 45:9-13. In the former poem Deutero-Isaiah clearly announced Cyrus as the new Moses, the anointed one to lead the exodus back to the promised land; this spirit is shared with all the poems about first and last. In the latter poem (45:9-13) the people argued against the prophet so that a serious rift developed. The separation became ever more pronounced in chap. 49-55.

⁴⁸The classical study of the "call narrative" is by N. Habel, "The Form and Significance of the Call Narrative," *Zeitschrift für Alttestamentliche Wissenschaft,* 77 (1965), pp. 297ff; these conclusions have been further refined by W. Vogels, "Les récits de vocations des prophétes," *Nouvelle Revue Théologique,* 95 (1973), pp. 3-24. The principal elements, though not all present nor presented in the same order with each narrative, are: divine encounter, introductory word, commission, objection, reassurance, sign, and acceptance.

⁶⁹This principle was stated and exemplified effectively by P.-E. Dion, "Les chants du Serviteur de Yahweh et quelques passages apparentés d'Is 40-55. Un essai sur leurs limites précises et sur leurs origines respectives," *Biblica,* 51 (1970), pp. 17-38, although I myself disagree on some applications and conclusions.

⁷⁰One of the fragments (48:22) is not associated with the Servant Songs; it rightly belongs, where it actually occurs again, at 57:21. It could have slipped in at 48:22 because of the disruption of inserting the Servant Songs. This could happen more easily if the collection of Deutero-Isaiah's poems were normally transmitted orally. Still other fragments, possibly associated with the Servant Songs, are 51:4-6 and 51:15-16 (cf., Antoon Schoors, *I Am God Your Saviour,* p. 127; p. 156).

⁷¹First published by myself in the Proceedings of the Theology Institute of Villanova University (see footnote 58), p. 120.

⁷²Translated from E. Vogt, "Die Ebed-Yahweh-Lieder und ihre Ergänzungen," *Estudios Biblicos,* 34 (1960), pp. 882-3.

⁷³Yahweh as creator of the cosmos is present: (1) in the overture to the Book of Consolation (40:21, 26, 28), probably composed by the editor or redactor from the prophet's poetry; (2) in chap. 41-48 only within transitional passages as 44:24; 45:12 & 48:13 (see footnote 67); 45:18 is a later addition; and (3) in chap. 49-55, only in 54:16; the other text, 51:13, is later. While Yahweh as Creator of the cosmos is found in only one text of the fragments (42:5), still this is a crucial text within the few available

fragments. Yahweh as savior of the nations is found in no authentic passage in the Book of Consolation: for 44:5 see footnote 64; 45:14 & 51:4-5 are later additions. In the fragments it occurs in 42:4; 49:6; 52:15.

[74]We draw attention to John of the Cross, *Dark Night of the Soul,* within *The Complete Works* (Burns, Oates, & Washbourne: 1947) I, pp. 347-8. John of the Cross' exposition follows.

[75]In the phrase, "the coastlands *wait,*" the verb *y-h-l* indicates some attraction and awareness towards the object (the servant's instructions), therefore to possess it *in germine*; the verb is very close in sound to *ḥil,* "have labor pains."

[76]We are dealing with difficult texts about which scholars do not agree. Hollenberg (footnote 64) identifies the coastlands or distant isles in 42:4 and 49:1 as crypto-Israelites. J. M. Miller, "Prophetic Conflict in Second Isaiah. The Servant Songs in the Light of their Context," *Wort-Gebot-Glaube.* Abhandl. zur Theol. des A & NT, 59 (Zürich: 1970), pp. 77-85, concludes to a conflict that rose not "between himself and his stubborn fellow Israelites [the position taken in my own study], but between himself, his disciples and the Babylonian authorities" (p. 82). We offer our own explanation for its value in putting the largest number of passages from Deutero-Isaiah into an understandable evolution of the prophet's ministry.

[77]Cf., Carroll Stuhlmueller, "Theology of Vocation in Jeremiah," *Thirsting for the Lord* (Alba House: 1977), pp. 45-53.

[78]Translation of this line is from *The Prophets. A New Translation of the Holy Scriptures.* 2nd ed. (Jewish Publication Society: 1978), p. 467.

[79]Cf., C. Westermann, *Isaiah 40-66,* pp. 226-8.

[80]Cf., P.-E. Bonnard, *Le Second Isaie,* p. 233; R. N. Whybray, *Isaiah 40-66.* New Century Bible (Greenwood, S. C.: Attic Press, 1975), p. 151; Westermann, *Isaiah 40-66,* pp. 227-8.

[81]Cf., Walter Brueggemann, "Weariness, Exile and Chaos," *Catholic Biblical Quarterly,* 34 (Jan. 1972), pp. 19-38. While this article sees a remedy for the weariness of the exile in the reestablishment of Yahweh's kingship, I see the Servant's answer more in humble silence and expiatory suffering of the innocent. Brueggemann's article is important for pointing to the theological value of the weariness motif and its association with earlier traditions.

[82]Two important words for weariness recur, especially the second: *yāʿep* in Is. 40:28-31; *yāgaʿ* in Is. 40:28-31; 43:22-24; 45:14; 47:12, 15; 49:4; 55:12; Jer. 3:24; 20:3; 45:3; 51:58. The only other occurrences of *yāgaʿ* are: Judg. 8:15; 2 Sam. 16:2; Hab. 2:13; Dan. 9:21.

[83]Cf., James Muilenburg, "The Book of Isaiah, Chapters 40-66," *Interpreter's Bible* (Abingdon: 1956), pp. 585-6; Bonnard, *Le Second Isaïe,* p.

235.
84David J. A. Clines, "*I, He, We & They.* A Literary Approach to Isaiah 53." *Journal for the Study of the Old Testament,* Supplement series, 1 (Sheffield: 1976), pp. 29-31, summarizes various positions. If the speaker is to be identified with gentile people and kings, they are "speaking voices" to give expression to the prophet's vision. R. N. Whybray, *Isaiah 40-66,* explains the "we" as the prophet's disciples (p. 172) who "identify themselves with the whole community" (p. 176).

85Clines, "*I, He, We & They,*" pp. 43-44.

86Cf., John of the Cross, *Living Flame of Love* within *The Complete Works,* III, p. 75, "For if the soul were to understand anything distinctly, it would be making no progress, for God is incomprehensible and transcends the understanding; and thus the greater the progress it makes, the further it must withdraw from itself, walking in faith, believing and not understanding; and thus it approaches God more nearly by not understanding than by understanding."

87A number of ranking scholars hold that the Hebrew phrases do not necessarily indicate death but "exposed his life to death" (53:12), "my grave was waiting," even before I was dead (53:9), "a hopeless situation" (53:8). See Clines, "*I, He, We & They,*" 27-29.

88Cf., J. A. Sanders, *Suffering as Divine Discipline* (Colgate Rochester Divinity School: 1955).

89Clines, "*I, He, We & They,*" p. 40.

90J. Hempel, *Hebräisches Wörterbuch zu Jesaja.* 3. Aufl. (Töpelmann: 1965), p. 56.

91C. R. North, *The Second Isaiah* (Oxford: 1964), p. 227, and Bonnard, *Le Second Isaïe*, p. 266, agree that the reading in the second person "doit être là le texte original; mais ces changements de personne, fréquents en hebreu, sont très mal tolérés par la traduction française." Even the new translation of the Jewish Publication Society (see footnote 78) reads "appalled at *him*" for stylistic reasons.

Chapter 4

HUMAN SUFFERING AND THE PASSION OF CHRIST
Dr. Arthur McGill

Let me begin with some preliminary remarks which will indicate certain directions that I will not follow.

First, there is something fundamentally misleading in any attempt to examine suffering in isolation. Suffering never occurs in and by itself, nor can we ever examine it properly as if it were an independent and self-contained experience.

Suffering always occurs in a *living context.* The agony is embedded in some project, some hope, some relationship. The physical distress of an injury occurs in connection with some striving on the part of the sufferer. The pain of betrayal belongs to the life of a relationship. Whenever we consider suffering in abstraction from its living context, we not only give it a false isolation, we also miss the way in which a suffering bears on the living situation.

Second, a distinction is sometimes made in discussions of suffering between what is called physical pain on the one hand, and mental or psychological agony on the other. "Physical pain" designates that which comes from the body, while "mental anguish" arises from decisions, attitudes, and experiences in the mind. These latter might include guilt, loneliness, separation, terror, etc.

I find this distinction not very helpful. It means to separate out the bodily suffering which befalls us from beyond the realm of our self-control and self-determination from that suffering to which our freedom contributes. I find, however, that this distinction disappears in real life. My mind will experience a bodily pain and draw it into its own frame of reference, finding it a reason for terror or despair, using it to avoid responsibility or win pity from others. There is never a moment when I endure physical pain by itself. Similarly, psychological afflictions generate and relate to various bodily illnesses. Suffering is a fabric that involves both the mind and the body, and efforts to isolate the one from the other constantly fail.

Third, I would also like to dissociate myself from relying very much on analytic reason to discover and verify some meaning connected with suffering. Today people expect that some intellectual expert will give them some teaching or some truth which will enable them to find meaning in suffering.

I consider this to be an illusion. It is only by passing in and through the actual experience of suffering that we have access to any meaning that it may entail. After doing this we may share our discoveries with one another. But abstract reason can give us only abstract meanings, and these unfortunately are too general to connect with the specificity of our suffering. Perhaps that is why the language of a novel or a poem can expose the meaning or meaningless of suffering much better than an intellectual discussion. However, such a discussion can challenge thinking which too easily ignores the difficulties of suffering.

Fourth and finally I will not pursue the question of how to free our lives in this world from all suffering. For instance, let us suppose that God might so interfere in situations that all our suffering would be immediately removed. At the first pain of hunger, for example, a meal would miraculously appear on the table. Upon cutting ourselves with a knife accidentally, we would be instantly healed. Upon being defrauded of our savings by some criminal, new money immediately appears in our possession.

We can appreciate the problems which would arise in this "ideal" world. First, much of human creativity and striving are directed to the overcoming of some bit of suffering. Hunger has provoked us to develop hunting skills and agricultural techniques. Against disease we have fostered medicine. The moral patterns we adopt warn us against the sufferings which we may produce in the lives of others. In any deep human relationship we discover how essential it is that the other rebuke and correct us at certain points. A real relationship always involves the suffering experience of being judged. What is a love that does not judge? It does not love us. It simply humors us.

Behind these circumstantial problems of a world devoid of suffering there stands a much more fundamental issue. When we wish for a life that never frustrates our desires, that never complicates our health, that never claims our moral restraint or encumbers us with social difficulties, we are asking for a world that lets us have our own way, that lets us be entirely centered within ourselves. It is against such narcissism that suffering may have a very significant effect.

Further still, when people dream of a world without suffering, they often forget that their suffering arises, not only from circumstances in their environment, but also from their own nature. The capacity to suffer is a measure of *human sensitivity.* Therefore we may realize our dream of a world without affliction, not by the rearrangement of circumstances, but by the removal of sensitivity from human nature. It is along these lines that we may long to possess a solidness that is immune to affliction, that we become heartless and steel-clad. Yet the very sensitivity that is lacerated in our suffering is the very quality that marks us as human.

In my remarks, therefore, I will not be concerned to free this world from all suffering. I will rather be concerned with the occasions of intense suffering, which, far from provoking people to striving and creativity, overwhelm and shatter them. I think here of the grim sufferings that afflict helpless children, though also of the famine and oppression and disease that crush adults.

In considering our suffering in relation to the suffering of the Christ, I will be particularly concerned with that dreadful degree of suffering which seems to stay with us through the centuries and which so lacerates the sensitivity of our humanity that it brings forth our destruction.

THE "PROBLEM OF SUFFERING" TODAY

The first thing which I wish to do is to get some bearing on the rather extraordinary status which "the problem of suffering" has acquired in our day. One can see this clearly if one reads the writings of earlier times. For instance, in the works of earlier theologians, like Athanasius or Augustine or Thomas or Luther or Ignatius, there is simply no mention of the "problem of suffering." Suffering seems to have been accepted as an immovable component of our present human life. No one developed it into a profound religious question.

That, however, is exactly what we do today. In contemporary Western literature no source of atheism is presented so insistently or so dramatically as the existence of suffering. Why is that?

We can begin our inquiry on this matter by observing how deeply we have been affected in our attitude toward suffering by two recent developments.

The first is the way in which technology has given us a control over our environment that was unknown to our predecessors. Much of that technological control we direct to the removal of the sources of suffering. Irrigation eliminates the dangers of drought. Advanced weapons defend us against our enemies. Drugs work against disease. This pattern of activity, however, creates in us a pervasive expectation: since technology has been able to remove so many kinds of suffering from our lives, can we not look to it to dispel all forms of serious suffering? We find ourselves directing that expectation, not only toward the disasters with which nature afflicts us, but also toward the psychological and interhuman sources of our suffering. If we are afflicted by economic adversity, if we are in conflict with our neighbor, can we not remove these problems by developing a better social order or by taking a drug to forestall our hostility?

That is the first development which has affected us. In many cases, however, we must endure a suffering whose source technology is not able to remove. In this eventuality we have recourse to a second help: the development of anesthetics and narcotics. By their effect on us we can dull the sensitivity in us which bears affliction.

We can readily see the bearing of these two developments upon our attitude toward suffering. While earlier ages looked upon suffering as one of the immutable givers in life, we no longer share that view. We look for the physician or the engineer or the political leader or the social conditioner to eliminate these conditions which impose our suffering. And insofar as that cannot be done, we will take an anesthetic or a narcotic to deaden our agony.

This expectation, this demand that suffering be removed, we not only direct to the agonies which we ourselves must endure directly. We direct this with equal insistence toward others, toward people who may suffer in our presence. We require that suffering also be removed from us. Therefore you will find no deformed beggars on the streets of our towns. The sick are sequestered in hospitals, and we can encounter their suffering only by "visiting" them. Moreover such care is taken in providing these hospital buildings with an attractive landscaping that when we drive by them no hint is given to us of the dreadful agonies that are being endured within those walls.

The demand to flee from suffering also has many subtle effects in the lives of middle-class Americans. For instance, in relating to one another they seem to feel prevented from obtruding their real afflictions upon the attention of each other. The lawn is kept mowed, the clothes are kept pressed, the smiles are kept boisterous, even while some difficult ordeal is being endured. On the street where I am living, one family has had their daughter run away. Another family is coping with the ravage of severe cancer in the husband's mother. Another family is being prosecuted by the Internal Revenue Service.

In every case, however, the afflicted families in these ways seem to go out of their way not to impose their pains upon their neighbors. It is as if there were a taboo against the social sharing of suffering, as if suffering should be kept a private matter, as if it were better to pretend to others that one is free from suffering than to relate others to one's agony.

The demand that suffering be removed is having a devastating effect on one situation in particular. What do we do when we face a suffering that no invention or drug is able to relieve? What does the physician do when his or her patient has passed beyond the reach of helpful treatment? In these situations we can understand how the demand that suffering be avoided pushes the physician and us all to withdraw, to abandon the suffering patient on the grounds that "we cannot do good anymore." As if the only order of good were the removal of suffering.

The work of technology and anesthetics has been somewhat successful. Some of the suffering that has haunted human life has been removed or at least minimized. Yet with regard to the success of this project we can only say "somewhat." People are still afflicted by terrible and widespread suffering; psychological forms of suffering are as intense as ever; and technological developments themselves are yielding their own fruits of difficulty. Nevertheless, people continue to expect the elimination of suffering with naive and single-minded commitment. Consider, for example, the pattern of education which is given to the children of the middle class. No child is deliberately directed to try out an experience of suffering; to learn the peculiar difficulties which his or her personality experiences along this road; to discover not only how to cope but how to maintain one's human ways under this duress; to develop the strengths of courage and patience in the face of suffering. No one is subjected to this kind of education. Our education is a one-sided development and reinforcement of all those techniques and skills and ambitions by which we hope to void suffering and live in happiness. Can you imagine a middle-class school providing an opportunity for children to "learn about failure?" Children are taught only to fear and flee from failure, and to condemn themselves for it. They are prevented from learning how to endure failure with a quiet mind.

Behind this kind of education, behind all the social constraints which work to keep us away from suffering, there runs a belief of utmost significance for Christian theology. This is the conviction that suffering is somehow utterly incompatible with being genuinely human. It is widely believed that no human growth and no human developments are possible in suffering. This is exactly the principle which shapes our education. Not only is it assumed that affliction enervates our humanity, it is also assumed that those who suffer have nothing of value to offer us. You know how tubes and masks and narcotics are allowed to obstruct the communication which a hospital patient may wish to make with others. The dominant belief seems to be that no significant humanity remains to be honored and listened to where suffering has taken over.

In other words, to many suffering has become the most

dreaded and the most overwhelming form of evil. While earlier ages were preoccupied with the moral evil that issues from the misdirection of human freedom, our time looks upon moral evil as secondary to the evil of suffering. In fact, the most heinous moral evils in the view of many are those which produce human suffering. Also, middle-class people tend to "explain" a flagrant moral evil which they find in some individual or some group as the consequence of some suffering or deprivation which has scarred that individual or group.

The reverse side of this perspective must also be observed. Since suffering effectively destroys our humanity, those who exercise their humanity to help the sufferers can only do so from a vantage point apart from suffering. Only because they stand outside of suffering are they able to work humanely and creatively, and thereby deliver others from suffering.

In the prevailing view, then, there are two domains, as it were. There is the domain of successful humanity, characterized by people who are healthy, confident, outgoing, and capable of serving others. We must also observe that these qualities are almost always made possible by the possession of enormous affluence. On the other hand, there is the contrasting domain of suffering, where the humanity in us is so thoroughly twisted and shattered that nothing very human is expected of us, and that we can only recover our creatively human possibilities by being taken out of this dreadful domain to the other.

Thus, in the prevailing attitude there is working a thorough-going dualism, with humanity in secure well-being on one side and dehumanized wrecks ravaged by suffering on the other. We can see a vivid example of this dualism in our hospitals. The staff who work there helping others do so in such a way that traces of their fragility and suffering are carefully hidden. The mask of "expertness" identifies each worker with a successful effectiveness that allows no room for his or her victimized agonies. There is an incredible pretense involved in this stance, but it is believed to be essential, so that physicians hardly ever present themselves as sharing in the same misery as their patients. Instead, they stand immune behind the facade of expertise.

The sick, on the other hand, are thought to have lost their creative humanity and to have become only "patients," passively being possessed first by their illness and then by the medical treatment which seeks to deliver them. It seems perfectly reasonable, therefore, that since the suffering sick have lost the power of their humanity no compunction is felt against denying them speech by putting tubes in their mouths, or denying them reason by keeping them comatose, or denying them the resources of courage by dulling them with drugs. What matters is the removal of their suffering. Until that is achieved, there is no point in so restraining medical treatment as to allow their humanity to function, because their suffering is thought to debilitate and destroy their humanity.

In speaking of the marked dualism—or mutual exclusion—which is believed to exist between being human and suffering, we must be careful not to overlook one peculiar feature of this dualism. For if suffering is able to shatter our humanity, that means that suffering has excessive *power* over humanity. Apparently a person's humanity is thought to have no resources within itself against the savagery of suffering. It is as if the sufferer's ability to maintain humanity, to exercise discriminations, to be responsive to moral demands was thought to be simply eliminated. It is as if suffering was thought to involve such a heavy and unredeemable evil that all factors within the sufferers which might qualify or transform its overwhelming destruction were automatically dismissed. Suffering has the decisive power, and any human gripped by it is in the position of total victimization.

To identify this extreme destructive powerfulness which is attached to suffering, we may say that in this view suffering is being seen as "demonic," not in the mythic sense of being caused by demonic spirits, but in the descriptive sense of having a destructiveness that can so transcend all human resources that in its presence we are utterly helpless and can see no positive meaning except by escaping from it. The only significant redemption, therefore, is the escape from suffering which technology provides. Why? Because in the prevailing middle-class view the really decisive form of evil is not our moral perversity or our self-engendered corruption of our human character or our act of personal sinning, but the imposition upon us of destructive suffering.

We can see the enormous impact which this prevailing cultural attitude has had on contemporary Western Christianity. We can see this impact operating in two opposite directions.

On the one hand, it has been adopted by Christians as illuminating the meaning of their Christianity. For instance, today many Christians identify the love of neighbor almost exclusively with the removal of suffering. Emphasis is given to Jesus' commands that we feed the hungry and clothe the naked and free the oppressed, and to His making our being approved or condemned at the final judgment depend on how well we have fulfilled these particular commands (Mat. 25). After all, Jesus calls us into the work of redemption, and what else can an authentic redemption be but the deliverance from suffering.

At the same time, since suffering is thoroughly antihuman, the Christians who seek to help others can do so effectively only from a vantage point apart from suffering. Their affluence (called by Christians "the blessings of God") or their faith is thought to put them in a position which should be immune from suffering and from which, therefore, they can hope to deliver the afflicted. Thus the pattern of love which prevails among the Christians of Western middle class represents an adoption of the view that sees full humanity only in the escape from suffering.

We can see how different this whole attitude is from the

viewpoint expressed, say, in the New Testament. For there, in addition to the feeding of the hungry and the freeing of the captive, that is, in addition to directing us to work for the removal of suffering, the New Testament writings seem to give equal emphasis to the work of simply *accompanying* the sufferers in their suffering. For instance, in the letter to the Hebrew, Christians were enjoined to "remember those in prison as if you were there with them, and remember those who are being maltreated, for like them you are still in the world" (Heb. 13:3). In this passage no stress is given to the elimination of suffering. The emphasis is rather "remember" the sufferers, in the sense of being with them mentally, because no one is immune from that suffering. The concern here is not on avoiding suffering, but on suffering with, that is, on "compassion," which originally meant to "suffer with." For the prevailing view today, of course, suffering with is seen as a very second-best activity. For what can be gained if one joins another in being crushed by the terribly destructive power of suffering? "Compassion" is, therefore, usually taken to mean that the person who stands outside of suffering is somehow able to reach across the dualistic gap emotionally, though not in actual life, and thus to empathize with the afflicted.

Adoption of the prevailing view, however, is only one impact which it has made on Christianity. It has also been decisive in providing a platform for the attack on Christianity. By stressing the perfection of life hereafter, has not Christianity had the effect of diluting people's struggle against present suffering? Has it not functioned like a drug to instill a kind of passive inactivity before this evil? Far from being in the vanguard to provoke people to strive against the sources of their suffering, it has tried to distract them, to lull them, in short, to serve the interests of those who profit from systems which afflict them. And if Christians today emphasize the removal of suffering, this is not because of Christianity itself, but because of the very different spirit of humanism and technology, whose abomination of suffering has been only recently adopted by Christianity. In earlier times Christians had no difficulty in believing that their God properly imposed the afflictions of hell upon the non-Christians, and that their duty was also to impose afflictions upon such available non-Christians as the Jews. The seeming hypocrisy of Christianity at claiming to be a religion of redemption while generally doing nothing against the dreadful evil of suffering outrages many today.

Equally vigorous has been the attack which has recently developed against the God that Christians claim to worship. It is a matter of comparison. After two centuries of making remarkable achievement against suffering, humanity by comparison makes the God who established and sustains this world seem morally grotesque. Why could not this God have originally created more provisions against suffering? Why could God not have originally provided an effectively anesthetic plant? Today there is no source of atheism so broadly powerful as the enormity and scope of human suffering.

We find this eveywhere today, inside as well as outside of the churches. Let me give one example from the novel *Catch-22* by Joseph Heller. In one scene Yossarian, the main character, is protesting against the prevalence of suffering in the world.

> "And don't tell me God works in mysterious ways," Yossarian continued . . . "There's nothing so mysterious about it, He's not working at all. He's playing, or else He's forgotten all about us. That's the kind of God you people talk about—a country bumpkin, a clumsy bungling, brainless, conceited, uncouth hayseed. Good God, how much reverence can you have for a Supreme Being who finds it necessary to include such phenomena as phlegm and tooth decay in His system of creation? What in the world was running through that warped, evil, scatalogical mind of His whenHe robbed old people of the power to control their bowel movements? Why in the world did He ever create pain? . . . When you consider the oppor-

tunity and power He had to really do a job, and then look at the stupid, ugly little mess He made of it instead, His sheer incompetence is almost staggering. It's obvious He never met a payroll. Why, no self-respecting businessman would hire a bungler like Him as even a shipping clerk."[1]

What Yossarian is doing is assessing God's activity by the prevailing ethic of removing suffering, and by comparing it with human achievements along that line. By that criterion God is grossly evil. Yossarian's castigation of God ends with the fury of moral superiority.

Yossarian snorted resentfully, "You know, we mustn't let Him . . . get away scot free for all the sorrow He's caused us. Someday I'm going to make Him pay. I know when. On Judgment Day. Yes, that's the day I'll be close enough to reach out and grab that little yokel by His neck."

For many today like Yossarian the Christian enterprise of believing in a good God who rules over this world makes absolutely no sense. Suffering is evil, is radically and profoundly evil. Therefore, as Yossarian says, the God who is responsible for this world which inflicts terrible suffering ought to be morally condemned and finally punished.

In these many ways we see how deeply the belief in the dreadfullness of suffering and the ethical striving to remove suffering works in every region of our culture. Therefore, from this point of view, if we ask about the meaning of suffering in relation to Jesus, we expect to learn how Jesus will take away suffering. Nevertheless, that exception has no support in the New Testament. There Jesus was not seen as removing suffering, either from himself or from his followers. He did not promise a way devoid of suffering. He did not teach a set of values that were supposed to produce the avoidance of suffering. On the contrary, Jesus is reported to have predicted that the world would persecute his followers just as it had persecuted Him (John 15:18-20), and that those worthy of Him would be taking up their crosses

(Matt. 10:38).

Therefore, in our approach to the issues before us, we will have to recognize that the belief in the intolerable evil of suffering and the single-minded quest to avoid suffering are peculiarly our own, with roots in our time. It was not the orientation of the New Testament nor of most of the Christian tradition. We belong to the age of technology and anesthetics, and that marks us as having a peculiar intolerance to suffering and an enlarged sense of its evil.

The Passion of Jesus

Let me now turn to the passion of Jesus as variously reported in the four gospels. The perspective which we find here differs so markedly from the view that now prevails in the Western middle class that it raises fundamental questions against that view.

The first thing which I will do is to call attention to the three surprises which meet us in the gospel accounts. These surprises will pinpoint what unusual attitudes toward suffering were called forth by Jesus' crucifixion.

The initial surprise is the one which I have just mentioned, that no hint is given in the gospel narratives that we may, or should, or must get rid of suffering. We know how some of Jesus' teachings emphatically point in that direction. The power of His miracles to relieve the afflicted reinforces his call that His followers do the same. Feeding the hungry, liberating the oppressed, and succoring the weak, therefore, become ways of continuing the redemptive work of Jesus and extending the kingship of God. Yet in the gospel accounts of Jesus' passion that theme disappears. In fact, He is presented as going out of His way to prevent the removal of suffering from Himself. Furthermore, the entire New Testament is unanimous in connecting His submission to suffering with His way of relating to God.

In other words, here God was not seen to work in such a

way that Jesus was "saved' from His agony. Something else was going on in the passion, something else by comparison with which the removal of suffering would have been not only secondary but a countervailing development. People have always found this to be a very difficult feature of the gospel accounts. How could it have been possible for Jesus to be the redeemer and yet in that very role submitted so completely to suffering?

By contrast the tendency in the early church was to resolve this seeming contradiction by minimizing Jesus' suffering. Hilary of Poitiers (300-367 A.D.) may be taken as an example of this early tendency. Hilary was a strong supporter of the council of Nicea, so that for him Jesus the redeemer meant that Jesus was a human nature assumed by the divine son of God. For Hilary this meant that Jesus had "a unique body as befitted his origin." "He was free from the . . . imperfections of the human body." Therefore, Hilary concludes, He could not have felt pain and could not have suffered as we do.

Hilary is very insistent on this point, in order to oppose the Arians. They had argued that because Jesus feared and felt pain and was infirm, we are prevented from treating Him as impassible and therefore must not assign to Him the likeness of God. Hilary took the opposite position. Since, in his view Jesus was the Son of God, since He became man without departing from the mystery of His divine nature, He must have had a human condition that befitted His divinity and therefore that was subject to no pain or sorrow or fear. How, asked Hilary, could He have been thirsty who redeemed by giving forth from Himself rivers of living water (John 7:38)?

The common tendency for many today is to give up the notion that Jesus Himself is a redeemer. Some find themselves having to reject all connections between the Jesus of the first century and their own lives. Others believe that Jesus exemplifies and arouses humanity to the work of love, but deliverance only comes about through that human work, not directly through Jesus. In any case the pattern today is to resolve the seeming contradiction between Jesus as redeemer and Jesus as sufferer by minimizing His redeeming role.

Then what of the gospel reports of His suffering? Hilary explained these by distinguishing between the infliction of cutting, piercing, and other actions upon Jesus (he called this *passio*, the being effected by another's actions) and the inner experience of suffering (he called this *dolor*), which he argued, that Jesus could never have felt.

> When he was struck with blows or inflicted with wounds or lashed with whips or lifted upon the cross, he felt the force of suffering (*passio*), but without its pain (*dolor*). When a dart cuts through water or pierces a flame or slashes the air, it inflicts all the "sufferings" which belong to its nature—it cuts, pierces and slashes. Yet the "suffering" which it inflicts does not have effect on the things that it strikes, for it is not in the nature of water to be cut or of flame to be pierced or of air to be slashed . . . So our Lord Jesus Christ "suffered" (i. e. received) blows, hanging, crucifixion and death. But the suffering which assailed the Lord's body, though it was "suffered" (i. e. received), still did not convey the nature of our suffering . . . for his body did not have a nature susceptible of pain.[3]

Most Christians today find this minimization of Jesus' experience of suffering impossible. Not only do the gospel accounts present Jesus as experiencing both pain and great distress—"horror and dismay" came over Him in Gethsemane (Mk. 14:33) to the point that His sweat was like drops of blood (Lk. 22:44) and on the cross He suffered thirst (Jn. 19:28)—but also that distress was reported as occurring at several levels. His most profound agony was the cry of dereliction, "My God! My God! Why have you forsaken me?" However, although today we have little sympathy for the tendency of many in the early church to dissociate Jesus from the agony and destruction of suffering, yet it is striking how restrained the gospel traditions were on this matter. Their own references to Jesus' own experience of suffering are few and far between. Their emphasis is on what was done to Jesus—He was flogged, mocked, abandoned, and crucified—but His own response to these assaults is mentioned with reserve and only occasionally. If His full submission to suffering is the first thing that surprises us, for the four gospels the agony of that submission was not the primary focus of concern.

Now we must consider the second surprise that awaits us in the gospel accounts. Jesus did not seek to remove Himself from suffering. He did not come down from the cross or conduct any kind of defense or seek help from the local committee for the liberation of prisoners. Yet in all this submission to suffering the gospels report on His part no viewpoint which construes His suffering as somehow good and significant. In other words, Jesus' passion was not presented as a vehicle by which suffering in itself and as such could become a positive good.

Efforts to construe it in this way have preoccupied many Christians since the time of the passion. Perhaps the two most recurrent themes have been the claims, first, that suffering is good because it functions as the punishment for sins ("Any transgression or disobedience has met with due retribution," Heb. 2:2), and second that suffering is good because by it the Christian is disciplined, tested, purged, and purified (2 Cor. 6:9; Heb. 12:6-11; I Pet. 1:6f; Rev. 3:18f). But these are later reflections. The gospel narratives do not report that any positive meaning is given to the suffering of humanity by the crucifixion.

In other words, in these accounts suffering is viewed as essentially evil. That is, in the mythic perspective of the New Testament, it is the effect of evil personal beings called demons, who victimize and impose torment. Like human sin, demons and their work may be "removed," or "conquered," or "driven out" by Jesus, but He never puts them in an interpretive context which converts their evil to good.

Suffering is a demonic evil, and that is as true for the crucifixion as for the instances of blindness and madness that Jesus healed. The fact that humans impose suffering does not change its character. This behavior only makes such people partners and servants of the demonic. As we are redeemed from sin, not by the thought that it builds character or has some other good effect, but by its outright removal, so we are redeemed from suffering, not by finding reasons to justify it, but by its elimination. Evil is evil. It stands opposed to God's purpose and will and nature. It is not the servant of God.

From this point of view, then, there is no satisfactory explanation for affliction, no vantage point that we can take in order to see its place in a meaningful scheme, no perspective by which we can transform its destructive and evil character. Redemption is by the removal of evil, not by its reinterpretation. The fact that the gospel accounts of Jesus' crucifixion do not emphasize deliverance from suffering as the most important event does not mean that suffering can somehow be justified and ceases to be thoroughly evil.

The religious bearing of this can now be seen clearly. So long as there is suffering, a demonic powerfulness is at large and therefore the rule (or kingship) of God is not complete. This is not yet my Father's world. On the contrary, in the way suffering imposes torments it seeks to repudiate God. The fact that affluent people can feel such unqualified gratitude to God for the blessedness of this world only means that their piety distracts them from hearing the cries of suffering that arise everywhere. The Lord's prayer makes the perspective of the gospels unambiguously clear: we pray that we may be delivered "from the evil one," that is, from being victimized by the demonic, for the demonic is very much still at large; and that "Thy kingship may come and Thy will may be done," because as yet this is not fully the case.

The third and final surprise for us arises from the fact that the gospel accounts of the passion show so little place for hope. That is how we ourselves usually endure suffering. We hope that it may be removed or that it may produce something valuable.

Hope figures in the New Testament and sometimes with great force. Yet, as reported in the gospel narratives, it plays no part in Jesus' suffering at the crucifixion. Jesus there gave no hint of looking to the future and thinking, "My suffering will prompt people to give us such dreadful practices," or "this agony is only for a moment, for I will be raised in three days." There are indications of the very different context in which Jesus placed His suffering, but that context was not one of hope.

THE CHALLENGE OF THE GOSPEL PERSPECTIVE   We now come to the heart of our problem: what do the gospel accounts portray as happening in Jesus' passion?

Emphasis seems to be given by the gospels to two activities on the part of Jesus. The first kind of activity is indicated by the saying in Luke's gospel which Jesus gave from the cross: "Father into your hands I commit my spirit." This may be taken in what may be called a weak sense or a strong sense. The weak way is to see Jesus as holding onto an agenda of His own hopes and values, and as committing Himself into God's hands in the confidence that now that He is dying, God will fulfill Jesus' agenda. Too often people have looked forward to resurrection in this sense: they imagine that in the resurrection God will do their will and fulfill for them their agenda of expectations.

The difficulty of such a reading is obvious: Jesus did not say that He was committing His values or hopes into His Father's hands. It was His spirit, that is, His central self that he committed, the self from which He could not distance himself. This weak reading becomes more unlikely if we remember that this saying by Jesus echoes the words of Psalm 31, and that there the weak meaning of the words is excluded.

> In you, O Lord, do I put my trust . . . you are my rock and my
> fortress. Therefore, lead me and guide me for your name's
> sake . . . Into your hands I commit my spirit. (Ps. 31:1-5)

The strong reading of Jesus' statement gives to the word
"commit" a much more unusual meaning. In this case His
act of commitment was not in His mind a means for the
realization of some other purpose, of some plan or hope. In
itself it was the final and decisive act. He gave himself into
His Father's hands, with a trust in His Father that reached
beyond His own knowledge, beyond His own expectations,
beyond His own grasp of His Father's purpose.

The reason for this is two fold. On the part of Jesus, extreme suffering so debilitated Him that He could no longer
proceed on the basis of Himself. Suffering may so violate a
human self that it cannot maintain its own psychic energy. It
is driven into helplessness. If Jesus was genuinely subject to
affliction at the crucifixion, that helplessness was His condition also.

The second and much more important reason pertains to
the status of God. It is not just that God is the decisive context which obtains for Jesus during His crucifixion, as in all
the moments of His life. God is the context in relation to
which Jesus did not need and did not use any reliance on
Himself. He passed over all His own strengths and virtues
and knowledge and hopes, and gave Himself into the care of
His Father. When the New Testament writers see Jesus' taking on suffering and death in terms of His *obedience* to His
Father (Mk. 14:36; Philp. 2:8), we must not reduce that obedience to the mere conforming of His outer behavior to
God's requirements. His obedience involved the inner con-
formity of His self to His Father's status as His Father, that
is, as the one who established Him and nourishes Him and
cares for Him. Therefore, in His extremity, as in His daily
life, He trusted His Father to the point of committing His
whole self to the Father. The inner content of obedience is
trust (Heb. 11:8).

We can now see the bearing which this strong reading of Jesus' words has on the question of suffering. Jesus may be seen as actualizing the way in which we may become authentically and fully human. To be a person means committing ourselves into God's care, means not trying to assert our own control over ourselves or our situation or our neighbors. It means living without maintaining a wall around ourselves. But the accounts of Jesus' crucifixion make perfectly clear what it means to live without a wall: it means letting oneself be *vulnerable*, be open even to destructive activities.

This is what takes precedence over the removal of suffering. In other words, the gospel perspective radically challenges the view which prevails among the Western middle class today. What primarily destroys our personhood is not suffering, but rather our way of holding ourselves behind a wall. If you love, if you commit yourself in trusting, if you open yourself in receiving or expend yourself in giving, then the walls which you hold around yourself must go. But in a world where the rule of God is not yet complete and where a demonic powerfulness still moves at large, this abandonment of walls means the acceptance of suffering. What emerges from the accounts of Jesus' crucifixion, then, is that sin and not suffering is the much more critical evil. Or to put this in somewhat different terms, suffering is primarily evil, not by causing immediate distress, but by provoking us to build a protective wall around ourselves so as to avoid suffering. This wall may indeed protect us from this enemy, but it also prevents our self-commitment to God or to our neighbors.

But why should things proceed in this way? Why should precedence be given to the removal of sin and not to the removal of suffering? Why should we be called to let go of the walls around us, before we are freed from the forces which torment us? Why must commitment to God involve our becoming vulnerable, not just to God and the good, but also to demonic evil?

At one level we can see this in terms of a comparison

between the *power* of God and the *powers* which bring suffering. If it were the case that, in order to be God, God had to remove suffering, the reverse of this statement would also be true: suffering had to remove God. Whenever powers would work to produce suffering, God would there be excluded.

In such a belief there is operating just that sharp dualism between the good and suffering that prevails in the middle class today. That dualism implies that God cannot be God, that God has no place wherever suffering is present. Wherever tormenting forces operate they are all-powerful. They wholly dominate. The only way for God to qualify their enormous power is by obliterating them altogether.

What emerges from the accounts of Jesus' passion is a very different notion. God exercised God's power and Jesus was able to keep letting go of all walls around Him, thereby stepping into vulnerability, *even while the evil forces worked their dreadful suffering.* Normally in human experience nothing provokes us to hold onto walls around us as much as fear and suffering. Yet even while He was afflicted at many levels, Jesus did not resort to walls. He maintained His openness to God. Even under that physical and psychic torment he continued to exercise what he exhibited as full humanity. He did not "fall" into the belief that His humanity could really operate only in affluence, security, vigor, and happiness.

Therefore, the dread of suffering as being somehow final and ultimate, as that before which humanity is totally "nothinged," becomes misplaced. Suffering has its destructive power, but that power is relativized by God's power to nourish and maintain our humanity even in the midst of suffering.

We can understand the failure of dualism in another way. If the removal of suffering had to be the first and most important thing, then the fundamental human attitude would be the fear of that evil. One often gets the impression that much work today against suffering is primarily motivated by fear. "Love" often becomes simply a name used when fear prompts us to work on behalf of others. In such cases help may be given, but it is not affection for victims which informs this help. It is primarily the dread of suffering.

The kingship of God is not grounded on fear, does not authorize fear, and does not call for a love that is essentially a form of fear. In the passion, therefore, Jesus was not controlled by fear and did not attribute to destructive forces a power comparable to God's. This comes through in that Jesus conformed to the will of His Father and therefore maintained His refusal to defend Himself with wall, even at the expense of being vulnerable to terrible suffering. The forces which inflict suffering are really evil, yet even in its most extreme action, evil is not able to exclude or overwhelm the work of God.

There is a second activity alongside of trusting in God which the gospel accounts indicate in Jesus during His passion. This is the activity expressed by the saying in Luke 23:24, "Father, forgive them, for they know not what they do," or by John's way of seeing Jesus' death as His decisive act of "handing over" His life to humanity (John 19:30). John used the word here of which the noun form is translated "tradition." In spite of the presence of suffering, Jesus also refused to place a protective wall between Himself and those humans who crucified Him.

The removal of walls between people and the vulnerability that results are a striking theme in many of Jesus' teachings. Love your enemy, turn your other cheek to receive the blows of others, have "com-passion" and accompany those who suffer even into their sufferings. Jesus seems to be warning us that we cannot be with any of our neighbors authentically without suffering. If we wish to avoid suffering, we must keep all of our neighbors at a distance, observing them, relating to them, even helping them, but holding off so as not to share with them in their actual suffering. As Jesus truly joined us in our agonies, He directed us to follow the same course with one another. In the passion where he joined us in our suffering, Jesus exhibited what "com-passion," or suffering with, really means.

Suffering normally forces us to self-preoccupation and self-pity. Then we are tempted to give up trying to reach beyond ourselves and to maintain our responsibilities. The wall of self-absorption takes us over. Jesus' direction to others is that they break through our wall, not just by their doing outer actions which enter our suffering lives in order to take us out of suffering, but by their actually sharing in the same suffering with us. For, in terms of the most important consideration, humanity is not genuine when it gives help from behind a wall that preserves it from suffering. This only makes the sufferer feel hopeless so long as he or she suffers. The helper serves merely to exhibit the conviction that there can be humanity only where suffering is avoided. For this reason passing assistance or strength from those who are well to those who are afflicted is a crucial Christian work, but it is not the primary form of love. In love, getting rid of walls is primary.

This bears directly on the ways in which we impose suffering on one another. Middle-class Christians sometimes believe that those who are affluent and healthy and effective are the ones who may deliver others from suffering, may liberate them from victimization. But do those with affluence or health or efficiency prove to be less cruel, less brutal, less pernicious than others? Not at all. Affluent and effective people seem to inflict even more suffering than other groups. For the problem before us is not enough, even with Christian motives, to stand on that healthy side of the dualism.

The reason is clear: affluent and effective people still enclose themselves behind walls. At their deepest levels they live as isolated selves in isolate societies. When they help the afflicted, they imagine that they are reaching beyond their own kind to "the unfortunate." They do not believe that they can live humanly with and for others while suffering.

Because the training in "com-passion" leads us into living without walls, it knows no limits. One thinks here of the suffering of infants or of the mentally deficient who cannot understand speech. Are they not cut off from the reach of compassion? Does not their suffering lock them within an isolation that compassion cannot cross? Does not Jesus' well-meant diagnosis that the decisive move is to remove walls collapse at this point?

The primacy of God becomes in practice very obscure in such cases. How can we know if our compassion ever reaches the infants or the mentally retarded? We believe that it does; that is, we believe that even on this frontier our humanity is not without meaning.

The work to relieve suffering and to deliver people from it is critically important and receives the full emphasis of Jesus. But it is not primary. First live openly, live to receive and to give, live so that you do not have to identify yourself in terms of what you are and have and do over against others, live by sharing even the agonies of suffering. When the separative walls are removed, when we have learned to suffer with and to let our commitment to others be stronger than our fear of affliction, then we may give our help with love and not out of fear. Then the passion of Jesus shapes and guides our own existence.

DISCUSSION

QUESTION: The question was asked about the theme of Christus Victor in the Patristic period, and I wonder whether the presentation of the crucifixion doesn't involve a hope that there may be or now is victory over suffering.

ANSWER: It seems to me that the Christus Victor theme was in the early Church identified with the fullness of God's reign. In other words, it really had a kind of eschatological contact, and one of the most fascinating things about the Patristic period is the fullness of life into the Eschaton with which Christians lived. I'm much less clear that the Christus Victor theme was thought to sort of be the rule of Christian practice in the sphere where God had not yet removed the powers of evil. There the work of victory was, of course, being advanced, and the work against suffering was emphatically emphasized by Christ and by a few of the early theologians, but at the same time, there was also the conviction that the forms of suffering are so various and so manifold, that suffering works in any human being at so many levels and in a whole society in so many dimensions, that the movement toward a genuine victory over suffering and not just provisional victories at this or that point—that that's really the eschatological fullness. That's when, well in one image, we will have a new flesh, and for that reason, therefore, it was not in the context of eschatological hope that I was speaking this afternoon, but the times between the times in which we are now living.

QUESTION: I want to express my utter gratitude for your presentation—it was a magnificent presentation and very helpful. However, you leave me with some problems because I'm a professor who teaches students to work in the field of therapy—psychotherapy and family counseling—and all that you said was really overwhelmingly beautiful and I am grateful and very moved. However, I'm left with the dilemma of one of the things that we deal with in training our students—the separation of the subjectivity and the objectivity and the necessity of a very real need to empathize, a very real need to hear and have compassion, but the need to control that so that one doesn't begin to intermix one's suffering, the client's suffering with one's own, and I heard you very well and I believe what you said. Could you enable me to find that bridge so that we can enable those who work with those who suffer not to take on that suffering so we do not, as we say, lend our strength and our ego and help our suffering clients out of their suffering by our own strength. Again, I want to thank you for what you've given me—you've given me a great deal, but you've left me with a dilemma. Please help me.

ANSWER: Well, it seems to me that those who are well ought to be most grateful and giving of their wellness, ought to have no reservations about their being well and, therefore, in relation to those who suffer work in every way to bring those who suffer into the state of becoming well. At the same time, I only suspect, I really don't know, that the psychotherapist also suffers—they're also well but they also suffer—and insofar as they suffer or any of us suffer, that also provides an opportunity for us. That also provides a group, a community, a suffering situation in which we can enter, not entering as a person with health or vigor or vitality or effectiveness, but enter as a companion in suffering; and it was not on the roles and methodologies and procedures and effectiveness of the first mode that I was talking about—how the well deal with the sufferers. But rather, it was an effort to open up a door that, at least in my experience is not opened up very much, that even when we are suffering, the work of Christian love, the work of participating in the Cross of Christ, the work of moving out of ourselves into the lives of others, being responsive and responsible is as vigorous and as real as on the side of—I must say in the light of your question about eschatology—the light of so-called well-being; what we take as well-being may be from another point of view just another form of sickness, so that the two sides are there and each may work and each should work and in each case the rule of God supports and encourages and elevates our work.

QUESTION: You mentioned our attitudes towards suffering and then Christ's attitude—that of His ultimate commitment to the Father—and that somehow we have to learn from His attitude, not putting more borders around us, but taking the walls away so that we could also become vulnerable. I can't argue with that point. Now the point I'd like to find more about is what kind of relationship there is between contemporary suffering and the suffering of Jesus? Are we to look at Jesus as just a model and example, or is there some kind of participation in His suffering wherever we find suffering people? How does the suffering of Jesus strengthen us and give meaning or give eschatological orientation? You might have touched on those and I may have missed them, so I would appreciate your giving me some explanation.

ANSWER: Well, in relation to us today, I mean—and this was dealt with a little—one of the bearings of the Passion of Jesus is that suffering may not be as immense, as paralyzing, as inhibiting of humanity as we think when we're well; that there are strengths which come into play in the face of suffering that don't come into play otherwise. But, I guess what I'm really also interested in is what I might characterize as the first moment in the act of service, and that is the moment when suddenly the suffering of the other is before us and begins to engage us, and at that moment there is the very critical decision to be made—do I psychically back away and observe this other from a distance so as to protect myself, or do I let myself be vulnerable to that suffering? And, for me I guess, one of the meanings of the Passion of Jesus is that in and through the sufferings that are right in front of me in the hospital or in the neighborhood, I am involved with and being gathered into Him, and the sufferings of the many that are beyond my eye, that I'm indifferent to, that I refuse to see, or, for the sake of effectiveness, don't see. And it's that sense of Christ as gathering in the sufferings, as taking on our sufferings into the horizon of the love of God and transforming their meaning and opening them up to creativity and communication and not just flight—it is in that sense that I would find the call to creativity as well as compassion, to effectiveness as well as sympathy, to be directed to us by the Lord. That's a very immense question you ask and it's immense because it bears primarily upon what I do rather than what I think, and unfortunately, those are not always on all fours with each other.

QUESTION: I wonder if you'd comment on an extrapolation of, I think, a method which you used in your talk, which I thought was excellent, namely to try and understand the meaning of suffering in what our response to it should be. You went back to Christ on the Cross, His Passion, His Death as the exemplar of what human suffering is, and how we should have an attitude towards it. And it seems to me also that Jesus isn't just suffering from some abstract evil; He's not just suffering in general, but all of His suffering is coming from sin on the part of men—He's being rejected; He's wept over Jerusalem; those He has come to show the love of God are not accepting it, and although they may think they are serving religion or God or the Roman state, they are, in fact, paralyzing God, causing God to suffer and, therefore, at the Cross we have not only the message of what is suffering and how we are to react to it, but also the relationship of suffering to sin; that is, on the Cross we learn that sin is precisely the rejection of God. Jesus is the Will of God and putting Him to death is putting the Will of God to death or contravening the Will of God, and that, therefore, the driving of the nails into His feet and the final act of piercing His heart with a spear is an image for us of the origin of human suffering, namely, our sin which is the rejection of God who has become Man in Christ. That's quite a development but I feel that flows organically from what you said in your talk and I'd just like to have you comment on that.

ANSWER: I made very minimal use of the term "sin," because it's a word with a number of different thrusts in it, and it would have been crucial to distinguish sin as imposing suffering, sin as breaking a law, and sin as being offensive to God, and sin as one's own rejection of God. So that with this variety of meanings—like any word, this capacity to have a number of different thrusts—it was really a decision of time not to go into the clarifications of my meanings of that word that led me not to use the term. Sin, in this context, is concretely the rejection of one's participation in not only the will of God, but the life of God, and since the life of God is communicative, loving—in the love of God. And in human existence breaking from the arena of God's life and God's love, the emergence of suffering or the meaning of suffering alters profoundly. One of the most obvious ways can be seen right away, for what is more decisive for suffering than myself, and what is more important to sin than myself, so that not self-centeredness, but self-preoccupation or an evaluation of one's self as the first and essential thing becomes one of the elements, both fostered by suffering and used in order to assess suffering, so that I have difficulty looking over there and finding a relation between sin and suffering, because the relation between sin and suffering I know best is right in here and there sin is a disengagement from the life of God and the love of God; this disengagement constitutes the glasses that I wear when I look upon suffering. And it's in that sense that sin and suffering are in our experience so profoundly interrelated.

QUESTION: As I take it, we can suffer good, as well as evil, as when Jesus said, "Suffer the little children to come unto me," and we must suffer not to come in and take over our lives if we put up walls against that—they are sin—and only when we have suffered the good, especially the good of God taking over our lives, are we able to suffer the evil, and in that way have the evil cured by the good.

ANSWER: One complication in that passage and in certain others in the first letter of John in the New Testament is that it seems as if the love of God breaks into my life through the love of the neighbor. God's love may be first in value but not chronologically first. That's the one qualification I'd make—that it's our responsibility to each other which and through which and coinciding with which God is the primary worker, but though God's work is primary and most valuable in the glory and the final horizon for everything, yet our work is in our specific way we live, in the specific way we suffer, the work we do for each other, and the particular person we go and visit. That's also, I would say, crucial in the very situation you beautifully express. Thank you.

QUESTION: Do you think that the Western middle-class resistance to suffering and the refusal to become companions in suffering has something to do with the contemporary ascendency of the euthanasia movement which represents the final obliteration of the suffering from the euthanasianist's point of view?

ANSWER: Well, the fear of suffering, certainly, I would have to say in the women I know who've had abortions, is often dictated by the realization, or at least the medical advice, that their expected child will be deformed or inadequate or suffering in some way, and that the most merciful thing to do in that context is to end the life of such a fetus. That, for me, is the most vivid example of the practice of wanting not to have suffering, and I'm trying to think of any physician I know who's talked to me about his own practice of euthanasia—I usually like to have it firsthand, rather than on somebody else's part. Lots of physicians talk about it, but never as if they'd done it. You know, my imagination would guess that one of the impulses that moves people to impose euthanasia upon others would be the desire that the other not suffer. And, again, it's profoundly a matter of education, not schooling, but of the education and the sense of strengths we have and weaknesses which we have, and in an extraordinary way the middle class strikes me as having a sense of extraordinary weakness before suffering. And, of course, those of you who work in hospitals know that that's not at all a case when people—even middle-class people—are actually involved in suffering; they can develop courage and they can develop fortitude and they can develop patience, as well as developing self-pity and other things.

QUESTION: You've spoken a lot about breaking down walls, tearing down walls and being vulnerable, and I guess I need more of a description of that.

ANSWER: The question is for me to be more specific about the experience of vulnerability, how it feels and what one does in that situation. Well, I think what one does is not merely to suffer; in fact, that's one of the most emphatic themes in my remarks this afternoon—that when we suffer, there's still much to be done and still much which we may do. So being vulnerable means that while you're doing something and while you're being open, the impact on you of suffering, the invasion into your life of another suffering, or of distress of psychic or motivational kinds, an experience of any kind of debility would be accessible to that which injures. I can only speak in terms of a medical situation with which I worked for three years, and I must say that the experience of vulnerability there was downright exhaustion. It was crucial for me and for the physicians involved in this—subjected to this exhaustion—not to let the exhaustion so surprise us and defeat us, that it get in the way of our doing what we had to do. So it was necessary there to—if you will—be open to exhaustion; the only way of not becoming exhausted is not to do what you had to do. But to be open to exhaustion, but not to let "Good Heavens, I'm being subjected to suffering! How outrageous! Where is my help? Where is my escape?"—because in that case I would make such moves and, I suppose, the doctors with me would have made such moves, in the effort to escape from our own suffering, that we would have involved really compromising or violating our work with those who suffered and whose suffering we were addressing. Now, you know the forms of vulnerability are really incredible. You're exhausted one day; you're overpleased the next day; you're confused the next day; you get a stomach ache. I mean I'm now convinced after my operation that it's only the healthy that can survive the hospital. If you could only know ahead of time what's going to be vulnerable in you, you could take all the precautions. But you never know and it's that element of surprise and dismay which I'm addressing. I'd like to encourage the work of resourcefulness, the sense of "yes, I can do it, not because I've got energy, but because I'm here, and even though I don't have much energy, I'm here, and there are not many here," or "I'm here and I've been put here, and there are others here who would have their humanity confirmed by my love." So, I really don't have, I'm afraid, a very clear sort of step-by-step procedure for how you cope with vulnerability, but I'm very concerned that there has to be the letting go of walls if we love, and if we love at all—we may not—but if we love at all, we let go of walls so as to reach; we also let go of the walls which protect. In other words, we become vulnerable, and I guess you know more than I do that love always suffers.

NOTES

[1]Heller, Joseph. *Catch 22*, Simon & Schuster, 1961. Dell Paperback Edition, 1978, pp. 184-5
[2]St. Hilary of Poitiers. *The Fathers of the Church,* Fathers of the Church, Inc., N. Y., 1954, p. 417.
[3]*Ibid.*, p. 415.

Part III

SPECIFIC EXISTENTIAL CONDITIONS OF HUMAN SUFFERING

It was felt that the Congress would not be complete without centering on certain major conditions of suffering in social systems and in individuals today. Four periti from quite distinct areas of concern provide superlative presentations. Dr. Robert Jay Lifton, of Yale, treats the phenomenon of numbing and apathy, relating it to his studies of Hiroshima, Vietnam, and Auschwitz. Dr. Henry James Young, of Naperville, Illinois, develops the entire history of blacks in this country, vividly portraying their sufferings as well as their religious understanding of it. Dr. Joel Gajardo, of Chile, develops similarly the whole history of Latin America from colonial times and the forces at work in that area now. Dr. Wayne Oates of Louisville, Kentucky, concentrates on the various forms of grief which are daily encountered in peoples' lives.

Chapter 5

APATHY AND NUMBING —
A MODERN TEMPTATION
Dr. Robert Jay Lifton

In 1962, I lived and worked in the city of Hiroshima for a period of six months in order to conduct a study of the psychological effects of the first atomic or nuclear weapon dropped on a human population. At that time, I interviewed a total of about 75 survivors—half of them more or less chosen at random from the city lists, and the other half a special group of people who had particular activity in connection with the atomic bomb experience, whether as political leaders or religious leaders, or writers, or doctors, or leaders of survivor groups. In both groups virtually all of the people I spoke to reported a particular experience which I heard versions of again and again. They would tell of observing the grotesque scene of the dead and dying right after the bomb fell—a kind of sea of death in which they were immersed. Very quickly, they would cease to feel. They would cease to feel very much about what they were witnessing, although they were quite clear about what they were seeing. They would say such things as, ''I saw everything but felt nothing," or "I became insensitive to human death." Or as one writer put it, "I experienced a paralysis of the mind." I came to understand this phenomenon as a form of diminished capacity to feel—what I came to call psychic numbing, or in its acute form, psychic closing off.

Under those extreme conditions, it was clearly a useful defense mechanism—a way of coping with experiences and images that were simply too threatening, too overwhelming to absorb, or to respond to in ordinary ways. Such images had to be warded off if one were to retain one's sanity. In that sense psychic numbing was a temporary deadening of the mind in order to prevent a death of the mind—that is, a kind of psychosis; or of the body, in the sense that psychic numbing helped one to take some measures toward survival.

Of course, as with any such defense mechanism, it turned out not to be so temporary and to outlast its usefulness. It could and did persist in many people into various forms of withdrawal, apathy, constriction, depression, despair, or bodily symptoms. In other words the numbing would give rise to these patterns long after the disaster itself.

I was also to undergo a more personal lesson in psychic numbing, and in a sense, professional numbing. When I arrived in Hiroshima, I discussed with various people there the human impact of the atomic bomb, and I was astounded, first of all, to discover that no one had ever made a systematic psychological study of that impact. There had been studies of the physical aftereffects, and there had been commentaries on various aspects of spiritual suffering, but nobody had carried through a comprehensive investigation of the human consequences of the bomb. I came to see that strange fact—and it was a very strange fact to me, the failure to address psychologically one of the most significant and threatening events in human history. I came to see that as a manifestation of vast professional numbing. Indeed, one has the impression that the more broadly significant an event, the less likely it is to be studied or professionally addressed. Because its very significance defies our existing professional categories, and we tend to prefer to address instead events of lesser significance to which we can more comfortably apply these conventional interpretive categories. Nor was I, myself, immune to these pitfalls on at least two scores. During my first days in Hiroshima, I talked to many knowledgeable people about the atomic bomb experiences in general. I listened, asked questions, and I learned a lot. I felt I was making a reasonable beginning in my investigation. But, when I sat down with individual survivors to discuss their actual experiences, things were very different. As they described in concrete terms the details of what they had undergone—details of suffering of an order beyond any I had known or previously heard about—I found that I, myself, was becoming increasingly agitated. After the first few interviews, in fact, my anxiety was such that I wondered whether I could be capable of continuing the study, and of seeing it through to its conclusion. But then, within a few days, certainly in less than a week, this anxiety diminished, and I found myself able to focus more effectively on the psychological behavior and on shared patterns of response to exposure to the atomic bomb that was being described to me.

I had experienced first, as I described, an impulse to flee—to hold on to the kind of professional numbing that distances one from massive death and killing. And then, in staying to do the study, and thereby exposing myself to that death immersion, I had to call forth what I came to see as selective professional numbing, a degree of numbing in myself in order to be able to carry out the investigation. But one can see the delicate balance between feeling and numbing involved in all this, and the pitfalls on either side of that equilibrium. The greater danger, I believe, in most of our professional life, as in our personal and social existence, is the danger of too much numbing and not enough feeling.

A concept of psychic numbing can only exist in association with one of its opposites: of the psychic experience of feeling. Without going into that in great technical detail, here I lean very heavily on the work of Suzanne Langer, a still neglected symbolic philosopher, who in the midst of a vast three-volume study of the subject of human feeling, put forth the idea that the entire psychological field (and these are her words), including human conception, responsible action, rationality, and knowledge, is a vast and branching development of feeling.[1] In this sense feeling can be viewed as both a physiological process and a mental one. This fits in well with recent work in neurophysiology, which emphasizes the *constant interposition of brain tissue* in all human thought. Putting this very simply in both psychological and physiological terms, we human beings are incapable of experiencing anything directly—we must inwardly recreate whatever we psychically touch. That's the wonder and the difficulty, I think, of human existence. It is what I call the symbolizing or formative process. Then consciousness, or the experience of feeling, becomes an emergent quality of the mind or the mind/brain—and this is now a kind of convergence of neurophysical views, symbolic views, and psychological views.

In my own work I've tended to pursue a changing psychiatric paradigm, moving from Freud's paradigm or model of instinct and defense to one of death and the continuity of life. And in that paradigm or model that I've tried to describe, I've emphasized that there is a proximate dimension, one we usually study psychologically—one's immediate psychological experience. This dimension I studied through issues of separation and connection, of movement and stasis, of integrity and disintegration—three parameters which start physiologically, become images, and then become symbolized. In this way one can take every basic theme and follow them through the life cycle. But what I add in this model or paradigm that I think is crucial for psychologists but very much neglected and left too much, I think, exclusively to the theologians and the philosophers is what I call an ultimate dimension (what Paul Tillich called ultimate concern)[2] and what I speak of as a symbolic sense of immortality. And by that I mean several modes in which we psychologically, as human beings, have to feel connected to forces and processes and human groups that existed prior to, and will continue to exist after, our limited individual life span.

There is the biological and the biosocial realm—the sense I have of living on in my children and their children in a kind of endless chain of human continuity—that can extend out to community and to people. There is a mode of works—the sense one has of living on in one's human influences, whether great or humble—works of science or art, or simply influences on other human beings, often as a teacher or as a therapist, or as a spiritual counselor. There is the theological mode, which may actually postulate the idea of a life after death, but more basically, I think, postulates a quality of spiritual attainment. There is the mode of nature—the sense one has of living on in eternal nature, which every culture in some way symbolizes. And, finally, there is a pure psychic state, one that I speak of as experimential transcendence, the classical mode of the mystics. This is the experience of a psychic state so intense that time and death disappear. And that state, as you know, has been in a way rediscovered in our culture in the last couple of decades. I think we've had a hunger for it, and I think it's a very necessary state to us whether in dramatic or ecstatic experiences or more quiet experiences of transcendence, that we require, I think, to experience our sense of continuity—or what I call symbolic immortality.

In the forming of the concept of numbing there has been interesting neurophysiological work (and this will be my last reference to neurophysiology), as many of you may be familiar with, on the lateral hemispheres, or the separate brains, the right and left hemispheres. Much has been written about that, which I won't try to recapitulate, except to say that it's been found that the left hemisphere tends to be more concerned with cognition and rational behavior and speech; and the right hemisphere with more holistic or gestalt experience. What people are coming to, and what I take to be my impression of the issue, is that the integration rather than the separate function of the two hemispheres is of major concern in understanding human mental and emotional functioning. Numbing, in a psychological sense, can connect with dissociation of that integration of the two hemispheres.

Generally speaking, numbing has to do with exclusion. This means that if we view it always dialectically, as I tend to do in most of my work, there are, on the one hand, the dangers of exclusion, when we are not feeling things that we need to feel. But, on the other hand, it has to be said that exclusion is necessary for the human mind. One neurophysiologist said the function of the brain and nervous system is to protect us from being overwhelmed and confused by this mass of largely useless and irrelevant knowledge, by shutting out most of what we should otherwise receive and remember at any given moment, leaving only that very small and special selection that is likely to be practically useful. That's a very pragmatic definition, but it's a way of saying that much of the brain's function is concerned with keeping things out. Freud said something similar, as have a number of observers.

It would seem that the mind, or the mind-brain, has to regulate a continuum of feeling and numbing in order both to receive and restrict stimuli from within and without. In general, psychic numbing can take two forms when it becomes psychic impairment (what Gabriel Marcel called "suppression of being").[3] First, it is a form of blockage, in the way that I described or inferred from those Hiroshima examples, blockage in the creation and re-creation of images and forms. When I spoke of the formative or symbolizing process in the kind of paradigm that I work from, that includes a constant creation and re-creation of images and forms—the mind is always active and always potentially transformative. Numbing involves a blockage of that process.

But another aspect of numbing is the absence of preexisting images and forms to which information can be transformed into experience. It isn't that we can experience anything around us. In order to know something, or feel something around us, we need prior images that can connect with it. And this becomes a real difficulty in connection with threats of massive annihilation that confront us, because we simply don't have the images in individual life experience to be able to image what a nuclear weapon would do, or what massive experiences of death might actually be in experiencing them.

Yet, we need further distinctions. As a kind of overview I should like to describe three kinds of numbing; this is work in progress, what I call the anatomy of numbing. The three basic categories are: first, a direct response to actual death, and especially to massive death immersion or holocaust. The second is the numbing of everyday life, so to speak, of the everyday variety, in response to both unpleasant or unacceptable ideas or events, to various kinds of bureaucratic and technological distancing, and to the simple need to limit experience, as I have been describing. And, finally a certain kind of selective numbing of enhancement—the situations in which partial desensitization is necessary to professional or creative function. I would like to think that was what I described in my own work in Hiroshima. It's certainly true of the skillful surgeon, for example, when he does an operation. In that sense one needs numbing of some experience to enhance other kinds of experiences—to free other kinds of experience.

In each of these categories of numbing it's useful to look at the relationship of that process to a death encounter or death imagery in symbolism and, therefore, to what is happening with what I call the formative process, or with mentation—with psychic process in general, the creation and re-creation of forms. It also is important to see it in operation in human centering and decentering, or grounding, as well as the relationship of what I call psychic action to the intensity, or the experience of psychic energy. Finally, numbing is central to issues of self-blame or guilt and shame, to issues of emotional leeway, to decentering, the capacity to step aside and take a look at one's situation from the outside, and to the experience of play, or what I call playful decentering.

Now, under the category of massive death immersion, numbing appears as psychic closing off in association with a sudden sea of death. Here I have addressed three examples of this kind of massive death immersion: one, the Hiroshima experience I mentioned to you; second, the chronic traumatic desensitization, as of inmates of Nazi death camps—those who survived; and, third, the sustained brutalization, or dehumanization, through certain kinds of activities, as in Vietnam veterans, whom I also worked with. What is common to all three, and to this category in general, is a radical dissociation of the mind from its own forms, a radical undermining of existing psychic constructs around death and continuity. What I mean by the mind being dissociated from its own forms is that the mind no longer has access to its own earlier modes of response. It no longer has access to its own history.

The complex symbol of death, one could say, takes over the self. And there is much imagery in all of these events—the sleepwalker, the ghost, the walking corpse, the walking dead—as those subsumed by death, as though living in death. In my Hiroshima work I wrote of the identity of the dead even among survivors. There is also imagery of the end of the world—of *everything* being destroyed. One could speak indeed of a cosmology of death.

Let me read to you two passages which illustrate this: the first,

The whole situation around me was very special. And my mental condition was very special too. About life and death I just couldn't have any reaction. I don't think I felt either joy or sadness. My feelings about human death weren't really normal. You might say I became insensitive to death.[4]

And the second passage:

We were all too exhausted to react, and almost nothing stirred our emotions. We had all seen too much. In my sick and aching brain, life had lost its importance and meaning. There was that hole (there is a hole he described where they piled in corpses and parts of corpses)—that hole full of guts, red, yellow and foul-smelling, piles of guts almost as large as the earth itself. Life could be snuffed out like that in an instant. But the guts remained for a long time stamped on the memory.[5]

The first quotation is from a Hiroshima survivor, and the second is from a soldier in the German Army during World War II, who wrote a book called *The Forgotten Soldier,* describing the experiences and sufferings of German soldiers on the Russian front. What you sense is the grotesque death around them—the mind itself ceasing to live, becoming itself deadened, as if dead—the kind of wiping out of life. And the mind severed, as I said, from its own psychic forms, a radical severance of awareness from emotion, of knowledge from feeling. That is what I mean by the self being divested of its own grounding in its history and in its biology. The self also loses its capacity for centering and decentering. Centering is the feeling at the center of experience balancing the immediate and ultimate dimensions that I mentioned, one's immediate experience with ultimate concerns, balancing one's time relationships with past and future—and also balancing one's emotional valence, the degree of emotion one gives to varying situations. All of that can be understood as centering. In numbing that function is destroyed, or at least, radically impaired.

There are equal impairments in image formation and certainly in psychic action—all of a radical kind, in a way that I can't go into in great detail in this chapter. Perhaps the epitome of this kind of process is the so-called *"Mussul-männer"* described in Nazi death camps (*Mussulmänner* means moslem in German; people don't quite understand how the word originated). The person kneeling down and falling dead because he had simply lost all capacity or will to live was totally numbed and usually emaciated. It's thought that the term was applied because of the appearance imitating a Moslem in prayer, or looking toward Mecca, or for reasons that aren't clear. But, in any case, that was the term for somebody who was among the walking dead and who was soon to die—either to be put to death by the Nazis or simply to die. And Primo Levi has written about the *Mussulmänner* in these terms: "They, the drowned, formed the backbone of the camp, an anonymous mask, continually renewed and always identical of nine men who march and labor in silence, the divine spark dead within them, already too empty to really suffer. One hesitates to call them living, one hesitates to call their death, death—in the face of which they have no fear, as they are too tired to understand."[6] In that kind of ultimate numbing psychic action ceases, centering and decentering are destroyed, grounding of the self and the formative process are no longer functional. One is simply overwhelmed by death imagery and by the cosmology of death.

Guilt is central in all this. The person who experiences a holocaust undergoes very often what I have come to think of as paradoxical guilt. There is something terribly unfair about the victim experiencing a psychological feeling of guilt or badness. Of course, that has to do with the survivor's perpetual and classical question: Why did I survive while he, she, or they, died? That imagery sometimes extends to that of organic interchange: If I had died, he or she might have survived. It also, though, has to do with having crossed a certain boundary between the living and the dying—having entered an area ordinarily taboo to mortal beings, having become part of a dreadful event that once witnessed must so permeate

206 THE MEANING OF HUMAN SUFFERING

one's being as to render one in some degree an accessory to it. Subsequent to that first moment of that exposure, there is a sense of participation in the holocaust, and also one has by that very act and by surviving, wronged or failed one's fellow human beings and oneself. That's the kind of unjust imagery that survivors often have. Also involved in guilt and shame later on is failure to enact the image. Putting it very simply, at the moment of exposure to massive death, one has an image of what's happening, but one cannot act on it in an ordinary way because of that interposition of numbing. One can't help people in most cases. One cannot combat the forces of evil that destroy and kill people. One has an image, and image always suggests enactment or action—the image is never completed. One goes through life with the image never quite completed, and in association with that impairment is a sense of guilt or shame. The guilt is particularly difficult and tenuous when it involves massive holocaust in this way, because many of the patterns I have described can occur in any ordinary death encounter where one loses an individual person one loves. But, one has more of an opportunity in such a situation to overcome patterns of numbing, and for the numbing to be less total—less permanent—and more susceptible to being overcome by the work of mourning, which is in large part—that is, the work of mourning—a work of recovery of feeling.

I mentioned as the last of the criteria the issue of emotional leeway and play, a special kind of formative spontaneity, a playful decentering. There's no playfulness at the moment of holocaust. Yet, it's interesting that people never give us some struggle toward humor, and of course, in these situations, it becomes gallows humor. One in-between example is in military situations, as in the case of Vietnam veterans, in the kind of chants they sing as they march which are passed along to men in their training experience. One of the famous ones in preparation for Vietnam was: "If I die in a combat zone, box me up, and ship me home." They sing in a kind of chant or shout it out as they march along in their training procedures. You can see them in this process addressing a terrible possibility, because just what they say may well happen, and did happen in many cases. They are both confronting it and not confronting it—keeping a certain distance from it, dealing with it playfully, and at the same time, at least touching it, at least transforming something in the experience of this humor. As I say, at the moment of holocaust, any kind of playful decentering is simply not present or possible.

Yet, there are glimmerings of atomic bomb humor. As I described in my book, there was one such case of a professional cremator whose home was right next to his crematorium, and he told me how relieved he felt upon making his way after the bomb had fallen, back toward his home despite his severe burns, because, as he told me with a kind of wink, "I thought I would die soon and it would be convenient to have the crematorium so close by." These are horrible jokes—they are not funny. They don't evoke wild laughter, but they are a way of mocking, of playing with a dreadful, otherwise unmanageable situation. And the mind is still functioning. At this point, he was over the immediate holocaust—he was struggling with balancing these emotions, and that kind of humor served in some degree a decentering or playful process. There were other situations in which that was simply impossible.

The second large category, the numbing of everyday life, concerns us particularly when we think of widespread apathy. I've mentioned the numbing of everyday life to protect us from being overwhelmed and consumed by a mass of largely useless and irrelevant knowledge (that's in the words of a neurophysiologist), so that only a very small and special selection that is likely to be practically useful comes through. Of course, a psychologist has to ask immediately how one determines what is largely useless and irrelevant, and what is likely to be practically useful—and that's where one's responses to what is threatening and what can be received by the mind become bound up with either numbing or feeling. What is useful or manageable for one person may be deeply threatening and unmanageable for another. But, at a time of threat of massive holocaust, there are certain issues that threaten us all.

In that sense, the relationship of numbing to survival is never merely biological, but it's always significantly historical. At a certain point, one can postulate how the normal numbing process being useful for individual survival may be dysfunctional for collective survival. And that, of course, has to do with how the threats of nuclear weapons or other forces of extermination, around which what might be called normal numbing, serves individual adaptation. But the very adaptation through numbing is a threat to us all.

The numbing of everyday life involves formative functions, as I have described. It also involves things like image-overload; being bombarded with images from all over that we can't absorb, especially with the media revolution, but also at a time when there is a breakdown of ritual and symbolizations. That is, the symbolizations around which cultures have functioned in premodern times, and until perhaps rather recently in historical time, have tended to be questioned—whether about the life cycle, about religion, about authority, about education, or about the rite of passage around which lives have been lived. And that means that the image-overloading comes at a time when we are not very firm in our symbolic connections, and this makes it all the more confusing, especially around issues of death and dying. Also related are ideological matters and bureaucratic matters which distance and which permit and encourage numbing in different ways, and above all, technological distancing—ways in which by mere high technology or low technology for that matter, we are kept apart from experience, and we can separate feeling from experience.

One can argue from this standpoint that the normal

person may be more dangerous to collective survival than people we see as incapacitated. People who become neurotic or psychotic are, perhaps, not particularly helpful to collective survival, but they are responding to something that they cannot deal with; whereas, the very adaptation of people under the claim of normality may be more dangerous given a certain set of external arrangements.

I mention that the combination of image-overload, and above all, the breakdown of classical symbolizations, creates problems about death and especially death ritual. Death ritual is crucial to the numbing process that I am talking about. In this connection, I want to tell a little incident that I came upon in some work I did fairly recently that seems to illustrate the dilemma very well. A few years ago, I was doing some work with a younger colleague with innovative young professionals who were trying to be professionals in different ways. One of them was a young lawyer who was experimenting with advocacy law, and living in a small commune. He was living with his girlfriend, and a close friend of both of theirs died—a young girl who was a medical student and who died suddenly from a very strange illness. It was very shocking to all of them, particularly because the physicians mishandled her psychologically and medically. A funeral was held for the girl in the Midwest by her family. Her young friends went there and were very displeased with the funeral because it was a traditional Midwestern Jewish funeral, which meant that a rabbi was called in who didn't know the girl and who said what appeared to these young people to be cliches. The whole thing seemed unauthentic to them, although some of the older people seemed to derive some solace from it. So they vowed to have their own ceremony for her in their own way, and they collected in New York City or Philadelphia, where most of them lived, a group of young people who had known her quite well, and they were all to come together and share this experience. But, somehow when they came together, they all felt awkward—they had little to say—and the evening was empty and painful for them. They felt very keenly the absence of ritual, and they had to conclude that whatever limited authenticity the funeral arranged by the girl's parents had, nonetheless, was more powerful than their improvised funeral. From this, one can see the necessity of ritual. The difficulty of improvising ritual on the spot, and the relationship of ritual to deep feeling, in connection with any sense of loss, is necessary for evoking the work of mourning.

During the Vietnam War, it was frequently said that the mass media perpetuated the country's numbing, because you would see the killing on news shows every night. It became inseparable from a John Wayne movie. On the other hand, what wasn't said so often but what I was struck by, was the extent to which once you began to have doubts about the war, or the sense that it was wrong or bad, every time you saw one of those images, those doubts would intensify, and you would get angrier and more upset because the images could connect with very powerful feelings. The mass media are always at least a two-edged sword. They can reach us very profoundly, as well as superficially, and they can be agents, both of numbing or breakout from numbing. One can say the same about the experience of some of the other emotions I have been talking about—about guilt and shame, and even anger. Sometimes one can cover over one's numbing and one's lack of feeling with both guilt and rage. And sometimes guilt can be a beginning opening toward feeling. The Vietnam veterans with whom I worked came to value their early experience of guilt—not just on an individual basis because they wanted the whole country and the people who had sent them there to share in the guilt, but because the guilt was an energizing force toward what I came to think of as the anxiety of responsibility and toward a recovery of their feeling. And, from the guilt came not just energy, but also action on their part toward making known their experience, and in many cases taking a stand against the war.[7]

I mentioned hierarchy and bureaucracy and their relationship to numbing. It's a large subject—probably to generalize one could say that in the past, in the premodern period, numbing was very much encouraged on a class basis. You wouldn't expect people in the nobility in various European societies to experience compassion for peasants or those in lower classes. It would seem that the shift has been from that rigid class structure, although class structure may still be more with us and not just in Europe—more than we realize—but, anyhow, a shift from class structure to the numbing of large organizations, the distancing of bureaucracy, and also, the numbing of high technology, as I mentioned before.

I mentioned ideology. I was very struck by various dimensions of ideology in my recent work in Europe, where I had been studying medical behavior in Auschwitz, and medical behavior under National Socialism, and interviewing both survivor physicians, who had been in Auschwitz as inmates, and former Nazi doctors, who had done various kinds of medical work, including work in camps and other places, under the Nazi regime. Very often, there would be a combination in this group of ideological numbing along with other elements, but certainly, the experience of strong ideological conviction. In the case of Nazi Germany, a kind of feeling had swept the country, particularly in the early years, that there was a cleansing, that Germany was recovering from its humiliation at Versailles, that Germany was having a rebirth around a new ideology of a sort of a premodern *Volk* society that the Nazis formed. It was crude, and yet, it was powerful for many people. This enabled many people in Germany simply not to receive very much of what was being said about the Jews—which was being said early and strongly, although, at some times, soft-pedaled and sometimes reemphasized. I asked each of these former Nazi doctors, as they talked about their early enthusiasms, how they felt about some of the statements and actions concerning the Jews. And they would say things like, "Well, I didn't notice it too much." Or else, they would use a kind of pseudo-psychological language and say, "I guess I repressed that." The ideological energies are a very great source of numbing, particularly around the process of harming other groups. And, of course, that becomes much easier and more a possibility when that other group is perceived as different—as of a different ethnic source, different racial group, and different religious group.

There is much of great interest (which I won't have too much time to talk about) in the work of Albert Speer. Speer talks about, in his writings and elsewhere, how he could only view the Jews as abstractions. He could never quite see them as people whose rights were being taken away, whose jobs were being taken away, and then, who were thrown into camps. He could never experience them as individuals, and they remained abstractions.[8]

In another ideological sense, the post-atomic bomb Japanese experience is instructive. One of the survivor missions—the ways in which survivors can derive some kind of meaning from an otherwise meaningless and unacceptable experience, by taking on a mission—in Hiroshima was the joining of peace movements and antibomb movements in survivor groups. But, as these movements became politicized, and, of course, people from the outside moved in and often controlled them, there would take place arguments: Is the American nuclear weapon a bomb of war, while the Soviet and Chinese nuclear weapons are bombs of peace? And then, of course, there were discussions about whether the Soviet or the Chinese weapons were bombs of peace or bombs of war. So, finally, we came upon this paradoxical and tragic situation of survivors of the first atomic bomb, who had come to that survivor mission, having the very idea undermined by a kind of ideological impulse in the opposite direction.

Sometimes, equally tragic situations can occur where the preoccupation with atrocity can become a source of numbing and a source of violence. I have in mind the development of the Weathermen during the 1960s and 1970s. One observant young writer wrote a little essay called, "Weathermen Going Mad in the Movement." His argument was that the Vietnam War drove the SDS mad. Their preoccupation with atrocities led to an impulse toward violence to the point that leading people in the SDS, and then, finally, the Weathermen, would post pictures of atrocities on their doors—not just to remind others, but to remind themselves and to energize themselves.[9] I understand that impulse because I had certain pictures of the Vietnamese situation up in my own office, but where one is preoccupied *only* with atrocity, and sees *only* a universe of atrocity—that can lead to equally radical expression of a violent kind.

I mentioned technological distancing. That's of the greatest importance—certainly, the atomic bombing from the standpoint of those who dropped the bomb is a case in point, and I've tried to address that subject in other places. In Vietnam it was significant that people had psychological experience in relationship to how close they were to the people whom they were killing. It's a very simple and, perhaps, not surprising principle. But those who were on the ground had a whole constellation of experiences of a kind that I and others tried to describe, by involving terror and guilt and a sense of corruption and unauthentic environment—counterfeit universe as I called it. Those who flew on helicopters very close to the ground shared almost a similar constellation. Those who flew medium-level planes saw some of this—saw some distant figures on the ground and had some explaining to do about what they were doing in order to avoid guilt or, at least, some questioning of the situation. But those on the high-level bombers saw nothing. They had no visual or other form of contact with the people they were killing, and for them to even mobilize a sense of responsibility or guilt would require an act of moral imagination rarely actually achieved.

One could also point to the Nazi experience, and Speer has written interestingly on this as well, in terms of the first

214 THE MEANING OF HUMAN SUFFERING

totalitarian state in which there was technologically arranged control over the people and over the mass media, with a high level of manipulation, and at times, a rather effective psychological manipulation, including the manipulation of their victims in the camps, whom they could deceive until the last moment about their fate. I would emphasize that these elements can go together, and these affect us and are very important for our life situations now, so that one can have elements of technological distancing, and also elements of extreme ideology. In one or two of the Nazi doctors, whom I came upon or hear about, although most of them were not extreme ideologues, there were one or two who had a very strange and destructive combination of extreme technicism or scientism. This was worship of technique and of science, together with a deadly romanticism. That is, a romantic vision of the Nordic race and of Nazi ideology, which tended to be very romantic in a sense. And those two would seem to be opposite ideological impulses, but they could very much go together, and they did.

Indeed, one doctor whom I interviewed, told me that he had first come to the Nazi Party when he heard a speech by one of the Nazi leaders in the early 1930s, before the Nazis came to power, in which the man said, "National Socialism is nothing but applied biology." And that was a vision the Nazis had of themselves. Now, in that statement we find a strong element of their ideology, plus a technicism of the biological process. The biological process is rendered a technical tool by which they have the right to manipulate populations and even destroy populations, in the name of maintaining the biological life of a single race, their own. In that sense, the numbing around technology can be of two related kinds: one is the worship of technology itself, or technicism; and the other is technological distancing in the way that I have described. And the two tend to go together.

Going back to the making of the atomic bomb, it's of the greatest significance that no voices of questioning or protest came from Los Alamos. When you read the literature on people's experiences at Los Alamos, they were preoccupied with getting the bomb made, and they wanted to end the war. But they were also fascinated with the question, would it work? They were struggling for months. They didn't know whether this thing would work, and the scientists' and technicians' curiosity took hold of them. Their main preoccupation became at a certain point: Can it work? Can we make it work? The voices of protest began at Chicago, where they had finished their work on the bomb. They had no more to do because the bomb had to be completed and assembled at Los Alamos. It was there that the scientists began to question—raise little questions and big questions—and there is one very moving passage in the memoirs of Eugene Rabinowitch, who was one of the leaders in Chicago, in which he describes walking down a street in Chicago on a hot summer day and suddenly having the vision of all the skyscrapers exploding, being destroyed, first in Chicago, and then, in all of the great cities of the world.[10] And, of course, he knew what that meant. He immediately went to his hotel room and began to draft the first draft of what became the classical scientist's statement—the very first—asking that the bomb not be dropped on a human population without warning. Of course, that protest didn't succeed, but it created a beginning orientation around which later protests and questions have been raised. Someone like Rabinowitch or other scientists had to break out of the technicism that surrounds nuclear weapons. It surrounds the making of them; it surrounds the scenarios back and forth about first strike, second strike, and various claims of the weapons killing 5 million, 10 million. These figures just dazzle the mind and become unmanageable until scientists reach out of that technicism and have a moral kind of vision, so to speak, which enables them, like Rabinowitch, to break through and initiate a moral act along with their colleagues. And it's that struggle to replace technicism with difficult questions of value that is the heart of numbing in relationship to nuclear weapons and other sources of potential annihilation.

Now, I would claim that the manifestations or ramifications of the existence of these weapons very much affect what I am calling the numbing of everyday life. A younger friend and colleague of mine, Michael Carey, has done an interesting study (an interview study) of people of his own generation, in their early 30s now, which started out exploring the drills that they went through for nuclear weapons attack in the 1950s, usually the late 1950s, extending to the early 1960s in some cases. Then it extended into an exploration of death imagery and imagery about the weapons. Although he hasn't yet put it all together or written it up, it shows certain interesting things. These youngsters were terrified by a force that they imagined could annihilate them. At the same time, their teachers told them, "Just put a little piece of paper over your head, and bend under the desk, and you will be all right." And they *knew* that was absurd—even six-year-olds sensed it was absurd. So they developed a sense of absurdity and a sense of considerable distrust for authorities and teachers. They had terrifying dreams over years, but then, at a certain point, usually during adolescence, they suppressed all this and went through the motions of ordinary life, it would seem maintaining a double imagery of ordinary existence, but other imagery of potential annihilation that never entirely left them and could be restimulated by the threats of nuclear weapons or other threats in the world, and restimulated by Carey's investigation. Psychologically speaking, one interesting and very dangerous aspect that the study revealed was that there came to be an equation of death and annihilation. They learned about death—after all, you begin to learn about death during your early years of life, and during your 4th, 5th, 6th, and 7th years, you begin to understand that it means dying for good—at the same time they learned about holocaust or annihilation. So, death became equated with annihilation, which is a very unhealthy kind of relationship to death, which you know should ordinarily be considered part of the rhythm of human existence. All of this derealization of death in ordinary numbing, the numbing of everyday life, has a malignant influence in its interference with our capacity to anticipate holocaust. It's like a vicious circle. The holocaust threats contribute to our numbing; the numbing interferes with our combatting of potential holocaust. And we then face ultimate dangers in a state in which we are unable to deal psychologically with an agent that emanates no feeling of death itself. These technological weapons threaten to do us in. The very inorganic, unfeeling technology, serves constantly to distance and befuddle us, as though we continually expect it to take some human form, to feel pain when it causes us pain, to be subject to some kind of reason or coherence, which it does not have. Sometimes the matter is even worse—even the point of worshipping these weapons. We want the weapons to deliver us, to save us. And we then get into a pattern I call nuclearism or the worship of the very agents of our potential annihilation. That, of course, is one aspect of scientism, the worship of science. It becomes, of course, grotesque and profoundly dangerous. Around nuclear weapons, one can see it in certain public figures. Certainly, Edward Teller expressed this in the reliance upon weapons to protect from every danger, and the insistence that we not restrict our making of nuclear weapons or our potential use of nuclear weapons.[11] And the weapons really become a deity—a deity that is expected to create, as well as destroy. And I think that some of our dangerous embrace of nuclear energy and nuclear power has to do with a strong desire that somehow the deity delivers something constructive as opposed to the danger of the weapon. It turns out that if you are dealing with irradiation, maybe nothing is constructive.

Other aspects of nuclear energy that are relevant here have to do with the technicist impulse to rely on the expert. And I can't resist saying something about that because of the dance of the experts at that Three Mile Island accident in Pennsylvania, where the situation was such that the experts didn't know what was happening—they had no prior knowledge of this kind of accident. They had different opinions of the possible danger of the accident or how to overcome it. The psychological side of numbing, and I think very much of the technical side of unprecedented technological developments, has reached a dangerous degree, and in that sense we may have had a valuable lesson at Three Mile Island.

In closing I want to come back to ourselves. Can we speak of a realm beyond normal numbing? Probably not, since all we have said points to the necessity of psychic numbing to life itself. And yet, I return to an element of gallows humor or our own struggle with our own playful decentering. In talking about some of these things I have told a couple of stories that say something about the Nazi experience—the Nazis and the Jews. Let me share them with you. One of them concerns the only Jewish survivor of a pogrom under the Czar, who was called before the Czar. The Czar says to him, "Look, you seem to be a nice fellow, even though you are a Jew. And just as a gesture of leniency, I would like to offer you the right to die in any fashion you choose." And the Jew thinks about it and says, "Okay. I appreciate your leniency, and to save trouble for everybody, I choose old age." The other one involves Joseph Goebbels, the Nazi propaganda minister, who makes an inspection of German primary schools to see whether the little boys are properly mouthing all the necessary patriotic slogans. He asked a group of young boys to recite their favorite patriotic slogans. The first one says, "Heil Hitler!" He says, "Very good." The second one says, "Deutschland über alles." He said, "That's fine." And the third one shouts, "Our people shall live forever," and he said, "Why that's magnificent! The best of all. What is your name, little boy?" And the boy replies, "Hyman Goldberg."

Part of my argument tonight lies in Heinrich Bölls'

observation: "The artist always carries death within him, like a good priest his breviary."[12] That is, one needs death in order to create. Or, to extend that principle slightly, one needs death in order to feel. One could also say that the widespread tendency toward numbing, however extensive, is not biologically ordained. We are beginning to sense that to maintain and extend the world we now inhabit, we must confront what I called our cosmology of death, in order to avoid being consumed by it, in order to try to transcend it. That is, we require the capacity to feel the deaths that stalk us in order to enhance our experience of life.

DISCUSSION

QUESTION: How would what you just told us relate to Victor Frankl's experience in the prison camp concerning his "will to meaning?"

ANSWER: What he speaks about as the will to meaning is very close to what I'm talking about. I didn't discuss very much the psychology of the survivor or my own ideas about the survivor, but I did suggest what I take to be very important, the survivor's overall task of finding some significance in his death encounter if he is to feel significance in the rest of his life. That quest for inner form, or what I call formulation for significance of meaning, in a way involves the entire survivor experience. He can't deal with his death imprint, with his death guilt, with his numbing, which is very central in a survivor, or with his struggles with the counterfeit (these are all categories which I see in the survivor), except in so far as he can find the quality of meaning. And that's very much in the spirit of what Frankl wrote too.

QUESTION: Are you able to apply the concept of numbing and technological distance to child abuse after birth and child abuse before birth, meaning abortion?

ANSWER: Yes, child abuse after birth certainly involves numbing, not necessarily of the technical kind, but somehow my whole sense of violence is as an expression of what one perceives as a threat to one's own existence. I suspect that in child abuse parents develop, however irrationally, the sense that the child and his own disorder, or behavior of whatever kind, is a threat to their existence in some way. This is speculation, but it is along the lines that I would think in addressing child abuse. Then when you feel a threat to your own existence, even though it's what I would call a passionate form of violence as opposed to numbed violence—numbed violence being from a technical/technological distance as opposed to face-to-face violence. Actually, the two merge and you need numbing for passionate violence and you need some kind of distancing or passion even for numbed violence. So there would be at least that degree of numbing involved as well.

As for abortion, well that's hard to say and I sense a somewhat loaded question. But my feeling is that there are different qualities of feeling and numbing in consideration of the abortion issue, i. e., there is some degree of technical distancing in the act of abortion. That's the gist of your question and I agree with that. I think from some experience I've had in talking with young women who have had abortions, there is no such thing as an abortion without some experience of loss and some kind of psychological pain. And it's also been shown by one interesting study of people who do abortions in a place that did a large number of them in New York, including nurses and some doctors, that these people are covering over certain forms of guilt and pain in the process. But I think it is also true that in liberalizing abortion laws there is some concern about feeling and compassion for young women who become pregnant under difficult circumstances. And in that sense one might say that there can be in some cases conflicts around what one feels and what one feels numb to—about where one's compassion is and where one's numbing is.

QUESTION: In my city there would be about 35 percent of the black youth without jobs, about 20 to 21 percent of the white youth without jobs. Would you comment, Dr. Lifton, on unemployment and numbing.

ANSWER: Yes, it is very much an issue. I thought of that when sometimes economists or political leaders project various economic policies around inflation or stabilizing the dollar or what have you, and they say, "Oh yes, we will of necessity have to keep 4 million, 5 million, whatever it is, unemployed—that can't be helped." That's what I would call numbing because they do not psychologically experience what it means for a young person or a not-so-young person to be unemployed, or for a particular racial or ethnic group to have the burden of unemployment, or a particular age group, too. They don't feel the pain of what it is to be unemployed and that's rather parallel to not feeling the pain of what goes on at the other end of the weapon, so to speak, in terms of numbing and weaponry. Now maybe all political decisions involve distancing and numbing and you need to be thick-skinned and not feel a lot of pain on the part of other people as a political leader. One could argue that but I again would say what I said at the beginning of my talk—that our society at all levels, including the professions and certainly political leaders, suffers much too much from an overdose of numbing and an insufficiency of feeling, and the employment issue would be a case in point.

QUESTION: I am interested in that you said that in order to function you must have some numbing. I transfer this now. Is there a theological distancing in the presence of the sufferer and therefore we don't really enter into their experience to bring out the God-life in them?

ANSWER: What you describe is very close to the whole pattern of professional numbing which I have been much concerned with in recent years. I think in all the professions we tend to technicalize them. And one can technicalize theology, I'm sure, as well as psychiatry or law or whatever. And that means having a certain body of ideas or cliches that one relates or reduces every single problem to, rather than opening oneself to the pain. I think ideally the professional, including the theologian, requires an equilibrium, a balance between technical skills or special knowledge. After all, as a theologian or psychiatrist, we are not exactly the same but we have certain parallels. We have a certain identity and a certain body of knowledge and experience that is special and that is sought after. So one still requires the technical and special features of that professional identity. On the other hand, one also requires an open and spontaneous advocacy of one's own and willingness to enter into that process. Martin Buber puts this very well when he speaks of "distance and relation." He has a famous essay on just that subject. We always need a combination; and again, I became interested in the whole concept of the professional and how the word derived into its present use because I began to feel as I looked around that a lot of professional behavior is deeply numbed, unfeeling, and that's what the young people, when they spoke about professionalism during the 1960s and 1970s, meant. In looking up the history of the word profession, as you know, it has religious origins during the Middle Ages when it meant a profession of faith or profession of belonging to a particular religious order. But very quickly within a couple of hundred years it did a 180 degree turn and became really a technical skill that one holds as it became almost totally technicized. Now we want to step back and not make it merely a profession of faith, but return to some older elements of value around being a professional around the technical or special skills. So that's the general model which applied very much to what you say.

QUESTION: How did you come to equilibrium in your own life?

ANSWER: I wasn't all that systematic or logical; it was painful. In fact, I didn't quite think it through until a little bit later. I experienced it as I described it and, much to my surprise, I felt all right and able to manage, and then I began to observe the numbing—or what I came to call numbing—in the people I was interviewing, in the way that I mentioned and in many other ways as well. I began to realize that what I had experienced had some relationship to what they experienced. And I also tried to think more about numbing on a broader level as I was doing the work. But it was sort of hit and miss, in bits and pieces. When you read about the reports of research studies, they sound very carefully done—"How I came to this; studied this; came to this conclusion; saw this didn't work." But it's really not that way. It's a whole mixture of feelings and pain and fear and then rather excited moments when you think you're learning something. Then you put it all together in a hit or miss fashion and put some order to it. Some weeks into the work I began to realize that I had that kind of process occur in me.

QUESTION: Comment please about racial numbing, and a Bishop closing an inner city school with mostly black students, for financial reasons.

ANSWER: I didn't go into the numbing around race and otherness but that's very important—take the Vietnam situation, the "Gooks," the non-whites. While that Bishop's closing the schools or doing something nasty about black education (if that's what he's doing), you can bet he's not feeling what's going on in those homes, with those kids, the parents, and so on, or the cost of his actions. In that sense he is numbing himself and it can be done more readily toward another race or a race that has been seen over a long period of time as a victim. Because one gets used to numbing toward them, racism and numbing in that sense go hand in hand. It isn't that it isn't racism; I'm sure it is—it certainly can be. The numbing process is rather essential to racism.

QUESTION: Is it easier to be numb in those sensitive issues than it is in the professionalism of the gun?

ANSWER: I think they both can be called forth in different situations. It is very easy to be numbed with the professionalism of the gun if you've had military training; you're taught to shoot the gun; you have a rationale of defeating the enemy until at times that rationale can break down as in Vietnam. On the other hand, the social-racial situation, as you describe, can be easily called forth, especially where there is a certain tradition for things of that sort in American cities, and there can be a habit of racism and numbing associated with it that can be called forth all the more easily because the institutional structures are there to do it.

QUESTION: How does one intervene; what does one do when one actually sees numbing taking place, especially in a professional setting—maybe among one's fellow professionals?

ANSWER: In a way, one direction of thinking about that is really the heart of this conference. The reason why people numb themselves or *an* important reason is to avoid experiencing the suffering of the people they are ostensibly serving. And the first act is to find ways of entering into that suffering. In my experience in working with a number of people from the holocaust or who have experienced mass death, the only people who do this work, who do what I think is useful work, are those who open themselves up to that suffering and who take it on in some way, who become survivors by proxy of that experience. I suppose there are concrete ways one can go about pointing up experiences of suffering or even pointing out what I implied in my talk. There are certain kinds of suffering that we as professionals don't understand and don't know about. A certain humility before suffering is useful. I remember listening to Vietnam veterans telling really dreadful stories of what they saw; sometimes they did certain things; and I began to think as I sat in this rap group, as we called them, "These people have been through things that I don't know about; I've never touched them; they know things that I don't know." At our wisest as professionals, we really just listen and give them the sense that they understand something that we don't know. By listening and not talking too quickly, not interposing our categories too quickly, this is a signal and indication that we are responding to their suffering and joining it in some sense. I think there are ways to do that. With other professionals it's hard to have a systematic procedure to overcome it, but maybe one can best influence by example.

QUESTION: You said one needs death in order to create. In the case of black schools closing, there is a real death. But how does the creative person function when there is such numbing that people cannot create?

ANSWER: I didn't make a distinction that has to be made. One is death as either simply part of the ordinary rhythms of existence in which people live lives and die, and to the extent that one creates, one has to live in that rhythm, including living in the acceptance of death and even in the experience of some of the equivalents of death in the confrontation of death. In that sense death can be called a constitutive symbol that can be a source of creative energy as Böll said in the little passage I quoted. The other kind of death, the closing of a school, is the death in life kind of death. It is the deadening, the numbing, and that's where death becomes the opposite of a constitutive symbol, but rather an indication of numbing. It becomes deathlike in the sense of numb. Death is a complex symbol that can have both of those sides and it's the first side I decided that's the souce of creativity, the second is the enemy of creativity, I would think.

QUESTION: Those of us who live close to Three Mile Island feel that there has been a surprising apathy on the part of those living within the Three Mile Island area and I'm wondering whether that would be part of the numbing effect. There's been a study done by the Associate Research Center at Elizabethtown College and it showed that 40 percent of the sample people evacuated; even so, that sample favors the continuation of nuclear power as soon as the NRC assures them that it is safe. There's another curious paradox in that study, and it is that 82 percent do not trust what the government is saying about nuclear power; about an equal number believe that the government is doing a good job in taking care of them. And then 4 percent of the sample are even more in favor of nuclear power than before, apparently because they're convinced now that safety has been improved. Any further comment you might have? *ANSWER:* It's a morass of reaction and it's hard to tease out what it all means, but some thoughts I have, which I'm sure are similar to yours, are these. Yes, I think there could be an apathy and a kind of numbing as a result of the accident because I'm sure you witnessed a certain amount of fear, terror. It looks as though people weren't in danger but nobody knows for sure about these things; no one can be certain. Maybe it's even more terrifying to lose complete faith in the "experts" because Americans, especially around these questions of high technology and nuclear technology, have become absolutely conditioned to depend totally on the experts. These are things that confuse all of us and the experts (we like to believe)—they know. We have to be able to trust them. I'm trying to think of what you said in terms of trusting and not trusting the government. One association (a kind of wild one, but it might apply slightly) is that a study was once done—it was called "When Prophecy Fails." Two rather innovative psychologists made their way into an end-of-the-world cult and wanted to study the reactions of what would happen when the prophecy failed, because this cult predicted a certain day on which the world would end and they went up to a mountaintop to experience the end of the world on that day. And they predicted that when the prophecy failed they wouldn't give up their views, but they would proselytize more and that's exactly what happened. The prophecy did indeed fail and the cult leaders were confused for awhile, but then most of them seemed to go out and proselytize all the harder and of course they said, "Well, we misread the *Bible*; it really means it will happen in 20 years from now or whenever it is"— another rationalization. And the proving of the prophecy false becomes an impulse to reassert it in oneself by convincing others. And that's a fairly classical psychological pattern in relationship to doubt. Finally, what I said before, I think that the American sense that we must go on, the real job issue, that I'm sure has always been very central for issues of nuclear energy—people have better jobs and more jobs and a lot of money invested on all levels. But there is also the faith in technological progress that we cannot turn back; we must go on. And I have a feeling that faith has been shaken. People want to reestablish the faith and push ahead and that gets to some of what I also said which could affect ordinary people—the hope and wish that the nuclear deity will produce something good for mankind.

QUESTION: It seems to me that many adopted people have numbed themselves to the pain of their abandonment and separation as children or infants. How does one live through that or come out of that, or is it healthy for the many adopted people who don't want to know who their natural families are?

ANSWER: The work referred to is my wife's first book called *Twice Born—Memoirs of an Adopted Daughter*, and it's about her personal experience but it is somewhat generalized; and then a second book just now published called *Lost and Found—The Adoption Experience*.

In these studies she's come to—and I've shared a lot of this with her and I've learned most of what I know about the subject from her—a sense that adoptees live on a numbed basis; and incidentally, this work has now been corroborated by a psychiatric team in California led by a man named Arthur Sorosky, and there's systematic evidence that it's quite widespread. The difficulty is not only the adoptee's pain of abandonment very early on, but also the lifelong adopted family situation in which everyone lives on an "as if" situation—as if that child was the natural child rather than accepting the rather special relationship of the child's being adopted and being open to knowledge about his or her natural parents. Probably there is more numbing in those adoptees who choose not to seek out information or even meeting their natural parents. My wife has come to a position that it isn't so much that she insists that everybody look for their natural parents, but rather they should have the right to do that and their own records shouldn't be sealed. There's a kind of rewriting of history, as you know, when the records are actually rewritten so that the adopted parents are put on the birth records; and there are even questions of possible inherited or genetic conditions that can't be known because there is no connection between the birth parents and the adopted parents. So, yes, there is more numbing, but maybe numbing that is serviceable to some adoptees who don't care to seek out their natural parent. There is a kind of breakout into a wider zone of feeling in the experience of those adoptees who do. They also experience quite a lot of pain in the process, but seem rather regularly to have a new depth of identity once they have found and identified their natural parents, met with them, and reasserted their lives, not disclaiming their adopted parents, but somehow feel more grounded and feel less need for numbing on that basis.

NOTES

[1] Suzanne Langer, *Philosophy in a New Key* (New York: Mentor, 1948; and *Mind; An Essay on Human Feeling*, Vols. 1 & 2 (Baltimore: Johns Hopkins Press, 1972).

[2] Paul Tillich, *The Courage to Be* (New Haven: Yale University Press, 1952).

[3] Gabriel Marcel, in Leslie Farber, *The Ways of the Will* (New York: Basic Books, 1966), p. 93.

[4] Robert Jay Lifton, *Death in Life: Survivors of Hiroshima* (New York: Touchstone Books, 1976).

[5] Guy Sajer, *The Forgotten Soldier* (New York: Harper and Row, 1971).

[6] Primo Levi, *Survival in Auschwitz* (New York: Collier Books, 1961).

[7] Robert J. Lifton, *Home From the War* (New York: Simon & Schuster, 1973).

[8] Albert Speer, *Inside the Third Reich: Memoirs of Albert Speer* (New York: Macmillan, 1970), and *Spandau: The Secret Diaries* (New York: Macmillan, 1976).

[9] Weathermen Going Mad in the Movement" (*unpublished manuscript*).

[10] (Eugene Rabinowitch) Alice Kimball Smith, *A Peril and a Hope: The Scientists' Movement in America 1945-47* (Univ. of Chicago Press, 1965); and Morton Grodzins and Eugene Rabinowitch, eds., *The Atomic Age* (New York: Basic Books, 1963).

[11] Edward Teller (with Allen Brown) *The Legacy of Hiroshima* (Garden City: Doubleday, 1962).

[12] Heinrich Böll, *The Clown* (New York: McGraw Hill, 1965).

Chapter 6

FORMS OF GRIEF: DIAGNOSIS, MEANING, AND TREATMENT
Dr. Wayne E. Oates

When I was nine years old, I read a book the title of which I cannot remember. I have never forgotten the substance of the book. The book told of a faraway country where the people's god had taken from them the ability to die. The whole fabric of their lives was shredded. People suffering unbearable pain lived on perpetually in that pain. People who had aged beyond any useful self-awareness continued to live in their loss of awareness. People injured in severe accidents could not die. People had less and less room in which to live. The book impressed me very early that death is a normal part of life. Without death, time, suffering, pain, and meaningless life have no end.

The substance of human existence is alpha and omega, the beginning and the end. The mind of persons imposes its own chosen meaning on the process of time between the beginning and end. To be able to impose these meanings is a form, a structure, a means of control. "Out of phase" endings either within life or in death are "out of control." They are experiences of grief and mourning for which some kind of meaning must be found in order that the work of mourning itself may have an end, an omega. "Having done with" grief calls for a new meaning for the rest of life that brings the loss of the loved one to a clearly positive meaning. Learning to live again asks for a new reason for being. Even in the event of a Lazarus-like restoration of life in time, a new *gestalt* opens and demands new meanings of living for the restored person. Likewise, the "Lazarus" has a crisis of meaning for the living out of his days to the deferred omega. Death, then, as Rollo May says, "is . . . the one fact in my life which is not relative but absolute, and my awareness of this gives my existence and what I do each hour an absolute quality."[1]

Death, then, becomes a prototype for the other sufferings of life. The critical issue in death is the fear of the unknown and the agony of separation from those whom we know, who provide security, love, and meaning to the process of life. Other separations between birth and death take on a protypical grieving process not unlike death. The "in phase" separations such as starting and finishing school, losing the undivided affection between marital partners at the birth of a child, the launching stage of parenthood, the event of retirement—all these have mourning aspects to them. More traumatic are those out-of-phase separations—a divorce, an abandonment, a war that pulls family members into combat, the loss of a job into which much of life's meaning has been vested. Birth thrusts us from the security of total dependence. Death confronts us with the end of a life that demands a comprehensive faith-courage for which each of the earlier separations are "staging operations" of preparation.

The developmental and traumatic crises of life call for "leaps of faith." The life of faith calls for the courage to leap into the unknown. As Paul Tournier says, we live in a rhythm between "finding a place and quitting a place." The community of faith provides—or fails to provide—a context of meaning, ritual, hope, and fellow suffering in the quest for "the city, which has foundations, whose builder and maker is God" (Heb. 11:8,10).

THE END AND THE MEANING OF THE GRIEF PROCESS

The very nature of the human psyche seems to insist on providing a meaning, even if it is maladaptive, to human suffering. Psychotic episodes are gross examples of negative meanings. Grief most often gives meaning by imposing a sequential order of both emotional states and social events. This sequential order takes time seriously in relation to the end siutations of life, the most imposing of which is death itself. Persons grieve differently. They must be diagnosed and treated differently according to the time and process differentials. In essence, as Ned Cassem says, "loss is a developmental showdown—to grow or else."[2] The priest, pastor, or rabbi has much to do with making the difference. Any professional seeking to bring a grief-stricken person or family into a growth meaning of grief can best do so by identifying different ways in which grief's meaning is patterned in process, guided toward a greater maturity, and set within the context of those who care—or fail to care—for the bereaved.

Several factors determine to some extent—not absolutely—the qualitatively different kinds of grief people experience. The towering influence of Elizabeth Kubler-Ross has served to awaken the professional outside the clergy to the meaning of death and dying.

One unfortunate side effect has been to produce a stereotype of grief based on a study of only *one* kind of grief—the long and drawn-out drying process of the incurably ill as they die. This is only *one* kind of grief. In our research and service, we have isolated and are describing at least six qualitatively different kinds of grief: anticipatory grief, acute or traumatic grief, chronic sorrow, "near-miss" grief, pathological grief, and the tragic sense of life itself.

My purpose is to describe each of these kinds of grief and to demonstrate how the quality of the preexisting relationship, the length of illness, the time interval between the death and the awareness of the death, unexpected reversals in the assumption of impending death, and the nonverbal and verbal power of the rituals of the surrounding community provide or deprive meaning to the experience of dying and being separated from one's loved person by death.[3]

The ever present awareness of finitude is the generator of the hope for self-transcendence in our offspring, in work whose results outlive us, and a resurrected life in which pain, tears, separation, and death are overcome in a new life. The Christian faith expresses the hope of life after death in three ways: first, that the early return of Jesus will fulfill the hope that we will not taste death before He comes again; second, that by reason of faith in Christ we will be given a new body in the resurrection, a new set of relationships that holds secure the bonds of love shared and yet transcends them with a new order; and third, that a heaven awaits those who suffer in faith and rewards the faithful with freedom from bondage to sin, suffering, and the power of death to destroy. These three projections about eternal life are akin, but not the same. Their behavioral patterning of the grief process varies, intertwines, and diverges in the reaction patterns of the dying and the bereaved. Add to these the non-Christian beliefs in the continuation of communication with the dead in necromancy, the pervasive belief in reincarnation, and the belief in the annihilation of persons in death. You can see how varied religious belief systems facilitate or impede grief work in the six types of grief we are about to discuss. Time is set within mankind's persistent search for eternal life. Selective deletion of these belief systems from behavioral scientists' explorations of dying and grieving persons' experience is as misleading to them as the neglect of empirical descriptive methods by theologians is to us. My suggestion is the inclusion of both in a comprehensive approach to the whole belief-behavior system of interaction of the dying, the dead, and the bereaved.

ANTICIPATORY GRIEF

The most prominent type of grief in thought, research, and literature is anticipatory grief. Anticipatory grief usually accompanies an incurable illness. The medical professions, dedicated to sustaining and extending life are caught up in research, teaching, and care of the victims of the killer diseases—heart disease, cancer, clinical depression, and degenerative diseases of the nervous system. The patient and the family and friends have a powerful way of "deadlining" each other through the patterned meanings of both subtle nonreligious and obvious religious rituals. One ritual follows another stamping the *gegenwarten* or "thrown situation" with the double imperatives of time—urgency and waiting. These rituals follow something of this pattern of interpretation of relationship, imminence or postponement of death, and the communication of both care and the sense of time. We are living in a time of collapsed or secularized ritualization of life and death. I am using the word ritual, not in any psychopathological sense, but with anthropological meaning. As Erik Erikson defines ritual in this way he says: "the anthropological meaning of the word . . . assigns 'ritual' a deepened communality, a proven ceremonial form, and a timeless quality from which all participants emerge with a sense of awe and purification."[4]

The Rituals of Urging. Symptoms emerge. They become impediments to work and family life. Social life is governed by them. Yet, the patient plods on—complaining or conceding his or her condition. Yet the concern of relatives, friends, and work associates takes the form of *urging*—urging the person to "take it easy," "to rest," to see the doctors. The urging becomes shrill, intense, demanding, authoritarian, or even angry. The patient being urged has a crisis of meaning: Shall he or she "let go," "let down," "give in," and "give up" to the unknown symptoms? As long as he or she does not *know* what is wrong, then to him or her "nothing is wrong." Furthermore, to give in to the symptoms is to become dependent, to take orders from others, to have others run one's life, to lose control. Such a swirling demand for a different and less desirable meaning to life has to be negotiated through love and care that sustains dignity in the face of frailty.

The Rituals of Diagnosis. When the patient gives in and goes for medical diagnosis, the high priests of medicine have their elaborate rituals of diagnosis. Getting the appointment with the physician presents the first ritual. Sometimes it takes political influence to get an appointment with the appropriate physicians! Once the patient arrives for diagnosis, the history-taking procedures, the laboratory tests, the X-rays, the physical examination, the follow-up tests, and periods of waiting are especially meaningless to the patient who has never been to a doctor or a hospital before. Even to the experienced patient, the maze of technology is often devoid of meaning. The critical ethical responsibility of the medical profession is to give an accurate and clear interpretation of what is wrong, and a positive evaluation of what is *not* wrong. The meaning of human suffering cannot be formed in a vacuum of factlessness, blurred and euphemistic language, and hasty assumptions that the patients' questions and private conclusions do not really matter. The priest interprets the rituals if he cares; the physician interprets the diagnosis if he cares.

The Rituals of Resistance. Let us assume that the clearly interpreted diagnosis is that of a severely life-threatening illness or a definitely incurable one. The therapeutic team, the patient, and the patient's family and friends now go through an internal and interpersonal set of emotional rituals. Elizabeth Kubler-Ross has described these rituals to a large extent. In her book *Death and Dying,* she describes the phases of emotional response in a sequence:

The First Stage:	Denial and Isolation
The Second Stage:	Anger
The Third Stage:	Bargaining
The Fourth Stage:	Depression
The Fifth Stage:	Acceptance

Kubler-Ross, it seems to me, omits an aspect of the fourth stage that makes all the difference. This stage is not pure depression but a struggle between depression and fantasy. If the person moves consistently toward harsh reality, then depression occurs. Rarely do dying patients and their bereaved families do this. The element of fantasy lays hold of faith cures, quack medicines, multiple reversions to different doctors for a "separate opinion," and into either acting out or psychotic behavior. At this point of the power of fantasy and withdrawal, I think Kubler-Ross's description of the rituals of resistance is in need of completion.

I have seen people who go beyond denial into elaborately built fantasies that replace the reality of their approaching death because the concept of death is too large to omit the rituals of a relatively complete break with reality. These psychotic breaks are, on occasion, so convincing that other family members are caught up in them in a *folie à deux, trois, quatre, cinq, etc.* Such families act out the fantasy past the death itself, much as Tennyson's poem "We Are Seven" describes. He speaks to a child of her two dead siblings:

> 'But they are dead; those two are dead!
> Their spirits are in Heaven!'
> 'Twas throwing words away; for still
> The little maid would have her will,
> And said, "Nay, we are seven!"

Dylan Thomas made a saga of the stage of anger. To him death itself was an enemy to be fought. He urged his father:

And you, my father, on the sad height,
Curse, bless me now with your fierce tears, I pray.
Do not go gentle into that good night.
Rage, rage, against the dying of the light.[6]

The Rituals of Family Gathering and Leave-Taking. As the time of death draws nearer and the patient's clarity of awareness and capacity to communicate becomes more scarce, the next set of rituals is for the family members to "come as quickly as they can." At best the purpose of this "gathering of the clan" is to communicate meaningfully, without deception, and without evasion with the dying person. To be able to reconcile old rifts, forgive old hurts, express unexpressed appreciation, admiration, and love is a family level of confession, not just of fault, but of love. Meaning is added to the dramas of leave-taking to know that good closure has been made and blessings are shared. I have seen patients seemingly decide to "stay alive" until they have seen important family members and friends. "Unfinished business" is a strong meaning for continuing to survive.

The act of pastoral confession is a very significant part of this gathering and leave-taking ritual. The more relational and less mechanical this can be, the more meaning is supplied to make death a real part of the total spiritual life. The pastor, priest, or rabbi often finds the person to be a total stranger, but the confession may be all the more profound *because* he is a stranger. Conversely, the patient may be a friend of such long standing that the clergy person's grief is mutual with the dying person. As one friend of 35 years said to me: "I broke down in tears on your last visit, not because I am all that unprepared to die. My tears came because we have known each other so long and the thought of leaving you, my friend, was too hard to bear without tears."

The Rituals of Prolongation. Medical technology, since the Quinlan case, has been both lauded and jeered because of its ability to prolong life through artificial means. Yet, the location of the patient in the hospital itself provides the medicolegal meaning of these rituals of prolongation of life in amount of time in spite of the quality of meaning life has for the person and their family. The patient who dies at home does not become subject to the legal responsibility of the physicians and nurses to extend life beyond the point of hope for a reasonably meaningful life. The basic issue at home, in the hospital, or at a hospice is *meaningfulness* of the life of the person.

I saw a 52-year-old woman whose 56-year-old husband had just died of emphysema and other complications of his lungs. Prior to being placed on oxygen therapy, he had suffered a psychotic breakdown because of anoxia. For 63 of the 65 days prior to his death he had lived entirely because of extensive artificial oxygenization. The patient asked to try to live without these means. His 13-year-old daughter asked: "Why can't Daddy breathe in his own way?" The oxygen was removed. The patient died in two days. The critical fact was his work: he had worked all his life in a cement factory. One asks: "What is the human cost of cement?"

The Ritual of the Death Vigil. "The point of death" ushers in the ritual of the death vigil. Families sleep in the waiting rooms, intensive care areas, and coronary care units. What meaning accrues to this vigil? What really prompts persons to want to be there at the moment of death? One person said she stood vigil to pray for the recovery of her husband. He did recover and lived two years longer. Another person stayed by "just to know that I was with him as long as he was with me."

The therapeutic team, particularly priests, rabbis, pastors, chaplains, nurses, medical students, etc., can make the vigil meaningful by including the family and friends in briefings, debriefings, and quests for meaningful interpretations of the loss they are suffering. Some instruction in the demands of the postdeath situation makes the rest of the grief process more easily borne with richer meaning. For example, to say to a family that after such a long illness, they have a right to feel relieved after the death really happens. The relief is a part of the grief, not a stranger to it. In addition, they need to be alerted to the need to build a whole new routine for their day and week when their loved one is buried. The routine itself will be a comfort. Patterned behaviors for each day will give a fresh sense of meaning to time. A clergy-person, a friend, a physician, a particularly wise person who has suffered loss also can help form a routine of work, diversion, worship, and conversation with friends, and "attending to the details" of the estate, the business matters, etc. They can be encouraged to defer drastic decisions about selling property, buying large purchases, etc. They will tend to remember these suggestions.

The Ritual of the Notification of the Next of Kin. As soon as the death occurs, the next of kin are to be notified. The physician can give the most factual and authoritative notification to the next of kin. Often the responsibility falls upon the nurse because the physician is not present at the time. Compassionate friends and professional persons can ask for a list of persons to be notified. Thus the burden of repetition is taken off the next of kin.

The Planning of the Funeral and the Funeral Itself. The funeral provides a projective screen for eliciting the meaning of the loss from the bereaved. Plans for the funeral reflect the values, the meanings, the belief structures, and the personal support system of meaningful persons. Community-to-community funerals are idiosyncratic ways of helping persons to begin and/or continue the work of grief. The critical importance of the family seeing the person as dead is often handled by an "open coffin" procedure—one that is very common in rural communities and in urban blue-collar and poverty communities. In hospitals, nurses are increasingly preparing the body while it is still warm so that the family can see the body in its most nearly natural state. This reenforces the fact that the person is dead. The formal funeral provides closure to the deceased's presence in the family and community; the interment or cremation brings finality to the kinship of all of us with the earth.

The Ritual of Visitation of the Cemetery. The length of the need to visit the grave, the placing of flowers, construction of monuments, etc. moves from the very transitory habit that does not persist to the morbid and pathological meanings attached to the visitation of the grave. Idolatry of the dead is one of the oldest forms of idolatry, which, as Paul Tillich says, is the absolutizing of the finite. August Comte, the founder of logical positivism, lost his lover, Clothilde. He and a group of her other admirers met regularly for many years to pay homage to her.

The Ritual of the Thinning of the Crowd. Many of the aberrations of meaning in the grief process are due to the over-saturation of the bereaved with attentive support during the crisis of death and the funeral, on the one hand. On the other hand, shortly after the funeral the crowd thins out. Not many persons continue the care of the bereaved through the phases of its time-bound process—numbness, a struggle between fantasy and reality, a flood of grief and catharsis, selective memory and bereavement dreams, and the reconstruction of a new pattern of relationship, after grief work is finished.

Rituals of the Division of Effects. Dead persons leave not only persons. They leave things, property, possessions. About the time the crowd thins out, the relatives are coming to terms with such matters as the will, personal mementos, who was included and who was not included in the will. The doctor may be called upon to testify as to the mental competence of the deceased, the clergyperson may be the interlocutor seeking to find a common ground between contending parties for the change of a will. "The Waiting Vulture Syndrome" has been related by Glen W. Davidson to the situation in which families "have processed their initial sense of loss after realizing that a patient will die, but *before* the patient's demise."[7] However, the title is more appropriate to the situation of relatives whose grief is a pretext for the greed for profit by the death of the deceased. They are indeed waiting for the spoils.

I have placed much emphasis on the shifting meanings of anticipatory grief for a reason. The process is more "in phase" and its shifting meanings are more identifiable. On these counts anticipatory grief, when understood, illuminates the other kinds of grief.

Acute or Tramatic Grief

Whereas Elizabeth Kubler-Ross has described the meaning of anticipatory grief, Erich Lindemann's extensive study of acute or traumatic grief is still an influential work. He studied the grief-stricken families of victims of the Coconut Grove fire in 1944. He observed 101 patients. My own observations both correspond with and diverge from his.

Acute or traumatic grief differs from anticipatory grief in the radical suddenness of the death or other loss. The sudden onset makes much difference in the meaning of the suffering to the bereaved. The *manner* of suffering is of paramount importance. Automobile accidents, completed suicides, homicides, freak home accidents, sudden death by heart attack, and sudden death in hazardous occupations such as police duty, firefighting duty, and plane accidents are examples of situations that prompt acute grief. The person has had no time to "prepare" for the loss.

Acute grief introduces important meanings not present in other kinds of grief. Let me identify them:

Physiological and Psychological Shock. The blow of the news of the sudden death "hits" the person. He or she may or may not go into shock of a physiological order. Physiological shock is an acute, progressive circulatory failure that causes damage to tissue. One constant feature is the failure of the blood to flow through capillaries. Thus an inadequate supply of oxygen and nutrients is delivered to tissues and metabolic waste removal is incomplete. The pulse may become "thready," arterial blood pressure drops, and an cold sweaty skin, deep and rapid respiration, mental confusion, dilated pupils, a dry mouth, and diminished urine flow occur. Fainting is not unusual. In some cases death occurs suddenly upon seeing or hearing about the death of a loved person. A drug store owner and his wife were at work in their store one evening. A gunman came in and demanded their cash on hand. The husband killed the gunman instead. Then he fell over dead with a heart attack. His wife had to be hospitalized from the shock. In anothter instance a woman's husband was killed instantly by their daughter's boyfriend. Then, she, the wife and mother, dropped dead from a heart attack. One can imagine the shock of her daughter—her father and mother dead and her lover in jail on a murder charge.

In such tramatic situations, physiological shock calls for medical management. Grief can kill both suddenly and slowly.

Psychological Loss of Feeling, i. e., Numbness. The word "numb" appears in the conversation of acutely bereaved persons repeatedly. Lindemann reports in terms of "marked sighing respiration," complaints of loss of strength and exhaustion, loss of appetite.[8] "The sensorium is generally somewhat altered. There is a slight sense of unreality, a feeling emotional distance from people, and an intense preoccupation with the bereaved."[9]

The religious expression of this numb detachedness comes in these forms: "I can no longer feel that God is near." "God is far off." "I cannot pray any longer." "I no longer have any spiritual feelings." These feelings are interpreted by the bereaved as if they will always be and never change. One emergency measure is to point out that the bereaved person feels this way in most cases, that the feelings toward God are similar if not the same as the feelings they have toward other people as well as toward the person of

God, and that they *will* change.

The Recovery, the Sight of, and the Identification of the Body of the Dead Person. The sudden loss of someone is, in a large majority of cases, different in that the body has to be located, recovered, and identified. The mass suicide of the Jonestown population is a dramatic example of this.

The recovery of the body of a victim of a fire may be easier than identifying the person who was killed. Forensic medicine and careful police work is often involved. Sometimes, as in the case of Jimmy Hoffa, the body is not recovered at all. Actually seeing the body and identifying it as a family member is of both legal and spiritual meaning. The identification by the bereaved gives them a *fact* to which to relate and grieve realistically. The "if" phase of grieving tends to capture persons who never actually *see* their loved one's body. Their fantasy life keeps operating on the "outside chance" that all of this is not so and their loved person will show up, healthy, alive, and safe. Grief then becomes a "waiting" on the basis of this chance of error. Other significant purposes of the person's life are drained of meaning by this shred of hope that none of it is so anyhow.

The Delay of Grief Work. Another characteristic of acute grief is the delay of the mourning or working through the grief. The intense emotional stress is avoided in behalf of a more mechanical, feelingless existence. Hence, emancipation from bondage to the deceased is delayed. The chance to bid farewell to the deceased was snatched from him or her. The family gathering, the leave-taking, the vigil were all missing. No putting of relationships and business matters into order was possible. There may well not have been a will of any kind. As a result, the bereaved person's mourning process is somewhat "set aside" in order to restore order after a catastrophe has occurred. Therefore, as Lindemann indicates, the personal judgment of the bereaved may become seriously impaired:

"There is a picture in which a patient is active but in which most of his activities attain a coloring which is detrimental to his own social and economic existence. Such patients with uncalled for generosity, give away their belongings, are easily lured into foolish economic dealings, lose their friends and professional standing by a series of "stupid acts," and find themselves finally without family, friends, social status or money. This protracted self-punitive behavior seems to take place without any awareness of excessive feelings of guilt. It is a particularly distressing grief picture because it is likely to hurt other members of the family and drag down friends and business associates."

The delay of realistic grief work or mourning, therefore, lengthens the process. Some authorities say that the acute phase of grief is over in six to eight weeks. Others contend that the grief is the central meaning of the person's life for as much as two years. Yet, this delay puts this population of suddenly and traumatically bereaved persons at risk for a higher incidence of physical and/or psychosomatic illnesses, for a profound depression, or a schizophrenic withdrawal into a delusional system all their own. In the case of the depressed person, the pattern of learned helplessness can be floridly present. Let me tell you of a patient I saw on consultation on the second hospitalization for depression in the three years since her son's death. She said: "My doctors say that I will begin to get well as soon as I can accept my son's death. But, if I accept his death, then he will be dead." I pointed out to her that she seemed to feel that not accepting hs death kept her in control of her son's destiny. "The need to control seems to be very important to you. Yet, you have—in reality—met an event in the death of your son you cannot control." She felt that this was a new thought to her. Yet, existentially, the main meaning of her life is that of being in control of all processes of life around her. Such a situation underscores the remark of Clifford Kuhn, M.D., when he says that *sudden* death puts the bereaved at a higher risk for an emotional break with reality leading to psychopathology.

Normally, in the case of acute grief, the dam of repression bursts and a flood of grief and tears is poured out to those near the person. In this instance, the flood of grief may be weeks, months, or even years after the fact of death. If the deep sobbing, mourning, and catharsis of feeling can be assigned the right meaning, and if the person affirms it as "making sense" then the person is ready to "get on with life" in its present and future hopes. Later contact will reveal periodic "flashbacks" on the grief when a realistic incident "triggers" a selective memory of the bereaved. More unconsciously, bereavement dreams appear. As they move from unpleasant to pleasant dreams in their after-waking effects, we have an index as to the completion of the grief process. The person by now is "living again."

The Reinvestment of Life in New Purposes and People. In both anticipatory grief and acute grief, the grief work is resolved in reinvestment of life in work and love. Freud says that life is at its best when *leiben* and *arbeiten* are at full tide of expression, love and work.

"No-End" Grief

Death is not the most difficult grief with which to cope. Some grief situations have "no end" in sight. "No-end" grief is the continuing necessity of living with a heartbreaking set of circumstances that are unalterable, unending, and ever demanding. Several examples serve to elucidate what is meant here.

A child is born with severe handicaps but with a relatively normal life expectancy. The Down's syndrome or mongoloid child will be chronically dependent upon its family of origin. The person injured in an accident of collision, fire, or gunshot wound and rendered quadriplegic, hemiplegic, or paraplegic grieves his or her own loss of function, searches for a new meaning in life as they "gather up the pieces." He/she is best treated in an existential manner of searching for meaning in human suffering, ways in which the suffering can be made useful to others, and learning to re-relate to both God and neighbor.

Another "no-end" kind of grief is the person who has decided *not* to end a marriage in divorce but to continue to function in a basically untenable marriage. Some longer meaning to marriage than happiness and some more self-transcending meaning than ending the suffering in divorce must be found. Even in the event of divorce itself being effected, the grief is jagged and uneven as contrasted with the definitive end of a marriage by death. This is particularly true when there are small and/or adolescent sons and/or daughters. The children become the channels for the continuing of the grief through recriminations, games of spite, vengeance, and nonperformance of promises, etc.

Another example is the unending grief of massive public embarrassment—such as often results in the loss of a job, imprisonment, etc. As these words were being written, former Attorney General John Mitchell was being released from prison after serving 19 months. His career as a lawyer is ended; his wife divorced him and then died. I do not know about the situation of his young daughter. Here is a compounded set of losses that have lasting and inescapable consequences of grief and suffering.

The Tempting Dilemmas of "No-End" Grief

The unending grief situation puts both the damaged person and his or her family into a set of severe dilemmas. The "unthinkable" thought keeps pushing itself back into the minds of both: "Why can't I die?" "Why doesn't he/she die?" The possibility of death as a blessing without disguise pervades the hinterlands of consciousness. The question as to why one is born is another version of the death wish. Questioning one's beginnings is the reverse form of searching for the end of one's suffering. The patient and family alike face the timelessness of their desperation as a stress unbearable. There is no light at the end of the tunnel.

Consequently, they seek to impose a time limit to the pain by means of their own choosing. Married couples who are the parents of the patient tend to "distance" from each other. Many of these marriages break up through divorce, desertion, or mutually agreed upon separation. They fear the eventualities of the birth of another child in the family. They may be tempted to neglect the handicapped person to death or even kill the person. As guilt recoils upon them, they may be tempted to commit suicide. They may ditch responsibility either on other members of the family or upon public institutions for the care of handicapped persons, even when the person still is capable of learning to survive independently through instruction and rehabilitation.

That the stress of a situation can be borne with less threat to one's mental stability was demonstrated during the Vietnam War. Combat personnel knew *when* their tour of duty would be over in 12 or 13 months. They had a "break," an R & R—rest and recreation—at the halfway point. Yet the persons caught up within an unremitting grief situation have no such assurances. As a result they seek to impose "ends" of their own in divorce, desertion, homicide, or suicide. The meaning of suffering is transcended by the self-elevation or hybris of their own making. They become their own God by taking matters into their own hands with neither wisdom, consultation, or humility.

A community of other sufferers, a search for accrued wisdom of professional persons, and a search for a fellowship of persons who can provide regular interruptions of the stress is a much more creative way of self-exertion. Such moves take a faith in oneself, in others—carefully chosen—and in God that amounts to courage. Paul Tillich states it this way:

"Healing power, coming ultimately from the Ground (of
Being) on which we stand in faith, can enter the personality
and unite it in an act of courage. . . . This courage is the inner-
most center of faith. It dares to affirm our being, while
simultaneously rejecting it. Out of this courage the greatest
strength emerges."[10]

My own faith would say confessionally that in Jesus
Christ's suffering we have the alpha and omega of the new
birth and the resurrection. Faith provides the courage to live
life a day at a time instead of imposing our own alpha and
omega on the necessities of a "no-end" grief situation. In the
depths of teachable moments of each day comes the revelation of fresh possibilities in the life of the handicapped child,
spouse, sibling, or parent for whom we are responsible to the
extent of their genuine helplessness, and no further.
Therapists find family members more often than not too
anxious to let the person do for himself or herself by tedious
effort, small successes, and inch-by-inch discovery or recovery of abilities they did not believe they could have.

"NEAR-MISS" GRIEF

Another type of grief is the kind in which a person
narrowly escaped being killed, recovered from an illness
which was supposed to have killed him or her, etc. The scythe
of the Grim Reaper barely missed this person. Examples of
this are: a 43-year-old businessman was diagnosed as an incurable cancer patient and "given three months to live." He
sold his business and prepared his wife and three daughters
for his death as best he could. Yet, two years and seven
months later he is still alive, the cancer is in an arrested state
if not nonexistent. One of the tasks of therapy focuses on the
acute pain he now suffers from three operations, one of
which was a neurocordotomy to stop the pain but which did
not succeed. Another therapeutic task was the gradual curb-

ing of the patient's incessant talking about his pain. At the same time a carefully "rationed" amount of time was given to *new* facts about his experience of pain. Once this was done, the theory centered upon the man's hostility toward the social security system and the Veteran's Administration for "dehumanizing" and humiliating his wife and himself about disability allowances. He then surfaced a fresh set of intentions to start a small business of his own and to rebuild his work identity and meaning. At the same time, he and his wife are concentrating upon helping reprogram their three daughters for a more austere budget and less indulgence of their slightest wish with money. In the spiritual relation of the man to God, he feels "delivered" from the pit, but wonders of God as to why he is one of two patients still alive out of the 18 in the oncology unit where he received chemotherapy.

Another example is a group of 11 families who were previously told that their infant or young child would surely die of a kind of leukemia. They prepared themselves for the death. In the meanwhile, new discoveries in medicine have actually cured these patients. Now the families are having to rebuild their life's projections to include the child as healthily moving toward adulthood. The child can no longer count on being the center of attention in the family, receiving the indulgences of friends and relatives, avoiding responsibilities of school work, etc.

Not much has been written on this kind of grief. Yet four physicians at widely different times and places have pointed to clinical cases of such grief. A new sense of having died and been brought back to life pervades some of these patients. Quickened senses of religious concern and gratitude appear. The premorbid life history is certainly necessary to appreciate the life style of managing stress as the person takes on the task of living to a normal life expectancy. Shall I find work to do or take disability options? Am I going to dominate my family as I did when I was ill? Can I see my illness as a thing of the past, or shall I keep it in the present by thinking, talking, and acting as if my illness was "forever?"

These persons have what I like to call a "Lazarus Syndrome." They still have to face the issues of life even though they were "as good as dead." They have to rebuild their life and face the obstacles that having a history of an incurable disease presents.

My own conclusion about "near-miss" grief is that it is more complex the older one is and the more options they actually have for meaningful work. Similarly, they may wonder if their spouses will be faithful to them and not abandon them. More research needs to be done on this kind of grief. My contribution is to identify it and to begin to develop hypotheses from such hunches as I have expressed here.

Pathological Grief

When does grief become pathological? Several factors prompt the observer to give a pathological name to grief. To decide that grief is pathological, one must make a diagnosis. That diagnosis is a fresh set of meanings of human suffering. A person may say: "As if it were not the end of things for me when he/she died, now I am being told I am crazy." He/she has assigned a new meaning to his/her life. Consequently, careful diagnosis and treatment accordingly is necessary. Several factors are relevant to such a diagnosis and treatment plan.

First, is the person's pattern and state of grief congruent with his or her community culture? If it is incongruent with a field knowledge of how the people grieve, one has a first cause to suspect pathological grief.

Second, how sudden was the loss around which this grief occurred? The more sudden and disruptive the loss was the more likely that pathology will appear.

Third, how long has it been since the loss occurred? Somewhat cross-culturally in social class and ethnic subgroups, one year is "allowed" for mourning. This was the wisdom of an earlier Episcopal ruling to the effect that persons getting a divorce wait a year from the date of divorce before marriage to another person. This gave time for some resolution of grief over the previous marriage breakup before one forms another marriage covenant. Thus the contaminants of the previous marriage and a subsequent marriage are reduced to a minimum.

Fourth, how much guilt, anger, and conflict characterized the relationship of the bereaved person? Unresolved emotions such as these make the person more vulnerable to an emotional disorder. These feelings need working through in order to let the dead be dead.

Fifth, how bizarre is the thought and behavior of the bereaved person? A father, whose son was suddenly killed in an auto accident, had the body embalmed and placed in an airtight casket with a glass covering. Then he had the encased body placed in a room in the parental home so that people could "always come and see him." That is bizarre!

Sixth, basic to all these criteria for examination and diagnosis is a thorough history of personal and family history for already existing illnesses, especially psychiatric illnesses, *before* the event of loss.

Seventh, how many other stress events accompanied the particular loss? For example, an 83-year-old woman lost her only son by suicide. Within a three-month period of time she had a recurrence of rheumatoid arthritis, the responsibility of nursing a daughter through a severe illness requiring surgery, and her financial security became much more threatened. As Clifford Kuhn, M.D., says: "Bereaved persons are at high risk for illness, accidents, or even death. Their immunological systems break down. Even cancer itself is thought to be related to such failures of the immunological systems."

From a therapeutic point of view, the patient suffering from pathological grief is to be given an opportunity to "regreve," or emotionally to relive the loss of their loved one. Regrieving amounts to directly intervening in the patient's circular thinking about the loved one. The objective is to deal with the now chronic hope to reunite with the dead person. No interview schedule can be followed mechanically in a therapeutic way. However, I find the following questions helpful to have in mind to be asked at the appropriate time.

1. When did you first learn about the death of _____, and under what circumstances?
2. Was_____ able to talk with you or you with_____before his/her death?
3. Were there any grievances between you and _____prior to learning of imminent death? Were these reconciled or left unresolved?
4. Did you have the chance to say goodbye to _____before he/she died?
5. When the family came together, were there any conflicts or other stresses? Was anyone unable to get there?
6. Who had the most to do with arranging the funeral? Any disagreements?
7. What was the funeral like to you? How did you feel?
8. What did you do about your own place to live, with whom to live, etc., after the family resumed life's activities?
9. Will people let you talk about the deceased? Do they change the subject?
10. Have there been problems about the estate, the ill, the division of personal possessions?
11. Do you think everything was done that could or should have been done to keep your loved one alive?
12. Did you have to place your family member in a nursing home? How did this affect you?
13. Do you have mementos such as pictures, rings, watches, etc. of your lost relative? What are they and what do

you do with them?
14. Do you dream about your loved one? How do you feel when you awaken?
15. What are some of the pleasant—even humorous—things you recall about your family member?
16. Had it occurred to you that your family member would want you to be living a happy and productive life or not?

The care of the total person who is pathologically mourning needs careful psychiatric appraisal as to the advisability of hospitalization and the viability of the use of medication. The psychiatrist may even be a confessor without *im primatur* to hear things the person could tell only to a stranger. Therapeutic team work is a "must" and not elective procedure in caring for the pathologically bereaved.

The religious form that pathological grief often takes is the compulsive, intense desire to be near to God but the complaint that God does not care, does not hear, or is nonexistent. Anger may be directed at God for "taking" the loved one. More often, however, defensive piety is the response: "He/she has gone to be with God. God is with me. Through God, he/she and I are in touch." Rituals of undoing old wrongs provide a neurotic person with a constant reenforcement of reunion with the dead. For example, a 10-year-old girl developed the obsession to do everything she did twice—putting each piece of clothing on, taking it off, and putting it back on again, etc.

The process of therapy is timed to recover memories of the deceased, test them against reality, enable the person to accept separation from the dead, and most certainly "to free himself from bondage to the dead."[11]

THE TRAGIC SENSE OF LIFE

No discussion of grief is complete without identifying the kind of grief that arises from the sense of being human, limited, and subject to death ourselves. No matter how many times we win in saving life, at some time, some place, and in some way everybody dies. Thus we are contemplating our own death at the same time we are comforting or guiding another person facing death and/or grief.

This kind of grief I name "the tragic sense of life," it is most intensely present in pastors, physicians, nurses, emergency medical teams, etc.; they often confuse this with depression. It is *not*, clinically speaking. To the contrary, the tragic sense of life is a normative condition for persons who function with feeling as well as technical competence. Wordsworth called this poignant and wistful awareness of the mystery of human suffering the meditative capacity to hear "the still, sad music of humanity."

The most vivid characteristic of this persistent wistfulness about life comes from having seen much tragic suffering, considerable portions of which are unnecessary. Therefore, the person cannot describe what he/she has seen because they have no mind-set for responding to him/her. For example, when I see a mother and her 16-year-old daughter in a severe quarrel, with the mother demanding that the daughter have an abortion or never come back home again, I am struck by the tragic sense of life surrounding the poverty-stricken mother, her daughter and her unborn grandchild. This tragic sense of life was doubled in intensity before the day was over when I was called to the pediatric emergency room to meet with a young mother whose *second* badly malformed child was brought in dead on arrival. As I traveled home, I knew that what I had felt could not be put into words. If it could, it could not be grasped easily or even at all by family members and friends. Persons such as yourselves have similar experiences. You can do as I am doing now, simply "pointing to" your and my sense of the tragic in life. We have "reentry" problems every time we leave our place of work, as if we lived on a different planet. We are prone to develop parallel lives with our own families. The fellow workers in such ambiguous tragedies I have mentioned become a life support system. As such, we and our colleagues may develop a tight-knit "in-group" that excludes the uninitiated. A spiritual bond with a larger community, with God, and within our own contemplation is imperative.

Dag Hammarskjöld developed this inner source of strength and renewal in God. He must have wept over Jerusalem, over New York City, over the memory of Hiroshima and Nagasaki. He recorded his thoughts in his *Markings*. He found communion with God through the Holy Spirit and an understanding of "groanings that cannot be uttered." On June 11, 1961, he wrote:

Summoned
To carry it,
Alone
To assay it
Chosen
To suffer it
And free
To deny it,
I saw
For one moment
The sail
In the sun storm
Far off
On a wave crest
Alone,
Bearing from land.[12]

SUMMARY

In conclusion, I have said that facing death is a parent-suffering of all other pains and losses. The human spirit demands of the parent-suffering a meaning. That meaning is developed by the imposition of a process of meaningful rituals on the time span available. The time span of the grief process differentiates types of grief that are diagnostically definable, creatively treatable, and open to wise and compassionate interpretation by the clergyperson, the physician, the nurse, and the family in their communication with the patient. These types of grief are: anticipatory grief, acute or traumatic grief, "no-end" grief, "near-miss" grief, pathological grief, and the tragic sense of life.

DISCUSSION

QUESTION: Regarding psychological grief and more particularly the control of the dead one over the family even after burial, the family does not seem to be able to bury the dead.

ANSWER: That's right. Professor Bowker is talking about primitive religions or historical religions. It's so vivid the way the spirit of the dead is taken seriously in the rituals of primitive life. We don't do that in our culture. But the spirit of the dead continues to control; even as in Hamlet, the spirit of his departed father was still walking the halls of the place. I say two things about it: after I have built an adequate relationship, to simply introduce the idea of the alpha and the omega of life, not only in this instance but in many instances, but also say, "How long do you plan to go before you really honest-to-God bury George or Jane or whomever?" I tell them that I would like for them to set a time as to when they are really going to have a requiem, depending on what their tradition is; but particularly to the Catholic I would say: "When are you going to have a requiem, your own requiem mass for this person and let the dead bury the dead?" If it gets to be too big a struggle, I'd say, "Well, who is God; let's discuss who God is." Now I know my temptation is idolatry. But then, again, I like the thought that has been conveyed: 'love me, but don't worship me.' I think this is something of the human or the theological approach to challenging the idolatry at stake. On the control side, here's another who labored through an anticipatory grief process, got stuck afterward, and would not accept the death of her son. For two years now she's been in and out of a psychiatric hospital. I was called into consultation and she said: "My psychiatrist tells me that if I accepted the death of my son, that I'd start getting better." I said: "Well, what do you think of that?" And she said, "Well, If I accepted it, he will be dead." And I said then, "You feel that if by not accepting his death, you could control whether or not he is dead, but the hard truth is you've run up against something you can't control. That is where the action is." I said: "Now, please don't hear me pointing my finger at you, because if you do, there are three more pointing at me. I like to control, too." And I confessed the situation—our son in the war—and that was a thing I couldn't control and I said, "Please know that I couldn't have known that about you if I hadn't known it about me. I may never see you again, but please don't forget this." Those are the two things I would say on that.

QUESTION: Some persons have children, or a spouse, or

loved one who is living physically but who has lost sensitivity and consciousness, etc. What kind of grieving or counseling can one offer to the person who has a loved one who is living only physically?

ANSWER: Yes, I see your point. Now we see so many coming in and going out of awareness like that. It becomes extremely painful when the person who is just out of it, not quite there, says or does something in a delirious state; that hurts their son or daughter or mother, whoever it is, and I have found one consolation. I think sometimes we need to put down some of the consolations that we found had helped. The one consolation I found that's been very helpful is simply to say to the person: "You know, I guess you know when the loved one is not *all* there—well, I'm not either. I lost that finger when I was a baby and my brother cut it off playing with a hatchet. I still have ambivalent feelings about it—we won't discuss that. What we are discussing here is that I'm not *all* here. A part of me has gone on to its 'reward,' which is a phrase I don't like. I've had to type the rest of my life without it. But in a very real way the consciousness is gone and the shell is there. And I'd like to say that there are just bits and pieces left. I believe in the Resurrection, and in the Resurrection we are given a new body. I'd like to trade this one of mine in occasionally, really, that it is a hope and that the end has already come, that's the consolation, that the omega was when he lost consciousness, not when the brain wave flattens out on the skull or whatever."

QUESTION: Could you help the person to grieve, then?

ANSWER: Yes, consciousness is a great gift. You can enable them to mourn the loss of this gift.

QUESTION: I wonder if you'd like to comment on the preventive aspects of grief. For instance, one of the things that we often work with is the guilt process around grieving. For instance, a month before my sister died, I knew we had unfinished work to do; there were many things that we had not discussed about our anger, our hostility that had not been resolved. I knew that I had better do this unfinished work with her and we discussed it during her death period. I try to encourage many people to deal with this before death, rather than having to work through guilt after. Would you comment on these preventive aspects of grieving?

ANSWER: I don't think I could do half as well as you've already done, namely that that's the importance of the family gathering, the leave-taking, and that we should tend to that, not let the sun go down on our wrath, nor give place to the evil one. Rather we should keep our spiritual house in order in terms of our relationships to people, so that as William Cullen Bryant says, when we do die, we go not as a quarry slave chained to his dungeon, but sustained and soothed by an unfaltering trust. And I think that's extremely important in setting our relationships to our loved ones in order. If we have done anything against them, we must confess it, seek forgiveness, and if they are not in a state of mind to forgive, put them in God's hands and live the kind of life that would be an example to them nevertheless. We're not requiring forgiveness of them or putting it as a condition of life. Then there's that business of forgiving them and of knowing that we don't forgive them once and have done with it. We know that the cycle of grief spins again and we go through the process again and we forgive 70 times 70. It's what I call the "Law of 490," that is, to keep washing it out—forgiveness is like cleansing our shirt; we felt washing it once would do, when in reality, human experience presents painful things again and again and we may have to wash it again, right? That's where our prayers come in; that's where our prayers keep us healthy. If we are angry about trying, tell God, because I think it was Jacob Boehme who said: "We cannot, by confessing our faults to him, add to his knowledge of us." Inasmuch as He knows them anyhow, I'd just as well talk it over with Him. But I think that is preventive care of the most profound kind. It's in the area of forgiveness. One of the things this controlling mother could not do was to forgive her son for going off and leaving her. After all, death is an abandonment. "Why did you have to go off and do it?" I feel very angry that I was abandoned by my doctor friend—he was not my physician, but my doctor friend. To admit that helps, keeps me from going and doing likewise.

QUESTION: When families are faced with making the decision about terminating extraordinary means—if you have a fair enough time to work up to that (in some cases you do and sometimes you don't)—how do you go about preventing grief about making a decision when they haven't anything to face but this traumatic decision of life and death so quickly?

ANSWER: And it's a new experience they haven't faced

before. Well, the important thing is that they know what the facts are about the procedure because some of these procedures are very mercurial in their results, such as pulling the plug on the Quinlan patient. She's still living; pulling the plug was irrelevant to whether she lived or died—it may or may not extend the life; it may or may not end the life. In other words, the factual data about the procedure are very, very important. The physician is, I think, under ethical responsibility to make that known to the person.

Another factor is that clinically the decision tends to get made by the intuitive wisdom of the family itself and more often than we give it credit. I saw a 52-year-old man who had died. He had emphysema. He also became psychotic three times in the course of 18 months. Finally, somebody came along and did a brain study. This man was suffering from anoxia—a lack of oxygen to the brain—hence, the psychotic behavior. They put him on oxygen and his consciousness cleared up, but he had to depend on oxygen in order to live. That went on for 63 days, the wife told me. I said, "How is it that you decided not to do it any longer?" She said, "We're just poor people, you know, but that's not what decided it." I said, "Well, what decided it?" She said, "Our little 13-year-old girl, who loved her daddy, said, 'Why does Daddy have to suffer so just because the doctors have oxygen?" And she said, "I decided then that she had more sense than any of us, and we took him off the oxygen and he lived three days longer." And that's what I mean by some intuitive wisdom. I think it's the work of the Holy Spirit myself, breaking through in their immediate, clinical situation. And I said, "Well, I'd like to ask you a question: What kind of work did your husband do?" She said, "He worked at Kosmosdale." Kosmosdale is a cement factory. And I rode back home on the freeway. It's made out of concrete. I had to ask myself how much concrete costs. Here's a man whose work had in it the shortening of his life. I don't know how to be any more specific, but I do know that a nurse, doctor, chaplain, pastor, friend, and/or relative at a time like this really should have a lot of respect for the gumption of a childlike wisdom.

NOTES

[1]*Existence, A New Dimension in Psychiatry,* edited by Rollo May, Ernest Angel, and Henri Ellenberger. New York: Basic Books, 1958, p. 49.

[2]"Bereavement is Indispensable for Growth," *Bereavement: Its Psychosocial Aspects,* Bernard Schoenberg, *et al.,* editors. New York: Columbia University Press, 1975, p. 12.

[3]John Schwab, *et al.* "Studies in Grief: A Preliminary Report." *Bereavement: Its Psychosocial Aspects,* edited by Bernard Schoenberg, *et al.* New York: Columbia University Press, 1975, pp. 80-84.

[4]*Toys and Reason.* New York: W. W. Norton, 1977, p. 78.

[5]Elizabeth Kubler-Ross. *Death and Dying,* New York: Macmillan, 1969.

[6]Dylan Thomas, "Do Not Go Gentle Into That Good Night," *Collected Poems.* New York: New Directions, 1957, p. 128.

[7]Glen W. Davidson, "The Waiting Vulture Syndrome," *Death and Ministry,* edited by J. Donald Bune. New York: The Seaberry Press, 1975, pp. 49-58.

[8]Erich Lindemann, "Symptomatology and Management of Acute Grief," *The American Journal of Psychiatry,* Vol. 101, pp. 141-148.

[9]*Ibid.*

[10]Paul Tillich, *The Eternal Now.* New York: Charles Scribner's Sons, 1963, pp. 152-153.

[11]Vamik D. Volkan, "Re-Grief Therapy," *Bereavement: Its Psychosocial Aspects,* edited by Bernard Schoenberg, *et al.* New York: Columbia University Press, 1975, pp. 334 ff.

[12]Dag Hammarskjöld, *Markings.* New York: A. A. Knopf, 1964, p. 211.

Chapter 7

SUFFERING COMING FROM THE STRUGGLE AGAINST SUFFERING
Dr. Joel Gajardo-Velasquez

PRAYER

Lord, forgive me for becoming accustomed to looking at children who appear to be 8 years old when they are already 13.

Lord, forgive me for becoming accustomed to sloshing through mud puddles which I can leave behind me; they cannot.

Lord, forgive me for learning to shut out the smell of open sewers which I can leave behind; they cannot.

Lord, forgive me for turning on my lights automatically, forgetting those who have no lights to turn on.

Lord, I can go on a hunger strike but they cannot even participate in a strike because of hunger.

Forgive me for telling them, "Man cannot live by bread alone" without joining in their struggle to have bread.

Lord, I want to love them for who they are; help me.

Lord, I dream of dying for them; help me to live for them.

Lord, I want to be with them when the light breaks through;
    help me.

Carlos Mugica
Argentina

Translated by J. Hill
January 14, 1975

INTRODUCTION

Nothing really great and important can be obtained without a certain amount of sacrifice; therefore, suffering is present in every human action that tends to transform and create new conditions for life.

Suffering is a fact in human life. Pain, as a specific physical sensation, may extend itself to the rest of the animal kingdom, but suffering is part and parcel of the mystery surrounding the human expression of life. It is related to our capacity for love and hate, to trust and fear, to hope and despair. To be ourselves and yet, at the same time, always becoming someone different.

Suffering will be understood in this paper as that state of our inner-being in which we deeply wish that our predicament were otherwise. This is not an attempt to deny the creative and positive role of certain kinds of suffering in human life. On the contrary, it is an affirmation that we could never have felt joy, never have had even an idea of love, if sacrifice had been impossible for us. "If there is meaning in life at all," says Viktor E. Frankl, "then there must be meaning in suffering."

The present chapter will neither attempt to elucidate the meaning and role of suffering in life from a psychological viewpoint nor try to explain it in a rational way. A theodicy is out of our scope.

Taking suffering as a given in human existence, this paper will attempt to analyze the special situation of misery and oppression that is present in Latin America today and the repercussions that this predicament has on people that, coming from different backgrounds and motivations, are involved in an honest struggle in order to put an end to unnecessary and meaningless suffering. Thus, here we are confronted with a testimony rather than with a theoretical analysis of suffering. The approach will be sociohistorical, though we recognize that many individuals experience suffering in their struggle against suffering in a more private way.

For obvious reasons, this paper cannot be all-inclusive. Not only does every minute add new dimensions to the suffering of Latin Americans, but it would also be impossible to give an appropriate account of the sacrifice and suffering that is present in that part of the world. There are too many unknown heroes, too many unknown martyrs to be remembered in silence and humble gratitude.

One thing, though, should be clear. Human beings can never accept less than human conditions of life without expressing their protest and aspiration for the recovery of their dignity and the right to create their own future. Thus, suffering coming from the struggle against suffering is one of the most dynamic forces of history.

BACKGROUND

There is no reliable information about life in this part of the world before the Europeans discovered it and inserted it into their particular history.

Anthropological reconstruction has been helpful in showing some of the basic trends of precolumbian society. There was plenty of space for everybody; land was held in common use, therefore, there was no need for private property; family life was an expression of the wider concern for the life of the tribe or clan. Work was oriented towards the satisfaction of basic needs, and authority and hierarchical power were exercised in such a way that everybody was protected and felt to be a full member of the community. People were aware of suffering through natural catastrophies, sickness, and death. Individual and social evils were present but they were not the main cause of personal suffering.

This situation was radically changed with the arrival of the first Europeans to the continent. After a painful and costly trip across the Atlantic, Columbus and his men landed on the island of Hispaniola. The moment of happiness for the newcomers would be the beginning of fear, suffering, and death for the residents of the island.

Was this an historical necessity for the improvement of civilization, or a disgrace, not only for the so-called "indians" but also for the decadence of some European countries? This debate is still going on among historians, but contemporary scholars have brought to light a forgotten theme: the impact of the New World in the old one. J. H. Elliott expresses it this way:

> From 1492 the New World was always present in European history, although its presence made itself felt in different ways at different times. It is for this reason that America and Europe should not be subjected to a historiographical divorce, however shadowy their partnership may often appear before the late seventeenth century. Properly, their histories should constitute a continuous interplay of two distinctive themes.[1]

This truth, which should have been quite evident, has been systematically ignored even today when socioeconomic themes are analyzed. America and Europe, the north and the south, are part and parcel of the same historical system. Europe got the best economic deal in this new relationship. America was forced to remain the provider of a free labor force and raw materials, and use the recipient of manufactured goods of poor quality coming from Europe.

Greed and plunder were rampant in the New World. Indians were treated as beasts, forced to work beyond their strength and in occupations that were not their own. They could not resist this type of oppression. They revolted time and time again. They were killed time and time again. Suffering was the birthmark of Latin America.

"Gold and conversion," says J. H. Elliott, "were the two most immediate and obvious connotations of America and those most likely to be associated with the name of its discoverer."[2] That is to say, the role of the Church during the conquest was to make sure that the gold would reach the pockets of Spanish and Portuguese nobility. Here the instrumentalization of the Church and the Christian faith is clear and evident. To be converted meant to be faithful to the powers that be, and to work harder than ever for the prosperity and well-being of others even at the expense of one's own life. What a contradiction with the real Spirit of the Gospel! What a denial of the One who came to proclaim, "Good news to the poor and liberty to those who are oppressed!" No wonder that the role of the church in those early days was one of ambivalence and lack of clarity.

But everybody was not willing to go along with the official attitude. Even if they were loyal to both civil and religious authorities, it was impossible for them to remain insensitive to the clamor and cry of the suffering majorities. Some changed sides.

The religious debate was intense and in many instances quite bitter. The best known defender of the Indians was Friar Bartolomé de las Casas, but there were many others who at great personal risk confronted the colonists and friars on how the Indians were to be treated justly, according to Christian doctrine. Friar Antonio de Montesinos was perhaps the first one to preach a truly revolutionary sermon in the New World when on the Sunday before Christmas in 1511 in a straw-thatched church on the island of Hispaniola he said:

> In order to make your sins against the Indians known to you I
> have come up on this pulpit, I who am a voice of Christ crying
> in the wilderness of this island, and therefore it behooves you
> to listen, not with careless attention, but with all your heart
> and senses, so that you may hear it; for this is going to be the
> strangest voice that ever you heard, the harshest and hardest
> and most awful and most dangerous that ever you expected to
> hear . . . This voice says that you are in mortal sin, that you
> live and die in it, for the cruelty and tyranny you use in dealing
> with these innocent people. Tell me, by what right or justice do
> you keep these Indians in such a cruel and horrible servitude?
> On what authority have you waged a detestable war against
> these people, who dwelt quietly and peacefully on their own
> land? . . . Why do you keep them so oppressed and weary, not
> giving them enough to eat nor taking care of them in their ill-
> ness? For with the excessive work you demand of them they
> fall ill and die, or rather you kill them with your desire to ex-
> tract and acquire gold every day. And what care do you take
> that they should be instructed in religion? . . . Are these not
> men? Have they not rational souls? Are you not bound to love
> them as you love yourselves? . . . Be certain that, in such a
> state as this, you can no more be saved than the Moors or
> Turks.[3]

Needless to say, Montesinos was forced to silence by his
superiors in Spain, but with him, the first great struggle for
justice in the New World had begun.

In spite of several men and women who, out of their
Christian faith and commitment, were willing to express their
solidarity with the Indians, poor, oppressed, and suffering
majority in Latin America, the hierarchical Church was
reluctant to move out of its comfortable relationship with the
crown, the local and national governments. Thus, sword and
cross, gold and conversion would remain together for many
centuries to come, perpetuating a situation of injustice and
inequality that persists even at the present time.

Right from the moment of its insertion into European
history, Latin America has been unable to work for its own

destiny. Given the role of raw material producer by the international division of labor and production, Latin America experienced the widening disparity between the price of its minerals and agricultural products, and the manufactured goods that it was forced to import.[4]

The injustices of this economic system were ignored by those who profited from it, and they remained unchallenged by those, especially the Church, who were supposed to be concerned with the well-being of the toal community. The situation is such that:

> According to the United Nations, the amount shared by six million Latin Americans at the top of the social pyramid, is the same as the amount shared by 140 million at the bottom, there are 60 million "campesinos" [peasants] whose future amounts to 25 cents a day.[5]

This reality is not only grasped through statistics and by economists, it is something that anyone with eyes to see can confirm. It is impossible to ignore the clamor that is coming with increasing force from the masses of poor and opressed in Latin America, the majority of whom belong to the Church and confess Jesus Christ as their Lord and Savior.

After a serious and honest analysis of this type of reality in which the Church is overwhelmingly present, the Second General Conference of Latin American Bishops was forced to declare that society was:

> . . . Faced with a situation of injustice that can be called institutionalized violence, when, because of structural deficiency of industry and agriculture, of national and international economy, of cultural and political life, whole towns lack necessities, live in such dependence that hinders all initiative and responsibility as well as every possibility for cultural promotion and participation in social and political life.[6]

The present can be understood as the reign of violence—structural and institutionalized violence. From a

Christian perspective, it is possible and necessary to speak with liberation theologians about the social expression of sin that condemns the great majority of the people to misery and suffering.

As long as the present economic, social, and political conditions prevail, it is hypocritical to speak about the respect of human rights in a world so sharply divided between the haves and have-nots, without a serious commitment toward the radical transformation of society's present structure of oppression. The time has come for such a commitment because, as it is again stated in the bishops' declaration:

> An outcry is rising up to the heavens . . . It is the cry of people who suffer and who demand justice, liberty, respect for their fundamental rights as persons and as people.[7]

WHEN ONLY UNDERSTANDING IS NOT ENOUGH

Karl Marx, in his famous XI Thesis on Feurbach, reminds the philosopher that it is not enough to interpret the world, but to change it.

Of course, this is not a rejection of the philosophical, scientific approach to reality. Marx himself was a great scholar who was able to penetrate reality with a seriousness and depth that few can match. Social sciences are essential tools in the search for a proper understanding of human predicament.

Attention should be paid to the fact that no scientific approach is immune to the temptation of distorting reality according to certain ideological preference. Nevertheless, the selection of the appropriate means for getting the best results in a sociological investigation is a step that should be done with utmost care.

Thanks to the importance of social sciences, gone are the days in which any given moment in the life of human society was attributed to the Divine Providence in an almost deterministic way. Now, the emphasis is put on human responsibility without necessarily denying transcendence. History is not a drama that has already been written and human beings act out, but history is the result of human decisions, it is the accumulation of the collective experience of humankind in its search for its true destiny. In this sense, history is always very concrete and particular.

The process of desacralization of society has been paralleled to the search for human liberation. Human beings are builders of history; there is a challenge to become actively involved in creating a future, and not only passively accept something predetermined from the past. There is a new dignity in being human, and therefore a greater challenge when one is confronted with the injustices of present day society which tends to deny all possibilities for being really human.

It is at this point that scientific analysis does not help us anymore to better understand the situation. It's not even of much value to know, in an abstract way, that history is and will be the result of human beings' trial and error, if such knowledge remains a theory without becoming a praxis, a commitment to action that will illuminate a new level of reflection that will again express itself in action. How is commitment really possible? In the Latin American context there are two forces that have proven to be strong enough to mobilize people: religion and politics. The fact that these are two different forces does not necessarily mean that they need to be in opposition. On the contrary, history has shown that in the majority of cases both elements have been together in the support of governments which very often have been quite insensitive to the suffering of the people.

Today, the desire for change is self-evident. Few people are willing to keep the world as it is. But, what type of society should emerge in the future? Where is the historical project that can gather together enough people to make sure of its success? Is the old and known always better just because it has been tried? Is the new always an improvement over the old? Where can people find some guidelines for the construction of a new society? All these questions are part of the intense contemporary political debate. Many people are willing to sacrifice and suffer in the struggle for political power, and concrete opportunities to implement a particular project for the future that will eliminate some of the causes of much suffering today.

If the "model" for society's future is not quite clear and so generates a bitter struggle that causes much suffering in the world today, then the problem of the way to achieve this desired end is also a complex issue.

In Latin America, those who are convinced of the absolute necessity of radical transformation of present unjust structures find themselves divided in regard to the methods that can be used. A basic difference is the role or use of violence in achieving the end. This is a particularly critical area for Christians in Latin America. Since the majority—including the Council of Bishops at Medellin and Puebla—will accept the fact that life is lived in a very violent context, is it realistic to speak of nonviolence? Furthermore, is it possible to make a decision for nonviolent means without postponing indefinitely the collapse of the present structure of injustice that impedes the dawning of a new society? How will the oppressive powers be replaced by the real empowerment of the people so that they—the substantial majority—can be free to write their own history, to be the shapers of their own destiny?

Dom Helder Camara, Archbishop of Recife and Olinda in Northeast Brazil, is one of the well-known apostles of nonviolence. He is afraid that violence will always generate more violence, thus creating what he calls "the spirals of violence." At the same time he is aware of the difficulties that his decision implies. He said:

> Yes. The nonviolent do not in the least underestimate the difficulty of the task. If I may speak personally, I could mention

my own half-failure, which forces me to struggle on and offers me new hopes.[8]

Out of his commitment to the transformation of society, Camilo Torres, a Colombian priest, was forced to take a different road. In his famous "Proclamation to the Colombian People" he said:

> I have joined the armed struggle. From the Colombian mountains I plan to continue the fight, gun in hand, until power for the people is won. I have joined the Army of National Liberation because in it I found the same ideals as in the United Front. I found the desire for and the realization of a unified base, a peasant base, without religious or traditional party differences. Without any spirit of contesting revolutionary elements of any other sector, movement or party. Without bossism. Which seeks to liberate the people from exploitation by the oligarchy and imperialism. Which will not put aside its arms so long as power is not totally in the hands of the people. Which in its objectives accepts the platform of the United Front.[9]

Both Dom Helder and Camilo are excellent examples of those who have been willing to accept personal suffering in order to avoid the suffering of the many. Dom Helder continues in the struggle; Camilo, although dead, is an inspiration and a challenge to many. For both, justice is not an option but a must. "If we are to be pilgrims for justice and peace, we must expect the desert."[10] Justice, not charity, is the real goal of society. As long as charitable institutions are needed, it is clear that justice is not the backbone of social relations.

The Church has been too much involved in a charity as a way of expressing Christian love. Charity, as it has been traditionally done, can be a poor substitute for justice, even worse, it depends on injustice as a prevailing situation in order to privilege a few with its "good works."

Camilo Torres, in his "Message to Christians" comments on the text: "He who loves his neighbor keeps the

Law" (Rom. 13:8) in the following terms:

> This love, to be valid, must seek ways to be effective. If
> benevolence, alms, the free schools, the few apartments, what
> is called 'charity' does not succeed in giving food to the
> majority of the hungry, nor clothing to the majority of the
> naked, nor teaching to the majority of those who do not
> know, we have to search for effective means of ministering to
> the needs of the majority.[11]

Injustice deprives human beings of their dignity and
rights, therefore, and is the main cause of human suffering.
Those who are committed to justice are the ones who in concrete terms are trying to avoid unnecessary and massive expression of suffering. No wonder that Jesus said, "Happy are
those who are persecuted because they do what God requires
(justice); the Kingdom of heaven belongs to them" (Matt.
5:10).

COLLECTIVE AND PERSONAL SUFFERING COMING
FROM THE STRUGGLE AGAINST SUFFERING

To be human means to accept and reject at the same
time, a given situation. It must be accepted because it is here:
it is real, it is the starting point of any new adventure. To
know the present—which certainly should include the
past—is a condition sine qua non to affirm human identity
and be able to express solidarity toward those who struggle
along the same historical process. But precisely because life is
an historical process, it can never be contained in any single
moment; it cannot be finished. Life, collective and personal,
is always becoming, is open-ended, therefore, cannot absolutize the now, but is able to recognize the finite, faulty
elements that must be corrected in order to create the conditions for a more humane existence. Acceptance and rejection
are part of the dialectical movement of history.

In the midst of a situation of extreme injustice, the elite

that profit from it tend to absolutize the present order and regulate it through legal means, thus attempting to paralyze any action on the part of the oppressed that will lead to change the correlation of forces to get rid of injustice. Under such circumstances suffering is mostly borne in silence until objective conditions permit people to see a chance of making a significant move in the establishment of a more just and humane order.

Historically, it is possible to distinguish two types of groups or individuals who have been willing to risk and sacrifice themselves in order to move history towards the road of justice, equality, and peace: (1) those who are part of the suffering masses and out of desperation, hope to challenge the establishment and its power, very often encountering barbaric treatment or death, thus moving from suffering to sacrifice; and (2) those who, although well-off (therefore members of the elite or privileged class) are aware of the injustice and sufferings of the many, and commit themselves to do something in order to create a society where their own privileges are going to end and a better quality of life will be possible for everybody.

These two groups are not all together separate. We could give good examples of personal cross-relations between the two. One thing is sure though: in the first group there is much more collective effort involved while in the second, it is usually individuals, here and there, that are willing to take an option that will be contrary to their vested interest.

Those Who are Part of the Suffering Masses and Move from Suffering to Sacrifice.

THE INDIAN MOVEMENTS.   As we have already stated, the native population of the region was—and still is—brutally abused and in many cases almost exterminated due to the forced labor that was imposed on them. Sometimes people will comment ·about the passivity of the Indians, their endurance to tolerate such inhuman treatment, without being aware of the many uprisings and revolts that were initiated by Indian movements in order to obtain their freedom and better living conditions. Since history has been written from the perspective of the winners, no wonder that Indians have such a small role to play in official documents. Nevertheless, modern historiography has been very helpful in showing the many plots and revolutionary movements that were organized against the existing powers.

The Mexican anthropologist, Miguel Leon Portilla, has put together a selection of accounts by the Indians of their confrontation with the Spaniards. It is a history told by the victims of much suffering and inhumanity but still with a tremendous sensitivity to what it really means to be human. Montezuma is depicted as a concerned king, afraid of what will happen to his people but still willing to do his best to protect them even as far as to compromise with the *conquistadores* (conquerors).[12]

After the fall of Mexico City (1521) a Mexican priest wrote:

> Nothing but flowers and songs of sorrow
> are left in Mexico and Tlatelolco,
> where once we saw warriors and wise men.
>
> We know it is true
> that we must perish,
> for we are mortal men.
> You, the Giver of life,
> you have ordained it.
>
> We wander here and there
> in our desolate poverty.
> We are mortal men.
> We have seen bloodshed and pain
> where once we saw beauty and valor.
>
> We are crushed to the ground;
> we lie in ruins.

> There is nothing but grief and suffering
> in Mexico and Tlatelolco,
> where once we saw beauty and valor.
>
> Have you grown weary of your servants?
> Are you angry with your servants,
> O Giver of Life?[13]

In spite of deep suffering and utter despair, the Indian population of Latin America has been able to express protest and inflict many defeats on their oppressors based on their traditional sense of community and love for the land. In the midst of much suffering the Indian people have been capable of maintaining, up to now, their determination to live according to their own values, and to respect and preserve their own culture and religious motivation. Their struggle has been a long and difficult one. Even today they have many problems vis à vis governments that, in the name of progress and development, are determined to put an end to any land that has been reserved for Indian use. It is to be hoped that such a long and immense sacrifice, in order to ameliorate the suffering of their own people, will not be in vain.

PEASANTS AND WORKERS. Although in some cases peasants and workers belong to the native population, still their place in the social system is different from the one of the Indian communities. Peasant and urban workers have been incorporated more or less to a degree into the mainstream of the exploitative system of the Western powers. This does not mean that they are enjoying the benefits of the system. Not at all. They are not on the receiving end of it, but rather on the giving end, without any more rights than the one to see their labor for insignificant or even nonexistent remuneration.

Any social and economic gain by the working class has been the result of a long and painful process of organizing, educating, and uniting the workers. The struggle to overcome suffering, misery, and exploitation on the part of the poor and oppressed has been against the elite that control economic, political, and military power.

Trade unions were always considered as a threat by the owners of land and industry; therefore, they struggle with all their might against them and especially against the leaders that arise from time to time due to the objective conditions of misery and humiliation.

The unjust structures that the Latin American continent inherited from colonial times were not modified, but utilized, by the modernizing sector of the capitalistic system of the West. In order to increase and accelerate the accumulation of capital into a few hands, salaries must be kept as low as possible, and therefore it is imperative to impede or delay the formation of labor unions.

The history of the *Movimiento Sindical* (labor movement) in contemporary Latin America is a clear recognition of the courage and determination of men and women to fight against the suffering coming from an economic system that will use their labor without granting them the necessary means for a real human expression of their lives. The personal and collective suffering that this work of solidarity has implied is very difficult to assess, but one can guess that it has been enormous. Each gain—shorter periods of work, no working children, physical conditions in the working place, holidays, remuneration, freedom of association—has been paid for with the blood and tears of the working class. Aware of their misery, they want to overcome it. Personal and communal suffering move them to sacrifice so as to create better working conditions for future generations.

The suffering of the poor—the working class formed by rural and urban workers—is far from being over. New needs in the economic system have forced new styles in government. Military dictatorships are much more efficient than democratic ones when repression of the poor is the work to be done. Gains, which the trade union movement in different countries thought as irreversible, have been erased all at once by military decrees. There is a clear-cut decision to turn back the clock of history. But surely the same courage, determination, and united power that the working class has shown in the past will allow them to overcome the dark hours in which obscure people want to force them to live.

Those Who, Although Well-Off, Are Aware of the Injustice and Suffering of the Many and Try To Do Something about it.

POLITICIAN. Politics has to do with the use of power in order to accomplish what is possible, at any given moment, through the structures of society. Therefore, any change in the social order must imply a political action, in the same way that maintaining the status quo is also a matter of political commitment. In the confrontation between conservative and progressive politicians, much suffering has been involved.

Although an increasing number of people have been involved in Latin American political activities, still, the leadership of the majority of political parties or movements is in the hands of those who have had opportunities for academic accomplishments and who have come from well-to-do-families. The parties with greater representation of the working class strongly emphasize popular leadership with a substantial degree of success. Popular movements in Latin America have been greatly influenced by Marxist thought; therefore, they are quite critical of the present capitalistic system and are engaged in the creation of a socialist alternative as a way of overcoming the shortcomings and abuses of the present system. There is no doubt that Marxist ideas have exercised a great attraction for many intellectual and middle-class people. It is also true that many politicians will become militant in political parties of the left, just to utilize the numerical power that exists among the poor and the oppressed. To stop opportunism is practically impossible, and this is not only true in the political arena. However, a fact that must be recognized is that the majority of political leaders in the popular organizations in Latin America have been genuinely and honestly committed to the cause of the poor, and have shown their solidarity with the suffering masses even at the risk of losing their lives.

The radicalizing element is reality itself. The ideological dimension is, in most cases, a second step. Confronted with so much misery, exploitation, sickness, and premature deaths, side by side with luxury, abundance of consumer goods, and sophisticated technology, reality asks the question: How long will this inequality be tolerated? Is there any other way in which society can be organized in order to avoid flagrant injustice and extreme suffering? In every country throughout the continent men and women have engaged in a search for alternatives through political action. They have done this at a very high price. To oppose the establishment can be very costly. But they could not do otherwise without denying their convictions. They have understood the impossibility of the predicament for both rich and poor coexisting in the same place. It is true that understanding others' sufferings is insufficient unto itself but it is the first step towards a more sure and permanent commitment. Someday a history of Latin America will be written in which due tribute and respect will be paid to all those politicians who have been fortunate enough to be born in the midst of comfort, but have disregarded their birthright and committed themselves to a common cause with the wretched of the earth.

SOCIAL REFORMERS AND RELIGIOUS LEADERS

What has been said for politicians can be applied almost entirely to social reformers and religious leaders. There is the same type of commitment, the same type of background, although initially they did not look for political power in the partisan sense, but rather tried to influence the decisions of responsible people in an indirect way.

Because most of the religious leaders, who have lived their commitment in favor of social change, can be considered "social reformers," it will be easier for the purpose of this paper to include both groups under the religious analysis. This is not an affirmation that only persons with religious persuasions can become reformers of the social order, but rather the recognition that this is the case in Latin America today outside of the partisan political realm.

The new situation of the Church in this region will be the main concern of the next section, so at this point I will give only a few concrete examples of individuals who have endured suffering and death in their struggle to overcome the suffering of the many.

The name of Camilo Torres has been mentioned earlier in this paper. He was born into an aristocratic family, a priest with excellent academic formation with a future that could have been bright if he had played the game according to the rules of the establishment. Instead he chose the way of humility, suffering, and death; the only way, according to his judgment, that could express in concrete terms his love for his neighbor. There is no doubt that Camilo Torres is a very controversial figure, but nobody can take his commitment lightly. His life and death have been an inspiration for many. A very popular song well-known in the whole continent says, "Where Camilo fell, a cross was born, not one of wood but rather of light."

The first page of this paper shows a poem by Carlos Mujica, an Artentine priest who was assassinated in May 1974, when he was leaving his church after mass. His crime? Being a member of a group of priests, nuns, and lay persons committed to the cause of the Third World people and in search of a better social expression for human community. His poem is a mirror of his soul. He felt a tremendous suffering because he was able to share the heavy burden of the downtrodden of his country.

In Guatemala on May 29, 1978, the army entered the small village of Panzos and opened fire on the men, women, and children who had gathered in the town to express their concern over the mistreatment of several Indian workers. Church sources reported that 114 persons were killed. Later, 24 Christian organizations and religious congregations issued a statement in order to protest a growing violence against Guatemala's poor. They said:

> As Christians we cannot keep silent, not stay indifferent when faced with this assault against the most humble of the people of God.

On July 1, 1978, one of the signers of the above statement, Father Hermógenes López was shot and killed by the military. The 50-year-old parish priest had long been a defender of the right of the campesino to have water from the region's rivers, the right to plant, the right to a decent shelter, and to human quality of life. As a Christian, identified with the poor and the oppressed, he struggled against local companies which were trying to displace the poor.

The archbishop's office in Guatemala City declared Father López a "martyr who will continue to be a sign of hope—hope in a church that, in spite of its errors each day might be closer to the gospel by being closer each day to the people, hope in a society where the causes of violence might disappear."

These are numerous examples of similar situations in recent years. These are enough to stress the point that those who are trying to correct the injustices that produce violence, fear, suffering, and death in present day society are bound to experience in their own life, regardless of their origin, profession, and persuasion, the unrestrained rigor of reactionary forces that are insensitive to the social and human cost of their policies.

A CLOSER LOOK AT THE PRESENT SITUATION IN LATIN
AMERICA AND THE ROLE OF THE CHURCH IN THE MIDST
OF SUFFERING

Pressure is coming from below—those who are suffering as a group—and the increasing awareness of some of those on top have created a very explosive situation in Latin America due to the reluctance of the privileged elite to accept the inevitable march of history.

Popular participation which was on the increase since the structural reforms of the 1930s has stopped. Economic and material interests blind people from seeing the real needs of others. National and international concern for the maximization of profits imposes drastic changes in the exercise of political power, violating the right of people to participate in the election of their authorities. In most countries the only institution capable of controlling popular demand for change is the armed forces.

The United States, the main beneficiary of these repressive measures, has helped Latin American countries, not only by actually training military personnel who will take over the government, but also provides the ideological instrument which serves as the rationale for so much excess and brutality: the ideology of national security. For the sake of national security, values are completely turned upside down. Human beings exist for the state instead of the state existing in order to serve and protect all citizens. The nation and government are one, anyone who disagrees with the government is automatically classified as being a traitor to the nation. In a Manichean fashion, citizens are either good or bad. The good are rewarded with material bliss, the bad are punished in the most incredible ways. Only the former deserve the respect and dignity of human rights. Peace and order are for those who work for and profit from the system; permanent war is waged against those who dare to dissent.

Extreme inequality demands extreme repression and it is

against this modus operandi that Latin American Christians and churches are challenged to stand up for justice and human dignity, in spite of the cost and the risk that is involved. When the right to speak is denied, the churches can become the loud voice of those who can barely whisper. In a time when the right of assembly is nonexistent, the churches need to be the place of those without a place. In a time of forced silence, the prophetic voice of the churches and the prophetic commitment of Christians must be heard and seen all over the continent.

The churches are trying to accept the challenge and grow to the occasion. It has not been easy and it will not be simple, for there is a long history of compromise and political accommodation in Latin America. Secular powers have gotten used to receiving religious legitimacy so they cannot allow the churches to change sides and be in the opposition. Of course there still are churches who continue to recognize their efforts to save "Western Christian civilization." This is one of the ironies of the present situation: governments that are repressing and killing people in order to establish Christian humanism are confronted by churches who, in the light of their Christian faith, denounce repression and the violation of human rights by these governments.

In order to discredit the opposition coming from the churches, the state accuses them of being infiltrated by/or at the service of an international Marxist conspiracy. This is an old trick but still very much in vogue. Almost a decade ago, Dom Helder Camara, a Brazilian bishop, wrote in the "Christian Century":

> All around me—in my diocese, in my country, in the whole of Latin America—I see millions of people who are ill and underfed, who live in miserable shacks and who have no opportunity to improve their lot. They suffer the consequences of an extremism—a massive, hysterical anti-communism which reaches such a point of blindness and hate that in some instances at least, it seems to be (and may God forgive me if I pass judgment) a new form of industry. Any new ideas

or suggestion aimed at improving the condition of the poor is instantly and efficiently labeled "communism." This attitude leads to deadlocks that in turn lead to repression, despair and terrorism. . . A privileged minority raises the banner of anti-communism and by resorting to slander and violence strives to prevent any change in the socio-economic, political and cultural structures that guarantee its own survival. So long as we remain obsessed with the fear of communism and avoid the real issues, we shall be far away from any real solution to the problems that plague us today. . . .[14]

This long quote is justified since this situation remains basically the same, in spite of the time which has elapsed.

The turning point for the Latin American Catholic Church was the bishops' meeting at Medellín, Colombia (August, 1968). In their final document, under the general title of "Latin American Scene," the bishops said:

1 . The Latin American bishops cannot remain indifferent in the face of the tremendous social injustices existent in Latin America, which keep the majority of our peoples in dismal poverty, which in many cases becomes inhuman wretchedness.

2. Within the context of the poverty and even of the wretchedness in which the great majority of the Latin American people live, we, bishops, priests and religious, have the necessities of life and a certain security, while the poor lack that which is indispensable and struggle between anguish and uncertainty. And incidents are not lacking in which the poor feel that their bishops, or pastors and religious, do not really identify themselves with them, with their problems and afflictions, that they do not always support those that work with them or plead their cause.[15]

The fact that the increase in Church-state confrontations between 1969 and 1970 did happen is not unrelated to the new awareness that crystalized at Medellín.[16]

In Brazil, the largest Catholic country in the world, an interesting study was published, "Repression Against the Church in Brazil." Because its findings are paradigmatic of other situations on the continent, it is worthwhile here to reproduce the different categories of activities performed against the churches by the state.

The registered aggression against the Church follow the following categories:

1. *Defamatory attacks*—emphasis is given to the content of verbal or press attacks against the Church and Church persons.

2. *Invasions*—the following events are considered as invasions: sieges, illegal entries, search and seizure, spying in the intimacy of residences, and Church meetings.

3. *Imprisonment*—all types of detentions for hours, days, months, or years are registered as imprisonments, with an effort to mention the motives and the dates.

4. *Torture*—special attention is given to explicit references of physical and/or psychological ill treatment.

5. *Deaths*—names and motives for death by assassination are listed, as well as death by "suicide" resulting from tortures or from street shootings; a list of *death threats* and their circumstances is included.

6. *Abductions*—this includes the disappearance of bishops, priests, and other personnel engaged in Church work that remained unexplained, even though said persons reappeared.

7. *Indictments*—inquiries that involve bishops, priests, nuns, and other Church personnel.

8. *Summons*—facts in which persons were obliged or invited to appear to make depositions only, whether or not there were judicial implications.

9. *Expulsions*—expulsions from the country are listed, from places of labor, whether by decree, official inquiries, or pressure; *threats* of expulsion and banishment of religious personnel are listed as well.

10. *Censorship*—public denunciations of censorship to newspapers, magazines, radio stations, and Church correspondence, as well as baggage violations.

11. *Prohibitions*—impediments to the exercise of

pastoral ministries are listed through vetoes of publications, grassroot projects, summons to Church authorities, and pastoral functions.

12. *Falsifications*—cases of false publications, letters, or identities of persons are noted.[18]

Impressive as this list may seem, in truth the attacks referred to in this paper fail to express all the violence that was regimented against the Church during this period and even less so those perpetuated on the population.

> A written phrase cannot contain the climate of persecution, the permanent fear, the hidden threats in many circumstances, the censorship to thought and free expression, the hours of terror lived by those who had to flee the country or by those persecuted, the pain of torture and of their families, the anguish of those who met death and of those who lost dear ones.[19]

According to the French publication "DIAL,"[20] an incomplete account of those killed in this drive of repression against the Church in Latin America is 69 persons from 1964 to 1978. Of course, this is a reference to bishops (1), priests (36), and prominent lay leaders (32)—only these have been mentioned in official publications. To keep track of how many Christians have been killed in the same period is quite impossible.

It is against this background that the enormous list of official documents issued by national episcopal conferences and Christian organizations during the last decade needs to be understood. The churches, out of their solidarity with the suffering poor and oppressed, have been found worthy of sharing in the suffering of Christ. Reality, once again, has called Christians to a better and deeper understanding of discipleship from the bottom up to the hierarchical levels. In this critical moment of Latin American history:

The Church is being true to its prophetic calling, adhering to what was announced at Vatican Council II and reaffirmed both at Medellín and at Puebla. The "why" of repression against the Church has its roots in mission goals, outlined by laypersons and priests, together with their bishops, in the face of poverty and misery. Misery and poverty are no longer objects for the "exercise of charity" but take a central place in the Church's action.[21]

The Church in Latin America is opting for the poor—for the suffering—in a renewed act of obedience to God and service to humankind.

CONCLUSION: SUFFERING AND HOPE

It was affirmed at the beginning of this chapter that suffering would be understood as that state of our inner being in which we deeply wish that our predicament were otherwise. In the analysis that followed, we tried to show the way in which an unjust and oppressive situation has forced people to an experience of suffering in their attempt to transform their own reality.

For those who were moved from extreme collective suffering to sacrifice, their sacrifice would have been in vain without their inner conviction that even in a desperate act there must be hope. For those who apparently opted for a sacrificial style of life, in order to express their concrete and effective solidarity with the suffering majority, hope was the dynamic force that helped them to question their privileges and reject their vested interests. If without faith it is impossible to risk, without hope it is impossible to preserve. Endurance in the midst of suffering must be the concrete expression of faith, hope, and love.

Hope can be demonstrated in different ways. Even if the word itself is not used or changed by a more contemporary concept, still, the inner human experience remains the same.

Without hope the vision of tomorrow fails, the horizon is closed, and suffering becomes meaningless.

Victor Jara, the Chilean poet and folk singer who was killed in the Chilean Stadium in September, 1973, wrote his last poem while imprisoned. At the end of it, in a way that resembles an "unfinished poem," he said:

> What I see I have never seen
> What I have felt and what I feel
> will give birth to the moment. . . .[22]

"Will give birth". . . In the midst of intense darkness and even despair, Victor was still able to see, through hope, the *new* that will be born in spite of, and probably especially *because of,* his personal tragedy.

In a Christian perspective this is the message of the cross. Good Friday would be meaningless without Easter Sunday. Suffering without hope is death without resurrection!

"The inner conquest of suffering," said Philip Potter, "is hope in action and is the indispensable preparation for fighting against the causes of suffering."[23]

This fight is here and now. Hope should never be the excuse for an escape from the present reality, but an incentive towards a more serious and radical commitment to the transformation of the present, according to the vision of the future that has been given in Jesus Christ in whom all things are made new, and by whom, even in the midst of suffering, it is possible to pray: "Thy kingdom come, Thy will be done."

Chile Stadium

> There are five thousand of us here
> in this little part of the city.
> We are five thousand.
> I wonder how many we are in all
> in the cities and in the whole country?

Here alone
are ten thousand hands which plant seeds
and make the factories run.
How much humanity
exposed to hunger, cold, panic, pain,
moral pressures, terror and insanity?
Six of us were lost
as if into starry space.
One dead, another beaten as I could never
have believed
a human being could be beaten.
The other four wanted to end their terror—
one jumping into nothingness,
another beating his head against a wall,
but all with the fixed look of death . . .

O God, is this the world that you created?
For this, your seven days of wonder and work? . . .

How hard it is to sing
When I must sing of horror.
Horror which I am living
Horror which I am dying.

To see myself among so much
and so many moments of infinity
in which silence and screams
are the end of my song.
What I see I have never seen
What I felt and what I feel
Will give birth to the moment. . . .

                            Víctor Jara, Septiembre de 1973

DISCUSSION

QUESTION: In light of the oppression that the Latin
American people are now experiencing, what is
your vision of what's going to happen to the
Church?

ANSWER: It seems to me that the tension between the

Church and State is going to increase in Latin America and I hope that this will not cause the Church to turn back, or cause it to be on good terms with the government because it is losing "membership." I feel that the only way the Church can remain, and keep a place for itself in the Latin American context, is by being on the side of the poor and the oppressed in more concrete terms than it has been able to show up until now. I envision more suffering for the Church precisely in order to avoid suffering, but eventually I think that the poor and oppressed, the majority of Latin America, helped by the Church as an instrument of expression, are going to get organized and they're going to take power. There is no doubt in my mind that it will not happen tomorrow, nor next year, but the majority are finally going to have the right to write their own history and speak their own words. For this reason, one of the most important activities that the Roman Catholic Church is carrying out in Latin America at the present time is what is known as the *communidades de base*, basic Christian communities. Many people were hoping that Puebla was going to condemn this movement because time and time again governments have accused these communities of not being Christian but subversive groups. Fortunately in Puebla, not only was this activity not condemned, but it was reinforced, and there is a substantial amount of detail about the way in which Christian communities should function in the future. In Brazil alone there are more than 50,000 Christian communities working. As an example of their influence, the National

Episcopal Conference of Brazil presented the authorities with a pastoral letter which they wanted published; however, the government denied the right to publication because it was too critical of the authority's actions. The bishops then informed the authorities that they would circulate it privately within the churches and communities. Permission was granted for publication.

QUESTION: Those governments—are they Christian, Catholic . . . Who are they?

ANSWER: A very good question. The repressive governments I'm talking about call themselves Christian, and in most cases they are Catholic. So we have a very interesting situation in Latin America where repressive Catholic/Christian governments are opposed to equally Catholic/Christian churches and this is causing much tension. In some cases governments are so blatant as to say that the Council of Bishops is not a competent authority which can interpret what it really means to be a Christian—they know better. So far the Church has been reluctant to use excommunication as a means to alleviate this tension, although in a couple of extreme cases it has done so. However, the time will come when the Church will need to make a clear-cut decision as to where its Christian position stands.

QUESTION: The task seems to be too big to cope with. What can we do as individuals in order to avoid the frustration of being aware but unable to do something?

ANSWER: Let me say that sometimes to be frustrated is not necessarily negative; it could be the beginning of something quite positive. We are so

geared to "doing" things that maybe it is good
to realize from time to time we can do nothing.
I sense that you feel that I should have a pro
gram for each of you to take home and to your
job, yet this is not the case; neither do I have
any rule of thumb against frustration. However, together with frustration comes an
awareness that not all is right, and it is this
awareness which needs to be constantly developed so that we can begin to relate or intercon-
nect one event here with another one over
there; and it will be this which will help us to
act at the appropriate moment, not as individuals but together with others who have
also developed an awareness of reality.

QUESTION: Could you say a word about what these basic
Christian communities are, where they are
located, and what they do?

ANSWER: The structure of the Roman Catholic Church
in Latin America is very large. A diocese can
have thousands and thousands of parishioners.
You can attend Mass any time from five
o'clock in the morning to seven o'clock in the
evening. You may go and participate at Mass
and then go home and forget about it. You can
belong to the same parish for years and never
know anyone else. There is no sense of
solidarity, no real communion. The basic communities are an attempt to break down this indifferent monolith into working units. Five to
fiteeen people in the same neighborhood
gather in each others' homes. When a group
becomes larger than this, they divide up and
form another group, and in this way multiply
themselves within a neighborhood, or even in
the same block. The idea is to try and reflect

what it means exactly to be a Christian in the
world, in my country, in my neighborhood today. In what way do my actions relate to my
Christian confession? When we talk about the
role of Christ, and that He came in order for
us to have life and life in its fullness, how do
we relate that fullness of life which the Christian Church talks so much about with the
miserable expression of life here and now?
These types of concerns, along with people
praying, reading, and studying the *Bible*
together, are the substantial elements of every
basic Christian community. Much creative
thinking and action has derived from this communal Biblical approach. We Protestants tend
to think that one needs a lot of understanding
and preparation in seminary before we can
comprehend the Biblical message. The
Catholics teach that the Magisterium of the
Church is the only one who can interpret the
Bible. It is absolutely amazing what people,
with no formal learning, have to say, for they
are not ignorant; they know more about life in
many instances than those of us who have been
domesticated through the educational process;
they react more instinctively when confronted
with the Word. The Biblical studies which are
coming out of this kind of experience are really
great. Brazil has published a couple of small
books as a result of these conversations around
Bible. It is out of this concrete sharing of
life's experiences that governments have accused them of being subversive. Yet, the whole
reality of Latin America is subversive. There is
nothing to eat—that is what you share. The
Brazilian Bishop, Helda Camera, once told us

in the Catholic University of Chile that he has been reluctant to repeat Psalm 23 ever since he visited a very poor parish where the people were repeating this Psalm. He asked them if they really had "no wants." They then started relating all of their needs, for they were living in extreme misery. I sincerely feel that the gift which these basic Christian communities have given to the Church as a whole is freeing the Word and Spirit of God from the bindings our traditions have held it in for so long.

QUESTION: I would like to ask for a survey report on the activity of Marxists in South America. I think the Pope at Puebla—while he restrained the Church from directly being involved in a sort of paramilitary liberation—I think he advocated that laypeople do something to stir things in the direction where there is a need to be stirred. I think because the Holy Father comes from a Communist country he knows that the Church can survive even if Communists make the moves. So I wonder now if it's too much a stress of the Christian imagination that perhaps, as Cyrus was the instrument to free God's people from oppression, perhaps the Marxists could be the instrument, and then the basic Christian communities would sustain the faith regardless of the external regime. Could you comment?

ANSWER: I think that that in itself is a very good comment, and it could very well be the case. The action and presence of some political forces, including Marxism, in the Latin American context, is a call to attention, a warning, to a Church that has been too complacent in the past, and was not really aware of the injustices

prevailing in society. It has been too much concerned with preaching a kind of acceptance
and resignation to the fatal elements in history
and nature, instead of providing a dynamic
force for people to transform their situation.
I think this could very well be one of the roles
that Marxism is playing at present, as the
Babylonian forces did in the past, as have
other forces done in our most recent history.
I'm not afraid of any political movement; I
think some are better than others, but it seems
to me that the Christian faith is strong enough
to sustain itself, and people, in the midst of the
most adverse conditions. If the Christian
Church, and the Christian faith, has been able
to make such an impact today, considering the
nature of the Latin American society, I don't
think that any political ideology can minimize
it. On the contrary, I think that maybe because
of the courageous witness by the Christian
people of Latin America, a strong, and apparently monolithic ideology such as Marxism
will be permeated and transformed. In the
future, whatever contribution this ideology is
going to have vis-á-vis the presence of the
Christian faith, I'm sure it's going to give us a
type of society that will completely change
present injustices, but always keeping the
values of the human person, the dignity of the
human being which is so dear to the Christian
tradition. I'm not afraid of what will happen
in the future as long as the Christian faith, and
the Christian Church, is willing to stand on the
side of the poor and the oppressed.

NOTES

[1]J. H. Elliott, "The Impact of America on Europe was Complex and Uncertain," in *Latin America, A Historical Reader,* edited by Lewis Hanke (Little, Brown and Company, Boston, 1974), p. 29.

[2]*Ibid.,* p.30

[3]*Ibid.,* pp. 43-44.

[4]Cf. Johnson, Dale L., *Dependence and Underdevelopment,* pp. 73.

[5]Galeano, Eduardo, *Open Veins of Latin America,* p. 13.

[6]*The Church in the Present Day Transformation of Latin America in the Light of the Council,* Volume II, Conclusions, p. 61.

[7]*Final Document,* Puebla 1979.

[8]*The Desert is Fertile* (Pillar Book, N.Y. 1974), p. 8.

[9]Mimeographed edition, p. 1.

[10]Dom Helder Camara, *op. cit.,* p. 23.

[11]Mimeographed edition, p. 1.

[12]Cf. Leon Portilla, Miguel, "The Grief of the Conquered: Broken Spears Lie in the Roads," in Lewis Hanke, *op. cit.,* pp. 56-62.

[13]*Ibid.,* pp. 64-65.

[14]Quoted in Quigley, Thomas, *Freedom and Unfreedom in the Americas,* (IDOC Book, N.Y. 1971), p. 72.

[15]*The Church in the Present Day Transformation of Lation America in the Light of the Council, op. cit.,* pp. 188-189.

[16]There are two documents that should be mentioned here: (1) The Rockefeller Report (1969) and (2) The Report of the Rand Corporation (1972) to the State Department. In both documents the Catholic Church received special attention. The first affirms that the Catholic Church is infiltrated by Marxists and, therefore, cannot be trusted, and the second is concerned with the Catholic critiques of the capitalistic system and liberal democracy.

[17]Centro Ecumencio de Documentacao e Informacao (CEDI), Rio de Janeiro, Brazil, Dec. 1978.

[18]*Ibid.,* pp. 8-9.

[19]*Ibid.,* p. 14.

[20]*DIAL:* Diffusion de l'information sur l'Amerique Latine, Paris, No. 497, Jan. 11, 1979.

[21]CEDI, *op. cit.,* p. 41.

[22]See *Infra.,* p. 28.

[23]"Global Perspective on Suffering and Hope," in *Testimony Amid Asian Suffering,* Christian Conference of Asia, 1977, p. 45.

Chapter 8

DOES CHRISTIANITY PROCLAIM REDEMPTION IN AND THROUGH OR DESPITE SUFFERING — SPECIAL EMPHASIS ON THE BLACK EXPERIENCE
Dr. Henry James Young

The question of redemption is a major concern of the Christian faith. Within the context of salvation, following the thought of Paul Tillich, redemption becomes the issue of "to be or not to be." The issue of what does it mean to be saved or redeemed has always been central in the Christian faith. There are at least two dimensions to this problem. One focuses on the fact that salvation or redemption is to be distinguished from both ultimate negativity and from that which leads to ultimate negativity. Ultimate negativity refers to condemnation or eternal death, the loss of inner telos of one's existence, exclusion from the universality of God's kingdom, and exclusion from eternal life.[1]

The historical context out of which black Americans have come has continually made the issue "to be or not to be" a fundamental dilemma. At one period in their history the slave owners had the power to determine the being or nonbeing of blacks. Blacks constantly lived under the threat and fear of death. The slave owners projected themselves as the masters and attempted to force blacks to conform. They projected themselves as divinely commissioned to stand between God and the slaves. How did they respond to eternal death, the loss of the inner self, the nature of God and eternal life in light of slavery and oppression? In fact, this chapter will examine these questions, seeking to show the various ways black Americans throughout their history have attempted to deal meaningfully with their sufferings from the context of the Christian faith.

Another dimension of this chapter will examine redemption in terms of its implication for the achievement of freedom and liberation of blacks in the present world. Blacks have never interpreted redemption in terms of a process taking place exclusively in preparation for life after death. In interpreting redemption they have maintained a balance between the quest for freedom and liberation in this life and the desire to reach fulfillment in God in life after death. Both dimensions of this dual redemptive eschatological experience will be interpreted from the perspective of black suffering. The social, political, and economic aspects of black suffering will be dealt with in the context of the Christian faith.

What were the social, political, and economic implications of how black Americans understood God and the redemptive process? Did they remove God-talk from the arena of social activism? Did they feel that God was responsible for their suffering? Did they maintain faith in God despite suffering? Or did they repudiate God because of their suffering? Beginning with a discussion of theodicy within the context of the black experience, this chapter will also provide a historical perspective of black suffering from the African slave trade to the present, showing how blacks have interpreted the Christian notion of redemption in terms of its implications for affecting social, political, and economic change within the black community.

Theodicy and the Black Experience

The theological category for all dimensions of evil, including the many ways of resolving it, is theodicy. Theodicy means God and justice. It refers to the attempt to defend the intrinsic love, justice, and righteousness of God in face of the manifold presence of evil in the world.

Based on the traditional Christian conception of God as infinite, absolute in goodness, all loving, perfect, merciful, nonpartial in justice, and omnipotent, the problem of human suffering becomes a dilemma. The dilemma is an apparent contradiction between the traditional Christian presuppositions about God and the presence of human suffering.[2]

One of the most pressing problems in the history of black religious thought has been the tension between the traditional Christian conception of God and the phenomenon of black suffering. This problem can be understood best in the form of the following dilemma: Either God wishes to eradicate black suffering and is unable; or God is able, but is unwilling to eradicate black suffering; or God is neither willing nor able to eradicate black suffering; or God is both willing and able to do it. If God is willing and is unable to eradicate black suffering, he is impotent. To think of God as impotent is not in accordance with the traditional Christian understanding of God's omnipotence. If God is able and unwilling to eradicate black suffering, he is partial. To think of God as partial does not conform to the Christian notion of God's justice. If God is neither willing nor able to eliminate black suffering, he is removed from the religious existential dimension.[3] If God is detached and removed from the dimension of black suffering, he has no relevance to the human predicament. This is not in keeping with the Christian notion of God. But if God is both willing and able to eradicate evil, then how do we explain the history of black suffering in America? This theological dilemma represents the focus of this chapter.

THE SLAVE TRADE AND REDEMPTION

The slave trade[4] was indeed a nightmare in the history of black America. It represents one of the worst human tragedies in American history. Historians are not sure exactly how many blacks were transplanted from Africa to America. And when one takes into consideration the number of slaves who were killed in the process of being captured, those that protested aboard ship and were thrown overboard to the sharks, and those who died aboard ship from disease and suffocation, the number becomes astronomical.

It is estimated that approximately 900,000 slaves were imported to America in the 16th century, 2,750,000 in the 17th, 7,000,000 in the 18th, and 4,000,000 in the 19th century. These were indeed conservative estimates. When the total picture is taken under consideration, including those who survived the importation and those who died en route to America, the figure becomes 5 to 15 million.[5] What was the slave trade like?

The slave trade consisted of pious captains holding prayer services twice a day aboard their slave ships; one captain is reported to have written the famous hymn, "How Sweet the Name of Jesus Sounds."[6] Africans were forced to desert their villages, families, and relatives. The slave trade consisted of "a bishop sitting on an ivory chair on a wharf in the Congo and extending his fat hand in wholesale baptism of slaves who were rowed beneath him, going in chains to the slave ships."[7]

The crowded conditions on the slave ships contributed to the incidence of disease and epidemics during the voyage to America. Smallpox was a common disease of the period and few slave ships escaped it. Another common disease aboard ship was flux. The symptoms of this disease were pains in the head and back, chills, fever, and nausea; it baffled many blacks and was fatal in most cases. Hunger strikes aboard ship created additional unfavorable health conditions and brought about more illnesses. The mortality rate on the ships was increased because of close quarters.[8] John Hope Franklin points out that

> Perhaps no more than half the slaves shipped from Africa ever became effective workers in the New World. Many of those that had not died of disease or committed suicide by jumping overboard were permanently disabled by the ravages of some dread disease or by maiming which often resulted from the struggle against the chains.[9]

How did black Americans deal with the slave trade theologically? When they became exposed to Christianity, how did they reconcile the tragedy of the slave trade with the love, mercy, justice, righteousness, and goodness of God? Nathaniel Paul, a black Baptist minister who served as pastor of a church in Albany, New York, spoke directly to this issue in an address he delivered on July 5, 1827. He begins in a poetic fashion by asking the question "Tell me, ye mighty waters, why did ye sustain the ponderous load of misery?"[10] He asks the winds, why is it that you execute the process of drifting the slave ships onward to the still more dismal state of slavery? And to the waves of the ocean, he asks, why did you refuse to overwhelm the slave ships and cause them to sink? What is the point of Nathaniel Paul's questions? He says, "Then should they have slept sweetly in the bosom of the great deep, and to have been hid from sorrow."[11] At this point, Paul seems to be entertaining the possibility that it would have been better for all the slaves to have perished on the slave ships, rather than to have experienced the cruelty of slavery. Does Paul really mean this? Or is he articulating an episodic experience of frustration, pessimism, confusion, and doubt?

In the above questions Nathaniel Paul is referring to an experience that many slaves on the slave ships came to grips with, the phenomenon of death. In light of the inhuman conditions they were forced to live under, death for many was perceived as a form of freedom and liberation. Many believed that the conditions of slavery were worse than death. This experience was more to the slaves than a mere act of suicide. It was "a primary disclosure of an elemental affirmation having to do directly, not only with the ultimate dignity of the human spirit, but also with the ultimate basis of self respect."[12] A spiritual which emerged from the black experience demonstrating that for many blacks, slavery was worse than death, says,

> Oh Freedom! Oh Freedom!
> Oh Freedom, I love thee!
> And before I'll be a slave,
> I'll be buried in my grave,
> And go home to my Lord and be free.

In spite of Nathaniel Paul's questions about death as an alternative to slavery, he accepts the fact that blacks did survive the slave trade. He then begins to challenge God's activity in light of the slave trade. He asks:

> And, oh thou immaculate God, be not angry with us, while we come into this thy sanctuary, and make the bold inquiry in this thy holy temple, why it was that thou didst look on with the calm indifference of an unconcerned spectator, when thy holy law was violated, thy divine authority despised and a portion of thine own creatures reduced to a state of mere vassalage and misery.[13]

Here Nathaniel Paul exposes the contradiction between slavery and God's nature.

Based on the Christian understanding of God, Paul knew that there was inconsistency between what blacks experienced during the slave trade and what God represented. When he says that God acted as an indifferent unconcerned spectator, he pushes to the core of theodicy. To accept this is to remove God from the dimension of human suffering, thus making him exclusively the God of intellectual philosophical speculation and not the God of religious human emotion. But Nathaniel Paul doesn't end here. He doesn't conclude with pessimism, confusion, and doubt. Neither does he attempt to avoid what he perceives as a fundamental religious paradox.

Nathaniel Paul concludes with an approach to theodicy which became very central in the development of black religious thought in America. He concluded his challenge of God with the words, "Hear Him proclaiming from the skies—Be still, and know that I am God! Clouds and darkness are round about me; yet righteousness and judgment are the habitation of my throne.[14] Paul did not feel that he could place the dilemma of theodicy completely into a rational framework. After he had exhausted his attempt to rationally show the contradiction between God's nature and the tragedy of the slave trade, he ended up with an affirmation of God rather than a repudiation of him. He concludes with a firm belief in the righteousness, justice, love, mercy, and goodness of God. And as a result, he argued that the enslavement of blacks would one day be eradicated. He makes this emphatically clear when he says:

> Did I believe that it would always continue, and that man to the end of time would be permitted with impunity to usurp the same undue authority over his fellows. I would disallow any allegiance or obligation I was under to my fellow creatures, or any submission that I owed to the laws of my country; I would deny the superintending power of divine Providence in the affairs of this life; I would ridicule the religion of the Savior of the world, and treat as the worst of men the ministers of the everlasting gospel; I would consider my Bible as a book of false and delusive fables, and commit it to the flames; nay, I would still go farther; I would at once confess myself an atheist, and deny the existence of God.[15]

SLAVERY, REDEMPTION, AND CHRISTIAN HOPE

When a small band of blacks landed in Jamestown, Virginia in 1619, the long and rugged enslavement of blacks in America originated. Every effort was made by the slave owners to systematically force blacks to abandon their

African heritage.[16] Blacks were forced to learn a new language, their family ties were destroyed, they were introduced to a new religious tradition, and their entire American cultural tradition was disrupted. As slaves they were not viewed as persons, but as chattel property. This gave the slaves no rights or privileges to be respected.

Slave owners used the *Bible* to sanction the institution of slavery. They made every effort to indoctrinate the slaves into believing that it was God's will for them to be slaves. They knew that if the slaves accepted this understanding of God, the future of the institution of slavery would be sustained. The slaves accepted Christianity very quickly and adhered to its principles as much as the slave owners would permit them. Since many of the slaves couldn't read, in large measure they were greatly dependent upon the slave owners for instruction in scripture and Christian principles. But there was something peculiar about what the slave owners taught the slaves about the scriptures and what they actually believed. Although the dominant trend suggested that most slaves did not believe the propaganda put out by slave owners regarding their version of the scriptures, some slaves accepted such teachings as God's will for them to be in bondage. Frederick Douglas said that he "met, at the South, many good, religious colored people who were under the delusion that God required them to submit to slavery, and to wear their chains with meekness and humility."[17] Not only did Douglas repudiate this understanding of God and refer to it as nonsense, but said that he lost patience when he found blacks weak enough to believe such stuff.[18]

The blacks who accepted the slave owners' teaching about God[19] dealt with the dilemma of theodicy from a compensatory perspective. Since accepting slavery was the will of God, they believed that God would reward them in the hereafter or in life after death, which was to them a redemptive process. E. Franklin Frazier interprets the body of black spirituals from this other-worldly redemptive outlook.

Frazier feels that the spirituals reveal a view of the world as ruled by the Providence of God.[20] If the world is ruled by God's Providence, then the slaves whom Frederick Douglas came in contact with asked, "Why doesn't God eliminate slavery?"[21] Douglas couldn't answer this and neither could the slaves. Therefore they resorted to thinking of heaven as the compensatory redemptive process of being liberated from the pains, cruelty, agony, despair, and dehumanization of slavery. A spiritual depicting heaven is:

> I've got a robe; you've got a robe,
>   All God's children got a robe,
> When I get to heaven goin' to put on my robe
>   Goin' to shout all over God's heaven.

Following the compensatory trend, slave owners taught slaves that whites ruled from God and that to question this divine right was to incur judgment and wrath from heaven. The immediate sign of God's wrath and judgment was for the slave to receive punishment. Slaves were taught that their condition was the fulfillment of the will of the slave owner and of God. Some catechisms for the religious instruction of slaves commonly bore such passages as:

> Q. Who gave you a master and a mistress?
> A. God gave them to me.
> Q. Who says that you must obey them?
> A. God says that I must.[22]

Many of the slaves did not adhere to the compensatory approach in dealing with the contradiction between God's nature and their social condition. If the majority of slaves had accepted the compensatory approach, it is highly possible that they would not have survived the institution of slavery. They interpreted Christianity in light of what they perceived to be the unchanging truths of God, on the one hand, and how these truths related to their particular condition, on the other hand. They perceived the unchanging truth of God to mean that slavery was morally wrong, sinful, and opposed to the will of God. The slave owners taught them one thing, but with their creative genius they believed the opposite.

Whereas the compensatory approach was to accept slavery and wait for a reward from God in the heavens after death, an alternative was to interpret redemption in light of freedom and liberation in this present world. The slaves were not docile, passive, and unconcerned about changing their social condition.[23] In fact, the black church was born in protest to the institution of slavery.[24]

In examining the origin and development of the spirituals it becomes apparent that in many instances when the slaves were singing about escaping to the North, the slave owners felt that they were referring to heaven or life after death. Frederick Douglas gives an example in the spiritual,

> O Canaan, sweet Canaan,
> I am bound for the land of Canaan.

Douglas' point is that this spiritual meant more than a hope of reaching heaven. It meant "to reach the North, and the North was our Canaan."[25] Obviously, this spiritual did contain a dual meaning for the slaves. At times it referred to heaven or life after death, and at other times it referred to the North.

Howard Thurman shows that even when the slaves used the compensatory model and looked for their redemptive reward in heaven, they did it in protest to the institution of slavery. How did the slaves do this? They had to employ a degree of reasoning about their social condition in contrast to that of the slave owners in light of redemption and heaven. They had often heard the slave owners considered themselves fit for heaven, but so did the slaves. The slaves reasoned, "There must be two separate heavens—no, this could not be true, because there is only one God. God cannot be divided in this way. [We] have it! [We are] having [our] hell now,"[26] but when we die we shall have our heaven. The slave owners were having their heaven, and when they died, the slaves thought that they would have their hell. In this regard, they sang,

> But everybody talking 'bout Heaven
> Ain't going there.

Thurman views the above spiritual as one of the authentic songs of protest emerging from the black experience. It was sung in anticipation of a time when there would be no slave row in the church, no slave gallery in the church, no segregation and discrimination, and no badge of racial or social stigma. It looks toward the time when there will be freedom and liberation. The mood of this spiritual is that "In God's presence at least there would be freedom; slavery is no part of the purpose or the plan of God.[27] Because they firmly believed that slavery was not a part of God's plan, they could hope and look toward freedom in spite of the experience of slavery. If they had believed that slavery was God's plan and purpose, they would have become defeated; they would not have been able to make sense out of God's love in the midst of slavery. In what sense did God love the slaves? Did he protect them from the slave owners? If slavery is contrary to the plan of God, then why did he permit it? The answer to these questions form the tap root of black religion, and is best expressed in the spiritual, "A Balm in Gilead,"

> There is a balm in Gilead,
> To make the spirit whole,
> There is a balm in Gilead,
> To heal the sin-sick soul.

Based on empirical evidence, the slaves had nothing for which to hope. The slave owners were not about to let them go free. The institution of slavery was based on economics and therefore was protected in every sense of the word. But because of their faith in God, the slaves were able to transcend their immediate situation and anticipate a day in this life when slavery would be no more. This is, as Thurman correctly puts it, the basic difference between optimism and pessimism. "It is an optimism that uses the pessimism of life as raw material out of which it creates its own strength."[28]

The foundation of this optimism and hope of the slaves was grounded in an understanding of the world or life itself as fundamentally just. They felt that life has its own restraints. They contended that there is a moral order in the world by which every person is bound. This moral principle they believed was inescapable, and applies to all people. The slaves then proclaimed the world as just in spite of the brutalities of slavery. This justice did not emanate exclusively from God. It was under the eyes of God. The slaves felt that the injustices of slavery occurred, but they didn't believe God was for them. God was not responsible for slavery. When the slaves came to this conclusion, they found a way of dealing with the dilemma of theodicy.

They knew that the institution of slavery was a contradiction to the nature of God. But the spiritual, "A Balm In Gilead," suggests "that the contradictions of life are not in themselves either final or ultimate." The slave owners attempted to indoctrinate the slaves into believing that life is fixed, finished, and unchanging. People are caught in the agonizing grip of inevitability, and all possibility for changing them is reduced to zero. The slave cannot change his social condition as a slave and the slave owner cannot alter his condition. With this theological understanding the slave owners tried to undermine all hope from the slaves. They attempted to create a situation in which the future for the slaves in this life would in no way differ from their present condition. They attempted to interpret the world in a manner that set conditions against the slaves, so that if they died in ultimate defiance of the institution of slavery, their death would only be a futile gesture and an act of fatalism and defeatism. But because the slaves believed that the contradictions of life are not in themselves ultimate, they were always able to have a growing edge of hope in the most tragic and barren circumstances. The slaves were never robbed of hope;[29] they refused to submit their will and spirit to the institution of slavery.

Although many slaves believed that redemption for them would come through the sufferings they were forced to encounter, the dominant trend which flows through the historical drama of the black experience is one that looks for redemption despite suffering. In other words, they didn't feel that they needed to endure the pain and cruelty of slavery in order to experience God's redemption. For this reason they always resisted slavery in every way. Resistance took many shapes and forms. Henry Highland Garnet and David Walker, both exponents of a theology of resistance, provide two classic examples of resistance found in the history of blacks in America.

David Walker published *The Walker Appeal* in 1829 and it became a focal point of resistance among the slaves. He begins with the contention that God is omnipotent, meaning that he rules in both the heavens and earth. God is sovereign and stands as the ruler of the world. Throughout *The Appeal* Walker refers to the justice of God very frequently. He doesn't think of God as being responsible for the condition of the slaves; he attributes it to the sinfulness of mankind; Walker takes great care in establishing the fact that slavery is unjust in that it goes against the justice of God. And because he thought of God as just and righteous, Walker felt that in the future God would intervene and destroy the institution of slavery. He says:

> They forget that God rules in the armies of heaven and among the inhabitants of the earth, having his ears continually open to the cries, tears and groans of his oppressed people; and being a just and holy Being will at one day appear fully in behalf of the oppressed, and arrest the progress of the avaricious oppressors; for although the destruction of the oppressors God may not effect by the oppressed, yet the Lord our God will bring other destructions upon them.[30]

In order for the slaves to experience redemption, Walker believed that they had to be liberated from the bondage of slavery. It was God's responsibility to deliver them. Since God was in control of the world and opposed to slavery, Walker felt that he would one day destroy slavery. He therefore appealed to America to either repent of the sins of slavery or encounter God's destruction. It was his thinking that if America repented of slavery, God would forgive them and redemption would be possible without an act of destruction. Buf if America refused to repent, he believed that destruction was inevitable. "Can the Americans escape God Almighty? If they do, can he be to us a God of justice? God is just, and I know it."[31] On this basis Walker exalted the slaves into believing that God would not suffer them always to be oppressed, but that their suffering will come to an end within history.

Henry Highland Garnet interprets the suffering of black Americans in terms of their Christian and moral obligation to resist slavery. In responding to the institution of slavery, he contended, "To such degradation it is sinful in the extreme for you to make voluntary submission."[32] He felt that the social, economic, and political conditions operative in the institution of slavery were not conducive to permitting blacks to adhere to the principles of Christianity. "The diabolical injustice by which your liberties are cloven down, neither God, nor angels, or just men command you to suffer for a single moment. Therefore it is your solemn and imperative duty to use every means both moral, intellectual, and physical, that promises success."[33] What did Garnet mean by this?

Garnet was not advocating physical violence in his attack against the institution of slavery as some thought.[34] After attempting to establish a theological justification for blacks to oppose slavery, he made an effort to mobilize their resistance. He agreed that redemption was not possible for blacks within the context of slavery. He called upon them to overcome the suffering of slavery because it hindered God's redemptive process. He wanted the slaves to organize a strike in protest. "Brethren, arise, arise! Strike for your lives and liberties. Now is the day and the hour. Let every slave throughout the land do this, and the days of slavery are numbered.[35]

Garnet did not put the freedom and liberation of blacks within the theological context of futuristic eschatology. Neither was his approach of a compensatory nature. He called for the immediate eradication of slavery and attempted to create a situation in which the slaves and slave owners had to make a radical decision. The slave owners were challenged to repent of their sins and voluntarily allow the slaves to go free. He said this was the mandate from God and that the slave owners were obligated to obey God's will. He challenged the slaves to refuse to work as slaves, organize a slave strike, and to demand remuneration for their labor.

CONTEMPORARY BLACK AMERICA: GOD, JUSTICE, AND SUFFERING

The theological questions raised by blacks historically about suffering recur among contemporary blacks. The tension between God's nature and the presence of black suffering has never been definitely answered. Each generation has attempted to provide viable answers to the problem, but none has resolved it. However, there are similarities in the ways in which each generation has dealt with the problem. The fundamental theme which seems to be operative in each generation is the effort to defend the righteousness, goodness, love, mercy, and power of God in spite of the manifold presence of black suffering. This is the strong faith affirmation which has been present among blacks ever since the origination of black religion in America. But this doesn't mean that the faith has been removed from doubt, frustrations, anxiety, dread, and suspicion of God's activity. Nathaniel Paul raised such questions, reflecting a sense of pessimism. And out of the pessimism emerged a reaffirmation of faith.

The questions that Nathaniel Paul raised to God, in a very similar fashion, recur in contemporary black America. W. E. B. DuBois, a black intellectual, raised critical questions to God in 1906 shortly after the famous Atlanta riot.[36] DuBois was in Lowndes County, Alabama, during the riot. When he heard about it, he immediately caught the train and returned to Atlanta. On the train he wrote his classic piece, *A Litany at Atlanta*. In it he raises some critical questions to God about justice in light of black suffering. Reflecting on the cruelty of the Atlanta riot, DuBois asked God, "Is this Thy justice, O Father, that guile be easier than innocence and the innocent be crucified for the guilt of the untouched?"[37] He wonders is the God of the Fathers dead. If He is not dead, then DuBois feels that He must be asleep. Or maybe the Atlanta Riot of 1906 was a divine act of justice for blacks. DuBois comments, "Doth not this justice of hell stink in Thy nostrils, O God? How long shall the mounting flood of innocent blood roar in Thine ears and pound in our hearts for vengeance?"[38]

DuBois continues with an assessment of the condition of the black experience before God. He describes it as bewildered, passion-tossed, mad with the madness of a mobbed, mocked, and murdered people. Pleading before the throne of God, DuBois said, "We raise our shackled hands and charge Thee, God, by the bones of our stolen fathers, by the tears of our dead mothers, by the very blood of Thy crucified Christ: What meaneth this?"[39] He tells God to sit no longer blind and deaf to the suffering of black Americans.

DuBois doesn't end with his feeling of pessimism. But within the tradition of Nathaniel Paul and the black experience, he ends up with hope and optimism. He uses the pessimism of the Atlanta Riot as raw material from which emerges a profound sense of optimism. He ends with an affirmation. "Thou art still the God of our black fathers."[40] On what grounds does DuBois make this affirmation? He doesn't make it on the grounds of how God demonstrated His love and mercy for blacks by delivering them from suffering. He realizes that he cannot reconcile the reality of black suffering with how the Christian faith views God. He concludes by saying "Vengeance is Mine; I will repay, saith the Lord."[41].

Continuing within the tradition of Christian hope as reflected in the black religious tradition, DuBois transcends the reality of black suffering and ascends to the conviction that God, through the help of mankind, will eventually eradicate black suffering. When DuBois says that vengeance belongs to God and He will repay, he is acknowledging God's ultimate plan for the elimination of suffering. Recognizing the fact that the injustice perpetrated by whites on the black community needed to be reckoned with, DuBois felt that God had a mandate based on His nature to alter the situation. At this point, DuBois is very similar to Nathaniel Paul in his analysis. This approach in part acknowledges the fact that there are aspects of God's activity which are incomprehensible. DuBois and Nathaniel Paul question things about the nature of God and His activity in the world, which contributed greatly to an affirmation of God that moved beyond the empirical reality of suffering.

VICARIOUS SUFFERING

A significant way in which black Americans have dealt with the problem of black suffering is from a vicarious perspective. The chief exponent of this theological orientation is Martin Luther King, Jr. This approach looks at suffering differently from the other approaches discussed. The other approaches discussed viewed suffering as an undesirable phenomenon that blacks should attempt to escape. Henry Highland Garnet challenged the slaves to reject suffering on the grounds that it is in contradiction to

God's will. W. E. B. DuBois opposed the suffering of blacks and called God to intervene and eradicate it. His hope was that eventually God would act in behalf of blacks and change their social, economic, and political conditions. David Walker felt that God had a mandate to ultimately act in behalf of blacks based on His justice.

Martin Luther King, Jr. interpreted black suffering in terms of its vicarious redemptive possibilities. Before fully understanding his approach to suffering it is necessary to examine his philosophy of nonviolence. Nonviolence for King was more than a strategy or tactic for effecting social change: it was a fundamental philosophical principle which he perceived as grounded in the truth of reality. He related black suffering to the cross of Jesus Christ. He believed that suffering, if properly understood, has redemptive possibilities for both blacks and whites.

King made it clear that nonviolence was not for crowds. He contested that if a person used the nonviolent method because he was afraid or merely because he lacked the instruments of violence, he is not nonviolent in the true sense of the word. Nonviolence doesn't mean that a person should submit to any wrong. It doesn't mean that a person has to use violence to fight the wrong. He referred to his approach as nonviolent resistance, and thought of it as ultimately the way of the strong. He made it emphatically clear that although nonviolent resistance is passive resistance, it is not a sort of do-nothing method. The method is passive physically, but strongly active spiritually. It is not passive nonresistance to evil, it is active nonviolent resistance to evil.[42]

Basic to King's philosophy of nonviolence is the principle of the inherent worth of each individual. It does not seek to humiliate or defeat the opponent but to win his friendship and understanding. The end of the nonviolence process is toward redemption and reconciliation. He viewed the consequence of nonviolence as moving toward the creation of what he referred to as the beloved community. But the aftermath of violence he felt would be tragic bitterness.

A third characteristic of King's philosophy of non-violence is that its attack is directed against the forces of evil rather than the persons committing the evil. "It is evil that the nonviolent resister seeks to defeat, not the persons victimized by evil"[43] He didn't view the tension as existing between blacks and whites but between justice and injustice, between the forces of light and the forces of darkness. If a victory emerged he felt that it not be one for blacks, but rather a victory for justice, righteousness, goodness, and unselfish love.

A fourth characteristic of nonviolent resistance is a willingness to accept suffering without retaliation. One has to be willing to accept inflicted brutality from the opponent without retaliation. He said to blacks, "Rivers of blood may have to flow before we gain our freedom, but it must be our blood."[44] The main principle operative in King's approach to suffering here is the notion of redemption. He firmly believed that unearned suffering is redemptive. "Things of fundamental importance to people are not secured by reason alone, but have to be purchased with their suffering."[45] He believed that suffering was infinitely more powerful than anything else for converting the opponent and making redemption possible.

King's philosophy of nonviolent resistance not only avoids external physical violence but also internal violence of the spirit. The Christian mandate, as he interpreted it, was for the nonviolent resister to refuse to hate the opponent. At the center of his nonviolent philosophy is the element of love. His understanding of love differed from both the Greek expressions of *philia* and *eros*. In Platonic philosophy *eros* referred to the soul in search for the divine; now it has come to mean aesthetic or romantic love. *Philia* refers to reciprocal or mutual love. King's approach to the Christian love ethic was grounded in *agape,* which refers to unconditional love.

He said that *agape* is not a weak and passive love; it is love in action. It seeks to preserve and create community.

Agape is a willingness to sacrifice one's self in the interest of saving the opponent. It is a willingness to go to any length to preserve and restore community. It is a willingness to forgive others to restore community. He viewed the cross as the eternal expression of the length to which God has gone to restore community. And the resurrection is the symbol of God's victory over the forces of evil which seek to block community.[46] At any cost, King felt that blacks were compelled by God himself to employ love in resisting the forces of suffering and evil. This he felt would facilitate and enhance the actualization of the beloved community. Therefore, one must always meet physical force with soul force, and hate with love. He says:

> He who works against community is working against the whole of creation. Therefore, if I respond to hate with a reciprocal hate I do nothing but intensify the cleavage in broken community. I can only close the gap in ʼbroken community by meeting hate with love. If I meet hate with hate, I become depersonalized, because creation is so designed that my personality can only be fulfilled in the context of community.[47]

Another aspect of King's philosophy of nonviolence which helps to illuminate his understanding of vicarious suffering is the conviction that the universe is on the side of justice. This provided great hope for the black community. Since God is on the side of justice, King believed that black suffering would one day be eradicated in this life. He maintained this hope throughout his life. It is very similar to the element of hope found within the history of black Americans.

King contended that faith in the future arises from the faith that God is just and good. In keeping with the black religious tradition, he says, "When one believes this, he knows that the contradictions of life are neither final nor ultimate. He can walk through the dark night with the radiant conviction that all things work together for good for those that love God."[48] He thought of history as the story of evil forces that advance with seemingly irresistible power, but ultimately they are crushed with the battle forces of justice. He argued that there is a law in the moral world—"a silent, invisible imperative, akin to the laws in the physical world—which reminds us that life will work only in a certain way."[49] This certain way is toward the ultimate eventuation of the good in spite of evil forces being continually present.

When Martin Luther King, Jr. was killed in 1968, segments of the black community took a different approach to suffering and redemption. Many blacks began to question whether America was capable of responding seriously to the problem of racism. They wondered whether America ever perceived herself as having a moral dilemma in reference to blacks. Many blacks felt that since the white community responded to the philosophy of violence by killing its principal exponent, Martin Luther King, Jr., they had to move at another level of dealing with suffering. Their approach was to move a step beyond the nonviolent approach of King. This approach resulted in violence which was the opposite of King's philosophy. King was able to pull all ethnic groups together around a common problem, namely, direct confrontative nonviolent resistance against injustices perpetrated upon blacks. The philosophy of King was based on inclusiveness, but the immediate theological orientation among many blacks following his death was exclusiveness. This led to the violence and social unrest that followed King's death.

The violence and social unrest of the 1960s came to a climax in the many race riots which literally paralyzed most major cities in America. After the riots the President of the United States asked the Commission on Civil Disorders to study the riots and make recommendations for dealing effectively with the existing problems between white and black communities. The Commission concluded that racism was the cause of the riots. They also concluded that America is polarized into two separate unequal communities, one black and one white.

BLACK THEOLOGY, SUFFERING, AND REDEMPTION

The agony, despair, frustration, and discontent of the 1960s gave rise to the development of black theology. Black theology was reflective of the increasing desire of black Americans to achieve freedom, self-determination, self-sufficiency, self-direction, and to participate significantly in the mainstream of American life. The orientation of black theology was to move black Americans toward an interdependent relationship with the white community as opposed to perpetuating the dependency complex blacks were accustomed to experiencing.

Black theology in its systematic formulation was launched by James H. Cone of Union Theological Seminary, New York, in 1969, upon the publication of his epoch-making volume *Black Theology and Black Power.* In it Cone sought to interpret the black power movement from a theological perspective. He believed that the black power movement was God's message to 20th century America, and that the task of the theologian was to interpret this message theologically. He challenged black and white Christians on the premise that black power was "Christ's central message to twentieth-century America. And unless the empirical denominational church makes a determined effort to recapture the man Jesus through a total identification with the suffering poor as expressed in Black Power, that church will become exactly what Christ is not."[50] Here Cone took a decided break from the theological approach of Martin Luther King, Jr.

King did not interpret the problem of black suffering in light of the polarization between blacks and whites. He viewed the problem as one of injustice manifested in black suffering and perpetuated by whites. Therefore, the issue for King was with injustice and the attempt to convert the sinful deeds of whites. But Cone developed an ontology grounded in a polarization between blacks and whites. Although Cone's theology begins with this polarization, it ends with a synthesis between blacks and whites. How does he do this, and what implications does it have for his understanding of redemption and suffering?

He begins by defining blackness from a dual dimensional mode. First, he views blackness as a physiological trait. In this sense, it refers to a particular black-skinned people in America who are victims of suffering inflicted upon them by whites. Because blacks have suffered unmeritedly throughout the history of America, Cone feels that they have the key to redemption and reconciliation between themselves and whites. Secondly, he defines blackness as an ontological symbol for all people who participate in the liberation of man from oppression. He argues that this is the universal note in his theology. Blackness then contains both the particular and universal dimemsion of Cone's theology.[51]

Based on his ontological analysis of blackness, Cone argues that the redemptive process for whites happens when they undergo the true experience of conversion when they first die to whiteness and are reborn anew to struggle against oppression. At this point, he contends that there is a place for whites in the struggles for black liberation. "Here reconciliation becomes God's gift of blackness through the oppressed of the land. But it must be made absolutely clear that it is the black community that decides both the authenticity of white conversion and also the place these converts will play in the black struggle of freedom."[52]

The chief critic of James Cone's theological orientation is J. Deotis Roberts. J. Deotis advanced his attack on Cone's theological program in 1971 with the publication of his *Liberation and Reconciliation: A Black Theology.* He argued essentially that Cone's theological program was too exclusivistic and narrow. He attacked Cone on the grounds that his position didn't include the dimension of reconciliation. He felt that Cone put too much emphasis on the liberation of blacks and whites. However, the underlying issue between J. Deotis and James Cone is a difference in their approach to liberation and reconciliation, not the fact that Cone doesn't include reconciliation in his theological position.

A concern that flows throughout Cone's theology is that blacks must establish the agenda for the black liberation struggle. This agenda for him was developing an ontological model of blackness which became the basis of his entire theology. On the one hand, J. Deotis Roberts agrees with Cone that blacks must write the agenda for liberation. He says, "Whites and blacks who desire to aid in the liberation of blacks must understand the new agenda. The new agenda is written by blacks—Cone is correct—only the oppressed may write the agenda for their liberation."[53] On the other hand, J. Deotis Roberts disagrees with the nature and content of Cone's agenda.

Whereas Cone makes his ontological symbol, which is the universal dimension in his thought, grounded in the category of blackness, the universal dimension in J. Deotis' theological program is colorless. For J. Deotis the universal dimension should be as existential to red, yellow, and black people as it is to white people. He opposes the affirmation of a black ontological model to the exclusion of a white ontological model in that it would exclude other skin colors.[54] Therefore, J. Deotis embraces an inclusive model in his approach to liberation and reconciliation, and James H. Cone tends to move toward an exclusive model.

The approach of J. Deotis Roberts to the problem of redemption in light of black suffering is that "We must use suffering creatively and redemptively; we must seek to render it unnecessary as a way of life."[55] He feels that in a white racist society such as America, blacks have borne a constant cross for centuries. And all of their suffering has not been an act of God; "neither has it been redemptive suffering." His contention is that much suffering which blacks have undergone has been a result of man's inhumanity to man and does not emerge out of the Christian understanding of providence. But at the same time he argues, "We seek to transmute suffering into victory; we must strive to transcend suffering that we as individuals and as a people may know the liberty of sons of God here as well as hereafter. At the same time that we seek reconciliation through our role as suffering servants we are to seek liberation from our suffering.''[56]

CONCLUSION

Black Americans throughout their history have used diverse ways of dealing significantly with the problem of suffering. Research in the field of black religious thought in particular and Christian thought in general reveals that there aren't any definitive answers to the problem of suffering. There are meaningful and viable ways of dealing with it in light of the existential circumstances in which a people find themselves. It is one thing to say that the problem of human suffering was resolved once and for all in the death and resurrection of Jesus Christ. In one sense this is true. But in another sense the problem of human suffering recurs in the life of any people. If this is the case, then, how do the death and resurrection of Jesus Christ offer power for people to eradicate human suffering? This is representative of the theological orientation that exists throughout black religious thought.

Black Americans in terms of their quest for genuine freedom and liberation represent an eschatological pilgrimage. God's activity has been expressed in various ways and in different periods of Afro-American history. Through the help of God they moved from slavery to the Emancipation. From Emancipation they moved through the period of reconstruction into the contemporary period. New understandings of God's activity in the world are reflected in each period. However, each period reveals a desire for redemption both in this world and the hereafter. This suggests that the dual eschatological dimensions are present throughout black religious thought. The desire for freedom and liberation among black Americans has never taken an exclusive, other-worldly eschatological orientation, nor has it ever taken an exclusive, this-worldly eschatological orientation. It has always maintained a balance between the two.

DISCUSSION

QUESTION: I might say that as a black person I appreciate the presentation. I had not met Henry until I met him here and heard many black theologians talk about this, but his presentation is, perhaps, the best I've heard yet. The thing that I would like—and I'm sure you didn't touch on it because of the fact of time—is for you to touch on the whole Black Power Movement and how it fits into this whole scheme.

ANSWER: There are many different ways I can do that. I guess it was a natural consequence of some of the agony that we experienced in the 1960s. So we followed the old dialectic, then the Black Power Movement is a kind of natural emergence in that system. Have you read Benjamin Mays' autobiography, *Born to Rebel?* You have, I'm sure. Here you find a person who is 84 years old and who really came through much of the agony that I talked about, and Benjamin Mays said he really could not understand the whole Black Power Movement because since he was five years old, he said he always knew who he was. He never had an identity crisis because his mother told him that he was somebody and he was important, and does black power mean any more than that? So, I think it represented more than that, but certainly I think the foundations of it is trying to understand one's identity; and many of the persons who came through as Benjamin Mays did had that identity clearly in place. But in the contemporary situation, many younger people did not have that identity, and as a result, they had to cry "Black Power," trying to find who they were.

Inquirer's Response: Yes, this answers my question. The thing that I have been concerned about since I've been here at this Conference is that no one has talked about the whole question of power, how it works in the whole business of alleviating suffering; and that's the reason why I asked that and why I was concerned. I had not heard anyone talk about the whole question of power and it seems to me that one of the essentials of the whole Black Power Movement is trying to identify the question of power as one of the elements which helps people to alleviate suffering.

Dr. Young: Yes, thank you—a very appropriate question and concern.

QUESTION: I wonder if you would comment on Malcolm X. I've recently read his biography and wonder how you would focus him and his excellent historical perspective.

ANSWER: I hate to talk about my own books, you know, but if you would allow me—the question is so appropriate that I'll have to refer to that book because that's where I deal with it. In the book that's coming out in October by Abington, I have a chapter on Malcolm X, and what happens is that I try to appreciate the great strength of Malcom X in the context of where he was at that time. And I see Malcolm X standing in the legacy of strong leadership that has been able to set some direction to the chaos in which we find ourselves. So I don't see Malcolm as being special, but I see Malcolm as being tied up in that legacy. I line up Malcolm X with King; I line him up with Elijah Mohammed; I line him up with Benjamin Mays, Howard Simon, and all the others to try to look at his life to see the tremendous strength and integrity that he represented. If I could just speak again—it's unfortunate that we did not really appreciate what he was about until after his death. I don't think blacks had really understood Malcolm until after he died, and that's unfortunate. You know, I must marvel that Alex Haley had such an intimate relationship with Malcolm, and he knew Malcolm closer than a lot of people. So, yes, I do see Malcolm in that context. Now I visited with Elijah Mohammed when he was alive, and I just mention him because of the association with Malcolm, and we were trying to find ways in which the nation of Islam could work with the black church toward social justice. And Elijah Mohammed took the posture that unless you became Muslim, there was no dialogue, and immediately I was turned off; and I say this in that book. I think there has to be a constant dialogue. No movement represents the total truth. And I think Malcolm, in his later years, had moved away from that orthodox narrowness of what Elijah Mohammed was about, and he was moving into a more holistic, universal approach, bringing all suffering people together under one umbrella; and I think that was a tremendous breakthrough for Malcolm.

QUESTION: Being a Deep Southerner, from poor whites in the cotton-mill culture of the deep South, the cotton-mill plantation offered ugly alternatives to black slavery—poor black rural people. Do you see yourself as a black person completely alone in slavery in the South?

ANSWER: I appreciate that question because what I really want to say now is that we're not alone.

Statement from Questioner: I've felt enslaved, and I felt my mother was enslaved.

ANSWER: And in a sense you were enslaved. So what we need to do now is to form a coalition.

QUESTION: Speaking of the great leaders: from your point of reference, would you give me what would be their summary of a conference such as this right now.

ANSWER: I think the summary would be—it has to be: the point by which we can realize that our destiny is tied up together and that it's not a black problem, it's not a poor white problem, but it's a human problem, and we are tied in it together. It is not for me to go back in my own little way to eradicate the problem since the redemptive process is a collective effort in which we commit ourselves to that human problem and work creatively towards its eradication. By working intentionally on an interdependent basis we create the kind of holistic model of how we are to work together.

QUESTION: You spoke of the ground of Christian hope. I'm trying to figure out what do you hold out or what was held out to the slaves of the past, or contemporary blacks who don't have a Christian ground of hope. Surely all the slaves were not Christian—all blacks are not Christian today. What do you hold out; what do we hold out for them?

ANSWER: There has always been—and the literature supports this—diversity throughout the black experience. You have elements of atheism; you have elements of humanism, elements of agagnosticism; and you have political ideologies that aren't undergirded with religious principles; you have materialism—you have all these elements there. I think that many adhere to various of these elements. But the dominant motif has been that Christian element. Even so, the literature supports the thesis that the Church has been the vangurd of all these other elements. The political, social, economic emerged out of that religious experience, and I think that's true even today.

QUESTION: Doctor, out on the streets, it seems to me that the legacy of Martin Luther King, which was moving toward the goals of friendship and reconciliation, has been overcome by the legacy of those who came after him. I think through the black movement towards goals of separation and alienation. Is that accurate and could you comment?

ANSWER: I think it's accurate. I think we are relatively splintered; we're splintered, and there is no singular motif that we rally around. One of the weaknesses of King, despite all of his dignity—and I'd be the first to bow on my knees and do whatever is necessary to respect his great contributions—was that he did not build around him support systems in terms of black leadership. Andy was close to him and Andy has moved very well into the political structure, and I think he's making a contribution there. Jesse Jackson has moved well into Operation Push in Chicago. Fauntroy is doing well in

Congress, in Washington. But the basic SCLC movement—no one takes it seriously. And there is not this figure that all blacks can look to. So I think your assessment is correct and I think we're in a period, a wilderness wandering, and I hope that emerging out of this will be some direction at which we can recommit ourselves.

QUESTION: Your description of King's position on nonviolence is pretty identical to my own. When I try to articulate that position, immediately, my colleagues talk of Niebuhr and his criticism of nonviolence. There is criticism of agape as foundation, saying that instead of an agape foundation, we must use some estimate of agape, always tending toward the goal. I was curious to see how you would respond to Niebuhr's criticism of nonviolence.

ANSWER: I'm glad you raised that question. You know Niebuhr was under that new orthodox influence and what that did was prevent Niebuhr from taking seriously the possibility for redemption within history, and because Niebuhr could not take that seriously, he could not move at the agape level because the agape level challenges us at the point that King pushed; and it was for that reason that King parted company with Niebuhr. I think I share that position and I share that critique that King had and that you have for Niebuhr at that point. King, a middle-of-the-road theologian, pulled together the liberal position with a kind of synthesis position, something which Niebuhr was not able to do. Now King was very much influenced by Niebuhr; he was influenced by the gradualistic approach that you find in Niebuhr. But he pushed beyond Niebuhr because he pushed to a momentum that challenged people at the point that the neo-orthodox stance of Niebuhr just is not capable of moving.

QUESTION: This conference primarily espoused the message that love leads to redemption. Can violence not lead to redemption? The thing that the Jews learned from their experience in the Polish ghetto was that to accept nonviolently that which was to be placed on them leading to death was not the proper solution. The Old Testament indicates to us about taking up our plowshares, turning them into swords, and defending ourselves. God in the Old Testament had instructed the Hebrews not to lie down and die, but to fight. And I think black history has learned that as well—that simply to have subjugated themselves and lie down and die was not the solution. Sometimes, taking up violent action, while in this world may not in the long run be the thing that God wants us to do, may be a solution. In the Masada, when the Hebrews were confronted with life or death, they took death with dignity by taking up arms and defending themselves unto their death. I just question, is there a possibility that violence may lead toward redemption?

ANSWER: You force me to take a position on that—you know, one thing theologians don't do. It's hard to pin them down and they'll avoid it every time. My response to that is that I cannot conceptualize the possibilities there are in redemption. Now if I choose nonviolence, that's one way I think God is speaking to me to behave. I don't want to close off the other possible ways by which redemption will occur. So I don't want to be judgmental on violence. I can just say that the agony of violence is something that I just can't appreciate. But if the situation becomes so demonic that it takes that to correct it, then we're all in trouble. And I take the position that we don't have to take the position on violence, but if we don't deal responsibly with the pain, then violence is inevitable. I can't stop it; you can't stop it; it becomes above that, so that our task is to commit ourselves to that struggle to offset it. And King believed this. You remember his speech in Washington was grounded in this. He said, "Unless we deal responsibly with the cries of the poor, the whirlwinds of revolt will shake foundations of the nation, and when this happens, I can't do anything." So, that's my point in that.

QUESTION: There are many different quotes from the Bible, different positions in the *Bible.* Would you see in this history a devotion to the *Bible,* a change, transition, and that the black people would be devoted to some parts or some attitudes of the *Bible.* In earlier days we were trying to reject those parts of the *Bible* and move somewhere else in the *Bible.* The *Bible* can be quoted by oppressors to justify themselves.

Dr. Young: And you're pointing to the various ways in which blacks have appropriated the *Bible*?

Questioner: Yes, can you tell us of any big change in the way in which black people have appropriated, identified with it, and then through the *Bible* responded to their like problems?

ANSWER: The reason I hesitate to say yes to that is that there are some dominant themes throughout the *Bible* that we merely rehearse throughout our history. You know: the Moses episode, the Jeremiah experience, the Jesus paradigm, and other motifs flow throughout our history. I think what we do is reinterpret those themes in light of our existentialist situation, but the same themes are there. Now Paul was critical—lacks took opposition to St. Paul in the 1960s—and that's something that I think was new from the past. Being a Biblical scholar, you would understand why they would take opposition to St. Paul. But I think basically the themes just recur and take different shapes.

QUESTION: About 10 minutes ago, I wanted to ask you in your beautiful presentation on redemption of the black people whether or not you wanted to speak to the black experience as being a redeeming process for the white people, and then you got into the universality part in regard to the fact that this is something that we have to have coalitions about, which was wonderful, so I put my hand down. And then we got into nonviolence again, and what I would just like to bring out now and get your viewpoint on is this: if I'm not mistaken, much of Dr. Martin Luther King's insights into nonviolence came from Gandhi, as well as from his own Christian tradition, and I wonder if at this point in time when we are becoming more and more aware, and as Christians being encouraged more and more to appreciate some of the insights of other major religions in the world, if in order to move with the perception of non-violence, if we, too, have to do something of what Martin Luther King did. I am thinking, not just stay with this or that part of the Old Testament, but see some of the dynamic, maybe of Jesus, in relationship to some of the other ways that the nonviolent movement has gained ground in our times. That would be, I think, appreciating something of the contributions in this regard from Eastern religions, and from Gandhi in particular.

ANSWER: Yes, very much. The only thing that I could say to that is Amen. Further elaboration would be a footnote.

QUESTION: I think that the basic problem is what we do with our anger. The God-given purpose of anger is to remove the obstacles to love in life. Most of the obstacles to love lie in the area of injustice. Because love is between equals, and as Aristotle said, "The work of justice is to establish equality so that equality is the last thing in justice and first thing in love." Can you put love primary in the way that Martin Luther King did? If you really want brotherhood and reconciliation and not just the removal of what's causing the injustice, then love will make your anger nonviolent and nonviolent anger comes out as the bigger of the two; it makes your love stronger.

ANSWER: I think that's a very well-said statement. I think what happens is that the nonviolent approach obviously puts your courage, your faith, at a level that other approaches have difficulty reaching, because when you are constantly oppressing me, then the human tendency is to retaliate and annihilate you. I can do that as a weak person and what we have is a perpetuation of self-annihilation and that contest for supremacy, power, and that demonic element in history just continues. But when you stand up in opposition to that whole historical process of violence, then that puts you at a very, very courageous level, and I would agree with you on that and challenge you and others to pursue that direction.

QUESTION: I'd like to touch on affirmative action, and speaking of coalition, I'd like to see what you think of the possibilities of the people who are taking a step in affirmative action, being able to have a dialogue with the people who seem to need it more. This is in line with this repressed anger which I see in the Bakke case and so on.

ANSWER: Yes, that affirmative action is a way of dealing in terms of the nuts and bolts of where people hurt, so that I see the affirmative action process as a way of dealing strategically and systematically within eradicating suffering at a level that makes a difference. So, if that connection is all right, my comment is certainly one that sees that affirmative action and that whole arena of trying to deal in diverse ways with eradicating suffering based on a theological conviction that our destiny is inseparable and by dealing with affirmative action and deating with other ways, then we are trying to, in a holistic way, get at the nuts and bolts of the social malfunctions that plague our existence.

NOTES

Paul Tillich, *Systematic Theology. Three Volumes in One.* Chicago: The University of Chicago Press, 1963, Vol. II, p. 165.

[2]John Hick, *Evil and the God of Love.* London: Macmillan, 1966, pp. 6-7. Based on the Process Philosophy of Alfred North Whitehead, many theologians are arguing that in order to give a meaningful and viable answer to the problem of evil and human suffering, it is necessary to modify the traditional Christian understanding of God's power. They have concluded that it is not possible to reconcile the contradiction between God's coercive power and the presence of evil in the world; the alternative is to view God's power as persuasive as opposed to coercive. See Lewis S. Ford, "Divine Persuasion and the Triumph of Good," *Process Philosophy and Christian Thought,* Delwin Brown, Ralphe James, Jr. and Gene Reeves, editors, New York: The Bobbs-Merrill Co., 1971, pp. 287-304; also by Lewis S. Ford, *The Lure of God,* Philadelphia: Fortress Press, 1978; David Ray Griffin, *God Power and Evil,* Philadelphia:The Westminster Press, 1976. John B. Cobb, Jr., *God and the World,* Philadelphia: The Westminster Press, 1976, John B. Cobb, Jr., *God and the World,* Philadelphia: The Westminster Press, 1969, pp. 87-102; also see Cobb's *A Christian Natural Theology Based on the Thought of Alfred North Whitehead,* Philadelphia: The Westminster Press, 1965. One of the earliest attempts to perceive God's power in light of persuasion was the philosopher, Plato. Whitehead employed Plato's notion of God's persuasive power in reconstruction, the Christian Doctrine of God. See Alfred North Whitehead, *Process and Reality,* New York: Harper and Row, 1957, pp. 519-523.

[3]*Ibid.,* p. 5. According to John Hick, the dilemma of theodicy was first formulated by Epicurus (341-270 B.C.)

[4]Although the first African slaves reached Jamestown, Virginia in 1619, the European slave trade began in the 15th century. See W. E. B. DuBois, *The World and Africa,* New York: International Publishers, 1965, pp. 44-80.

[5]John Hope Franklin, *From Slavery to Freedom,* New York: Random House, 1967, pp. 58-59.

[6]Jerome Bennett, Jr., *Before the Mayflower,* Chicago: Johnson Publishing Co., 1964, p. 31.

[7]*Ibid.*

[8]Franklin, *From Slavery to Freedom,* pp. 56-58.

[9]*Ibid.,* p. 58. For additional sources on the slave trade see W. E. B. DuBois, *Suppression of the African Slave Trade to the United States, 1638-1870,* Cambridge: 1896; Daniel P. Mannix, *Black Cargoes: A*

History of the Atlanta Slave Trade, 1518-1865, New York: Viking Press, 1962.

[10]Nathaniel Paul, "An Address Delivered on the Celebration of the Abolition of Slavery in the State of New York, July 5, 1827," in Carter G. Woodson, ed., *Negro Orators and Their Orations*, New York: Russell and Russell, 1969, p. 69.

[11]*Ibid.*

[12]Howard Thurman, *The Negro Spiritual Speaks of Life and Death*, New York: Harper and Row, 1969, pp. 15-16. A further treatment of death and life from the perspective of slavery and the black experience can be found in the authoritative study of black music by John Lovell, Jr., entitled *Black Song: The Force and the Flame*, New York: The Macmillan Co., 1972, pp. 306-310. Lovell says the fact that death for the slaves was an undercurrent symbol for the road to freedom on earth makes it in many instances a positively welcomed reality.

[13]Paul, "Abolition of Slavery," p. 69.

[14]*Ibid.*

[15]*Ibid.*, pp. 72-73. Benjamin E. Mays provides a helpful insight into Nathaniel Paul's approach to theodicy in his *The Negro's God*, New York: Atheneum, 1968, pp. 41-44. I also provide an assessment of Nathaniel Paul in *Major Black Religious Leaders 1755-1940*, Nashville: Abingdon Press, 1977, pp. 16-24.

[16]A major issue in the history of black America has been the controversy concerning whether the conditions of slavery forced blacks to completely abandon their African heritage or whether expressions of Africanisms survived the institution of slavery. E. Franklin Frazier took the position that Africanisms didn't survive the institution of slavery. His contention is that the systematic process of social and cultural assimilation that blacks were forced to endure led to the abandonment of Africanisms. Frazier's position was set forth in his *The Negro in the United States*, revised edition, New York: 1957, Chapter I; and *The Negro Church in America*, New York: Schocken Books, 1969, pp. 1-19. W. E. B. DuBois differed with Frazier. DuBois took the position that Africanisms survived in black religion and black music. See his *The Souls of Black Folk*, Connecticut: Fawcett Pub., 1961, pp. 181-190.

Dubois believed that the black church originated from an African background. In his study *The Negro*, reprint 1915 edition, New York: Oxford University Press, 1970, pp. 113-114, DuBois says, "At first sight it would seem that slavery completely destroyed every vestige of spontaneous movement among Negroes. This is not strictly true. The vast power of the priest in the African state is well known; his realm alone—the province of religion and medicine—remained largely unaffected by the plantation system. The Negro church . . . was not at first by any means a Christian church, but a mere adaptation of those rites of fetish which in

America is termed obe worship, or 'voodooism.' " For further details on the survival of Africanisms in black religion and black culture see Melville J. Herskovits, *The Myth of the Negro Past*, Boston: Beacon Press, 1958; Henry H. Mitchell, *Black Belief*, New York: Harper and Row, 1975; Henry Krehbiel, *Afro-American Folksongs*, New York: G. Schirmer, 1914; and John Lovell, Jr., *Black Song: The Force and the Flame*, pp. 24-126.

[17] Frederick Douglas, *Life and Times of Frederick Douglas*, London: Collier-Macmillan, 1962, p. 85.

[18] *Ibid.*

[19] Eric L. McKitrick, ed., *Slavery Defended: The Views of the Old South*, New Jersey: Prentice-Hall, 1963. This volume is very comprehensive in its compilation of data.

[20] Frazier, *The Negro Church in America*, pp. 12-15.

[21] Douglas, *Life and Times*, pp. 85-87. No other source in a more comprehensive manner deals with the compensatory aspect of the religion of the slaves than Benjamin E. Mays in *The Negro's God*. Although the compensatory dimension is not the only category of black religion examined by Mays in this volume, it takes the dominant interpretative approach.

[22] Benjamin Quarles, *The Negro in the Making of America*, New York: Collier-Macmillan, 1969, p. 71.

[23] Pioneering sources that correct the distorted image of slaves as docile, passive, submissive, and fast to accept the institution of slavery are: Herbert Aptheker, *Negro Slave Revolts in the United States*, New York: International Pub., 1939; also by Aptheker, *American Negro Slave Revolts*, New York: International Pub., 1943; Kenneth M. Stampp, *The Peculiar Institution*, New York: Alfred A. Knopf, 1975; John Lovell, Jr., "The Social Implications of the Negro Spiritual," *Journal of Negro Education*, Vol. VIII, October, 1939; Miles Mark Fisher, *Negro Slave Songs in the United States*, New York: The Citadel Press, 1953; and Raymond A. Bauer and Alice H. Bauer, "Day to Day Resistance to Slavery," *Journal of Negro History*, Vol. 27, October, 1942.

[24] The most authoritative sources on the origin and development of the black church are: Carter G. Woodson, *History of the Negro Church*, Washington, D. C.: Associated Press, 1921; Benjamin E. Mays and Joseph W. Nicholson, *The Negro's Church*, New York: Institute for Social and Religious Research, 1933.

[25] Douglas, *Life and Times*, p. 159

[26] Howard Thurman, *Deep River*, New York: Kennikat Press, 1969, p. 43.

[27] *Ibid.*, pp. 43-44.

[28] *Ibid.*, pp. 27-28. The setting of the spiritual, "There Is A Balm In Gilead" is the book of Jeremiah. The slaves changed Jeremiah's question "Is There A Balm in Gilead?" to a note of creative triumph; this was an

element of faith which transcended the pessimism of slavery. And not
only did it sustain them through slavery, but enabled them to rise above
it.
²⁹*Ibid.*, pp. 56-61. The element of Christian hope flows through much of
Thurman's writings. See his *Jesus and the Disinherited*, Nashville: Abingdon Press, 1949; *The Luminous Darkness*, New York: Harper and
Row, 1965; *The Growing Edge*, Indiana: Friends United Press, 1956;
Deep Is the Hunger, New York: Harper and Row, 1951; and *The Creative
Encounter*, Indiana: Friends United Press, 1972.
³⁰David Walker, *The Walker Appeal* in Sterling Stuckey, ed., *The
Ideological Origins of Black Nationalism*, Boston: Beach Press, 1972, p.
43.
³¹*Ibid.*, p. 60.
³²Henry Highland Garnet, "An Address to the Slaves of the United States
of America, Buffalo, N. Y., 1843" in Earl Ofari, ed., *Let Your Motto Be
Resistance. The Life and Thought of Henry Highland Garnet*, Boston:
Beacon Press, 1972, p. 147.
³³*Ibid.*, p. 148.
³⁴The address Henry Highland Garnet made in 1843 was pivotal in the
history of Black Americans. It was one of the most forceful and revolutionary documents produced during the abolitionist period. It was
delivered at the annual National Negro Convention in 1843 and was interpreted by some as advocating violence. Although Garnet's address was
well-received by many people present at the convention, it was opposed
by a person who was as articulate, influential, knowledgeable, and
charismatic as Garnet, Frederick Douglas. Frederick Douglas opposed
Garnet's address on the grounds that "there was too much physical force,
both in the address and the remarks of the speaker. . . . He was trying for
the moral means a little longer; that the address, could it reach the slaves,
and the advice, either of the address or the gentleman, be followed, while
it might not lead the slaves to rise in insurrection for liberty would, nevertheless, and necessarily be the occasion of an insurrection." Howard
Holman Bell, ed., *Minutes of the Proceedings of the National Negro
Conventions 1830-1864*, New York: Arno Press, 1969, p. 13. In spite of
Douglas' opposition, Garnet's recommendation for initiating a national
slave strike was put in the form of a motion before the convention. The
motion lost by one vote.
³⁵*Ibid.*, p. 152.
³⁶The Atlanta Riot began on Saturday night, September 22, 1906, and extended through Tuesday, September 25. Many blacks were mobbed,
whipped, brutalized, and killed. For details see Benjamin E. Mays, *Born
to Rebel*, New York: Charles Scribner's Sons, 1971, pp. 17-18; and
Charles Crowe, "Racial Massacre in Atlanta, September 22, 1906," *Jour-*

nal of Negro History, LIV, No. 2, April 1969.

[37]W. E. B. DuBois, *Darkwater*, New York: AMS Press, 1969, p. 25.

[38]*Ibid.*, pp. 36-27.

[39]*Ibid.*, p. 27.

[40]*Ibid.*

[41]*Ibid.*

[42]Martin Luther King, Jr., *Stride Toward Freedom*, New York: Harper and Row, 1958, pp. 82-83.

[43]*Ibid.*, p. 84.

[44]*Ibid.*, p. 85. Further discussion of King's understanding of vicarious suffering can be found in Joseph R. Washington, Jr., *The Politics of God*, Boston: Beacon Press, 1969, pp. 173-177; Kenneth L. Smith and Ira G. Zepp, Jr., *Search for the Beloved Community: The Thinking of Martin Luther King, Jr.*, Pennsylvania: Valley Forge, 1974, p. 61.

[45]*Ibid.* In terms of its emphasis on the willingness of blacks to suffer in the quest for freedom and liberation, King's emphasis is very similar to that of Frederick Douglas, the influential black abolitionist. Douglas does not focus on the redemptive aspect of suffering as Martin Luther King, Jr., but both agree that blacks accept suffering as a necessary means toward liberation. Douglas' famous statement in this regard is titled, "No Progress Without Struggle, 1849." "If there is no struggle, there is no progress. Those who profess to favor freedom, and yet depreciate agitation, are men who want crops without plowing up the ground. They want rain without thunder and lightning. They want the ocean without the awful roar of its many waters. This struggle may be a moral one; or it may be a physical one; or it may be both moral and physical; but it must be a struggle. Power concedes nothing without a demand." See Frederick Douglas, "No Progress Without Struggle, 1849" in Floyd B. Barbour, ed., *The Black Power Revolt*, New York: The Macmillan Co., 1968, pp. 36-37.

[46]*Ibid.*, pp. 85-87.

[47]*Ibid.*, p. 87.

[48]Martin Luther King, Jr., *Strength to Love*, New York: Harper and Row, 1963, p. 49.

[49]*Ibid.*, pp. 103-107.

[50]James H. Cone, *Black Theology and Black Power*, New York: Seabury Press, 1969, pp. 1-2.

[51]James H. Cone, *A Black Theology of Liberation*, New York: Seabury Press, 1970, p. 32.

[52]James H. Cone, *God of the Oppressed*, New York: Seabury Press, 1975, p. 42. For some assessments of Cone's theological program see William R. Jones, *Is God a White Racist?* New York: Anchor Press, 1973, pp. 98-120; Peter C. Hodgson, *Children of Freedom*, Philadelphia: Fortress

Press, 1974. Hodgson wrote this entire volume in response to James H. Cone; see also Peter C. Hodgson, *New Birth of Freedom*, Philadelphia: Fortress, 1976, 208-216; and Gayrand Wilmore, *Black Religion and Black Radicalism*, New York: Anchor Press, 1973, pp. 290-306.

[53] J. Deotis Roberts, *Liberation and Reconciliation: A Black Theology*, Philadelphia: The Westminster Press, 1971, p. 32.

[54] *Ibid.*, p. 139.

[55] *Ibid.*, p. 59.

[56] *Ibid.* See also J. Deotis Roberts, *A Black Political Theology*, Philadelphia: The Westminster Press, 1974, pp. 205-222.

Chapter 9

THE MEANING OF SUFFERING—
—A PERSONAL WITNESS*
Catherine De Hueck Doherty

Suffering is the kiss of Christ. Did you ever stop to think about that? It says in the beautiful Jewish song, the song of Solomon, "He kissed me with a kiss of his mouth." Do you realize that when God deigns to lower Himself so that He can kiss you, you will know what suffering is? The Crucified God, the God who is in love with men, leads men in His footsteps, inevitably, and they experience what He experienced. This tremendous experience has to be accepted in faith, in the darkness of faith, total darkness; you won't be able to see a precipice or a crevice or anything. You have to follow God wherever He leads without asking any questions, without asking where He's going; like a child, you put your hand into His

*By design, several special guests at the Congress were men and women who have been outstanding for their identification with suffering people, and are those who give meaning to suffering by their very lives. A foremost witness in this respect for almost 50 years has been Baroness de Hueck Doherty. We were honored to have her share with us this most personal testimony of her own history and spirit.

hand and you go, and He leads you to strange places, my dear friends.

It makes no difference what your religious affiliation is—Buddhism, Protestantism, Catholicism, or Judaism—whoever believes in God in whatever way, experiences the kiss of Christ. The person can reject it; he can leave it alone; he can forget it. But he won't be able to forget it, because suffering will walk with him always. Where there is love, my friends, there is suffering. Without suffering, there is no love. That is one of the first things one has to understand, and it should be the yardstick of any young person who is looking for love, and for all of us, who are not so young.

But today I am asked to talk to you about my journey, the journey of a woman in love with God. I am not ashamed to say that I am in love with God, and because I am in love with God, I follow Him wherever He leads. Sometimes He leads into strange places, as I have learned in my life. As a young girl, my faith was tested, and was made strong when everything around me fell apart. I watched relatives die one by one, and sometimes several. I saw my city of St. Petersburg become an empty city. Do you know what makes a city empty? It's not the people; the people were there. But there were no priests, no rabbis, no ministers of religion. They were all killed. Only one Catholic priest was left. Everybody who directed your soul was dead except this one person. You suddenly knew that something strange had happened, something incredible.

We used to go to Church hugging the wall in the darkness. To go to Church in those days meant that you could be killed in that Church. But who cares about being killed alongside the Hidden One—God! One day, at Church, this priest had just lifted the consecrated Host, and was placing it on the altar, when a shot rang out. The priest dropped dead, and the Host rolled, and an old man said very clearly: "Lord, forgive them for they don't know what they do." Somehow it had an effect on those atheistic communists; they left. They left the Host, and the old man picked it up and gave it to us. We buried the priest, washed the place with holy water, and then walked into St. Petersburg—an empty city. Although there were 2 million people in it, it was tragically empty.

I was one of the early refugees (but it shames me to speak of being a refugee when I think of the boat people, going from port to port and nobody gives a damn about them). I left Russia weighing 82 pounds. We were starved for seven months. I traveled from Russia to Canada with my husband, who was shell-shocked and suffering from poison gas. We had a child. I had to earn a living for us. My salary was $7 a week. How can you feed anyone on that? That's why I became so interested in labor and its struggles. Do you know what it is to hear a child cry from hunger? Sometimes today, I hear those children on the water, trying to go to Hong Kong, or whatever place, and suddenly I hear them cry. Do you?

After awhile, I came to the United States and worked as a waitress, a laundress, a maid. Suffering pursued me there. My soul cried out: "Lord, out of the depths, I cry to Thee. Hear my voice. Hear the voice of my supplication. Don't abandon me." Did you ever know what it is to go up Fifth Avenue in New York, or Chicago, or any place, and smell the bacon from the restaurants and you haven't got a bean to buy it? You look around; you're young; it's so easy to sell your body or your soul for a beer when you are young. But there is something bigger—the pain of Christ within you, and His lips overpowering you. You almost want to run away, you don't want to touch them, you don't want to listen to Him, but you can't help it, you are too much in love with Him.

I became a lecturer and soon was giving lectures all over. Things went better. But then there came another kind of suffering. You have talents; you have this and that; you can make your way; you can marry (or remarry) and can do a lot of things. But something happens: those two lips come close to you and a voice whispers: "Follow me . . . Arise; sell what you possess; give to the poor and follow me." So you do, and then you become a beggar. Have you ever begged, but I mean begged, really begged? Have you ever been in a group of beggars? I don't mean getting a couple of bucks from the government. No. I mean, you're hungry, you're so hungry, so terribly hungry. And you ring a bell and you ask for a piece of bread, old bread; but never, never ask for an egg. You're absolutely sure that if you ask for an egg, they are going to get the cops after you!

Then came the founding of Friendship House and Madonna House. You know what the greatest suffering in my life was? You would not believe it (not with Monsignor Egan giving me such a good introduction!). It was the suffering I endured from priests! They damned me from every side; only a few of them understood what I tried to do. And when I went to Harlem, I remember one of them said to me, "You're going to hell, mixing negroes with whites, you're going to hell." How do you think that feels? I, who loved priests beyond anything. I don't understand why I love them so much, but I do. I mean it's true. I really do love you. (Incidentally, I wrote a book about you; it's called, *Dear Father.* If you get hold of it, you're going to have a lovely retreat for priests; I really love you terribly.)

It all started when I was 12. I was in Egypt in those days, and there was a good Jesuit giving a retreat for kids, and he said, "When you grow up, you should pray for priests." And I said to myself, "Oh my God, grow up? I'll be old! Twenty years old!" I said, "I'll go in and talk to him." So I talked to him and I said, "Father, can I pray for priests now? I mean it." He said, "Catherine, do you really mean it?" I said, "Yes, I do." I did not know what I was saying, but I have prayed for priests ever since.

When I look back, the funniest thing about this is that the archbishops, bishops, and cardinals were very good to me. But, oh, did I have trouble with priests! They really put me down. And, of course, the nuns too. I'm sorry to say that;

they were very, very severe in those days. I remember talking to some nuns about Christian negroes. They asked me to leave the auditorium. Well, that's old stuff. But, can you imagine? Is your soul sensitive? Do you feel what it was to be penniless because of God, to be founding an apostolate when you didn't know what an apostolate was? Your bishop said, "Well, Catherine, you're going into Catholic action." I said, "What's that?" I didn't know what it was.

They used to say to me, "Oh my God, you're living in Harlem, aren't you afraid of dying?" I said, "No, I think it's a lovely place to die, don't you?" Ha, if I die at the hands of an enemy or by someone like that, I become a confessor. That's something to think about. But I never did become a confessor, so why should we remember that?

There was the ridicule of the Communists, the ridicule of the poor, the ridicule of the priests, the ridicule of all the people who belonged to what you call my "strata of society." This ridicule armed itself with terrible weapons—was it knives? was it pistols?—I don't remember anymore. Debts had to be paid; I was like one dead. I held on to God and God alone. Yes, to God alone. It's an inner intuition, the intuition of faith. When you are at the stage where I was, there's only one thing that can sustain you—faith. Faith that is as strong as whatever strength there is on this earth. Faith that believes notwithstanding when everything is against it. Faith that is like a child, for after all, Christ said that only children will go to Heaven. Faith that puts its hand in the hand of God and says, "Live." What is the yardstick of pain, my friends? What is the yardstick of pain when you set yourself against a whole, not only generation, but a whole civilization? You are compelled. All night and day in your ears you hear, "Friend, come on higher, follow me, come on, follow me." You follow Him, you follow Him until your life is extinct because you love Him.

Yes, maybe I haven't given you any of the things that you wanted to hear, but I have given you a life, a life lived amongst the loneliest people. But is it sufficient to tell you the suffering of one person? Would it be better to tell you about the suffering of all the negroes, all the second-hand citizens who are Czechoslovakian, Russian, or what have you? What about these people? I am not talking about the ones that are being taken care of; I'm talking about the ones that go with the little bags to eat from garbage. They are the ones I know. There are the refugees, the minority groups, the forgotten, the children. There are 1 million children, so your Chicago paper says, that are homeless. How much suffering can one lay out on the carpet of this beautiful house? How much? The answer is very simple: it's according to how much you love. It is high time to simplify this, to enter into the heart of Christ—all of us, whoever we are, and begin to love. We love superficially, I am sorry to say. I often want to cry out: "Put your feet where your words are!" Let us praise God. Yes, to praise God is wonderful. But don't praise Him unless you act according to His command to love—that is His Father's Will. This is the nakedness of the one who gives himself to God totally. He is naked before the Lord. There is nothing of him or her that is hidden from God.

And that, my friends, is achieved by prayer. I don't care what aspect of suffering we discuss, or what denomination you belong to. Prayer is the answer. It is through prayer that we reach God; yes, pray to reach God, and then suffering becomes possible, in fact, joyous, in union with Him.

I said suffering is the kiss of Christ. Well, ladies and gentlemen, look at the woman who has been very well kissed by Christ!

Final Prayer by Dr. Colston

O, thou God, who in Thy mercy looks upon us in our suffering and pain,
Who lifts us rejoicing from where we have fallen, to put us on a new plane.
Let Your gift of love be with us as we depart from one

another, knowing that we are not leaving our friends, but taking them with **us in** our hearts and in our minds.

Give us greater understanding and sensitivity, O Lord, to respond to those around us who hold their hands out to us, asking for ministry to them; let it be wise and discerning, let it be full of hope and meaning, and let us show in our own lives the gift of Your love to us.

You, who constrains us, who reconciles us, and who sets our feet upon a new way,

Guide us day by day, that whatever we do or say will be to Your glory,

Through Jesus Christ, our Lord.

Amen.